# YOUNG ELIZABETH

# YOUNG ELIZABETH

## The Making of the Queen

*Kate Williams*

PEGASUS BOOKS
NEW YORK LONDON

Young Elizabeth

Pegasus Books Ltd
148 West 37th Street, 13th Floor
New York, NY 10018

First Pegasus Books paperback edition December 2016
First Pegasus Books hardcover edition November 2015

ISBN: 978-1-68177-253-0

10   9   8   7   6   5   4   3   2   1

Printed in the United States of America
Distributed by W. W. Norton & Company, Inc.

'It almost frightens me that the people should love her so much. I suppose it is a good thing, and I hope that she will be worthy of it, poor little darling.'

*The Duchess of York to Queen Mary, autumn 1928*


'Never mind, Margaret,' said Elizabeth, while watching her parents and the Court wait to enter the throne room. 'One day you and I will be down there sharing all the fun. And I shall have a perfectly *enormous* train, yards long.'


'*History* is so thrilling.'

*Princess Elizabeth*

# Contents

# *Prologue*
# Abdication Day

*Princess Elizabeth in 1936*

ON THE AFTERNOON OF 10 December 1936 the ten-year-old Princess Elizabeth of York was at home with her younger sister, Margaret, in the family home, 145 Piccadilly near Hyde Park. She became aware of people collecting outside her front door, cheering and shouting for her father. Mystified, the young Princess wondered if the crowds might dispel – but instead they only swelled. Over and over they were calling for the Duke. Others were shouting 'God Save the King'.

Life had been unsettled for some months in 145 Piccadilly, the Yorks' town house. Elizabeth and Margaret were used to spending time with their mother and father, giggling in their room in the morning, playing in the garden and throwing water over each other at bath time. Their governess despaired of ever instilling a sustained education, such was the family's enjoyment of each other's company. But their cosy life had been much changed since the death of their grandfather, King George V, at the beginning of the year, and since the autumn their father had been shut in his study, buried in his papers. He had had no time for horseplay with his daughters; instead, trains of dignitaries had arrived to see him, including the Prime Minister and bishops in their full regalia. When their father was free, he had been tired and strained, and recently her mother had been terribly unwell, confined to bed with severe influenza. Their grandmother, Queen Mary, had sometimes looked cross and Elizabeth's beloved Uncle David, one of her favourite partners for tea-time games of Happy Families and Snap, had not visited for some time – and he had even forgotten a few engagements. But, she supposed, he was King now and perhaps too busy to play cards with his nieces. What exactly the problem was she had little idea. She and Margaret had been devoting them-selves to their swimming lessons at the Bath Club. 'You look like an aeroplane about to conk out,' she had shouted at Margaret when she slowed down. The two girls splashed and jumped about under the tuition of the engaging Miss Daly. It was easy to forget the cares at home when there was so much fun to be had at the baths.

Finally, that December morning, Elizabeth decided to ask a footman the reason for the noise. He told her that the King had abdicated his throne and her father now ruled. She hur-tled up the stairs to tell Margaret the news: 'Uncle David is going away, and isn't coming back, and Papa is to be King.'

'Does that mean that you will have to be the next Queen?' came the response.

'Yes, some day,' answered Elizabeth.

'Poor you,' said Margaret.

There was no reply.

Then, refusing to be daunted by world events, Elizabeth sat down to write up her report about the last swimming les-son. At the top of the page she wrote 'Abdication Day'.

For Princess Elizabeth, maintaining a strict routine was the way to control, even negate, the painful vicissitudes of life. It was a policy she would retain throughout adulthood, often to her disadvantage and, in 1997, to the severe detriment of the reputation of monarchy.

Lilibet wrote her notes on swimming class in the bold, clear hand George V had insisted she learn, but her future was irrevocably changed. She was now the heiress to the throne of Great Britain and its dominions. Unless her mother had a son, an event that seemed unlikely, she would take up the crown of one of the oldest and most influential monarchies in the world. As a mere Princess of York, her parents' sole ambition for her was that she should be happily married. But now her future was one of power, international influence, fame and great wealth, for which she would have to sacrifice privacy, intimacy and a family life. It was a role for someone able to hide her feelings and respond to duty. 'Isn't it lucky Lilibet is the eldest,' said Margaret.

'If I am ever Queen,' the ten-year-old Lilibet once declared, 'I shall make a law that there must be no riding on Sundays. Horses must have a rest too. And I shan't let anyone dock their pony's tail.'

In 2012, the year of her Diamond Jubilee, the Queen is less than four years away from superseding Queen Victoria as Britain's longest reigning monarch, and she has been one of the most popular queens in history. It is hard to see the Queen fulfilling her duties at Parliament, opening ceremonies and touring the Commonwealth, and imagine that she was not born to the role. Yet as the daughter of the second son of George V she was never destined to touch the orb and sceptre at all. She was brought up to be a good aristocratic wife and her education was to be very much like that of her mother, Elizabeth Bowes-Lyon: casual, loving, unintellectual. As the Duchess of York said, 'After all, I and my sisters only had governesses and we all married well – one of us *very* well.'

'Give me a child of seven ...' runs the Jesuit motto. For Elizabeth, the age of ten was when her life changed. The decision of Thelma Furness, lover of the Prince of Wales, to leave for America in 1934 and ask Wallis Simpson to look after her amour had fateful ramifications. It caused shock in the country, gossip in high society, distracted the government from the rise of nationalism in Europe and led to diplomatic problems between Britain and America. Most of all, the abdication changed the life of a precise, methodical little girl whose favourite activities were playing with toy ponies and weeding the garden with her doting father.

# I
# 'A lucky fellow if she accepts you'

*The Duke and Duchess of York*

'I DO HOPE THAT YOU & Papa are as delighted as we are
to have a granddaughter, or would you sooner have another
grandson?' Prince Albert, Duke of York, wrote to his
mother, Queen Mary. 'I know Elizabeth wanted a daughter.'
His wife, the Duchess of York, had given birth by Caesarean
section to their first child at 2.40 a.m. on the morning of 21
April 1926. Elizabeth Alexandra Mary of York was a plump
infant princess, a blessing on a happy marriage and, although
officially third in line to the throne, seen as little more.

Crowds were cheering outside the house, but for others
the monarchy was a hated symbol of privilege and repression,
tottering at the top of an unfair system. Britain in 1926 was
seized by worker unrest. In the previous spring, mine owners
had informed their employees that wages would be lowered
and hours increased. The union threatened industrial action.
Stanley Baldwin's Conservative government authorised a
royal commission into the matter and it found for the mine
owners. The TUC declared a general strike for 2 May, calling out other workers including railwaymen, printers and
dockers. It was a stand-off and they were determined to win.

In such turmoil, the advancing pregnancy of the twenty-
five-year-old wife of the second son and third child of
King George V, Albert, Duke of York, was an unwelcome

9

distraction for the Home Secretary, Sir William Joynson-Hicks. Called early on 21 April, not long before he was due to attend a vital meeting between the Prime Minister and the coal owners, he hurried to the home of the Duchess's parents, 17 Bruton Street in Mayfair. There, Elizabeth Alexandra Mary was born; he assented to her legitimacy and dashed back to his papers.

The King and Queen arrived to visit their first granddaughter (the Princess Royal already had two sons). Queen Mary declared that the child was a 'little darling with a lovely complexion and pretty hair'. The Duke and Duchess were equally happy. 'We have long wanted a child to make our happiness complete,' the Duke wrote. They had waited three years – long by the standards of the time.

'We are so anxious for her first name to be Elizabeth as it is such a nice name & there has been no one of that name in your family for a long time,' the Duke wrote to his father. Victoria was summarily discounted. 'He says nothing about Victoria. I hardly think that necessary,' George V said of his son to Queen Mary. The name 'Elizabeth' was chosen because it was her mother's, not to recall Elizabeth I. The Princess took her names from her mother, her great-grandmother and her grandmother and, indeed, her initials were identical to those of her mother: E.A.M. She was named after consorts and wives, not ruling queens. Her destiny was to make a good marriage, possibly into a foreign royal family, and become a supportive wife and mother, just like her mother, the Duchess of York, her grandmother, Queen Mary, and her great-grandmother, Queen Alexandra. The heir to the throne would be the child of her as yet unmarried uncle, Edward, Prince of Wales – 'David' to his family.

'The House of Hanover, like ducks, produce bad parents,' said the Royal Librarian to Sir Harold Nicolson, biographer of George V, 'they trample on their young.' George I, the Princess's great-great-great-great-great-great-grandfather, had arrived to rule in 1714 and began the Hanoverian line. He had made scant effort to speak English and his son, George II, had been reclusive. Despite losing the American colonies, George III had been a widely popular king both for his engagement with the country and his lengthy marriage with Queen Charlotte, and his sufferings from porphyria only increased sympathy for him. His seven sons and six daughters did not follow his uxorious example and before the arrival of Princess Charlotte, daughter of the Prince of Wales, in 1796, they had managed to produce between them over fifty-six illegitimate children – and no legitimate heir.

George IV separated from his wife, Princess Caroline, after three days and returned to his Mrs Fitzherbert, the Catholic widow he had married in contravention of the Royal Marriages Act in 1772. William IV had ten children with the celebrated actress, Mrs Jordan, and none with his wife. The reputation of the royal family was low when George IV's niece, Victoria, daughter of Edward, Duke of Kent, succeeded to the throne at just eighteen in 1837. The tiny Queen began summarily to rescue the monarchy's reputation, assiduously engaging with the duties of court and politics, and carefully showing herself off to the public as dignified and hard-working – the polar opposite of her misbehaving uncles. With her husband, Albert of Saxe-Coburg, she instigated the notion of the virtuous royal family, and prints and portraits disseminated images of the monarch and her brood around her great Empire. By the end of her reign Victoria's position was unassailable and her disreputable predecessors were a colourful memory. She ruled a quarter of the world's population, her nine children married into European royalty and the British aristocracy, and her grandson by her eldest child, Victoria, Princess Royal, was the German Kaiser Wilhelm II.

Victoria's son, Bertie, later King Edward VII, rebelled against his mother's iron morals as a young man – but he deplored the same lassitude when it manifested itself in his own eldest son, Prince Eddy, Duke of Clarence. The young Prince could not settle to life in the navy and muddled his way into the seedy corners of London's underworld. His father consulted Queen Victoria on the matter. 'A good sensible wife – with considerable character – is what he needs,' he wrote. 'But where is she to be found?'

The ever-resourceful Queen had her eye on the young Princess Victoria Mary of Teck, always known as May, the twenty-two-year-old daughter of her cousin, Princess Mary Adelaide, whose father had been younger brother to the Duke of Kent. The family were lacking in funds and dignity, and really hardly royal, for May's father was the product of the morganatic marriage of Duke Alexander of Württemberg. Shy Princess May had spent her teenage years in an agony of embarrassment as fellow royals looked down on her family, and her gigantically fat mother sallied forth, pretending not to care. Queen Victoria was more interested in May's restrained character than her lack of funds (and, indeed, the latter was perhaps desirable, for it made the family very unlikely to interfere). For her, the twenty-two-year-old Princess was a 'superior girl', steady, sensible and lacking in frivolity. May and Eddy were quickly betrothed, her trousseau was ordered and then, in January 1893, a week before the wedding, Eddy died of influenza. May's bridal wreath was laid on his coffin. 'The dear girl looks like a crushed flower,' Victoria wrote.

Princess May was the object of great public pity (and her hopelessly indebted family were in a state of terror over the expensive trousseau they had ordered). Stranded, with no other suitors, it seemed to many that her marriage prospects were ruined. But the plump and resolute Victoria was not about to let May slip through her fingers. The Queen decided she should marry the new heir, Eddy's brother, twenty-six-year-old Prince George. Princess May herself was distressed by the idea and decided to leave England. The Prince of Wales and George later visited her and her family at Cannes – and the two young people began to forge a genuine friendship.

Prince George was simple, disciplined, fond of the navy and very conscious of his duty. Four months after Eddy's death, George proposed to May and the wedding took place the following July. 'Princess May is the ideal bride,' declared the *Lady's Magazine*. 'I am simply devoted to you,' George wrote to his wife a few months into their marriage. In 1910 her husband ascended the throne and the young girl from a rackety family became Queen Mary, famously dignified, calm and severe, as impressively regal as Queen Victoria had been. The role took its toll, however. At the height of the Second World War she stayed with friends in Gloucestershire and wept when she was told she could return to London. 'I shall have to begin being Queen Mary all over again,' she said.

Prince George was reminiscent of George III, a submissive man of straightforward interests and tastes who gained the esteem of his people. His first child with May, Prince Edward, known as David, the last of his seven Christian names, was born in 1893, large, healthy and handsome. After David, his father had hoped for a girl. Instead, eighteen months later on 14 December 1895, came a boy, Prince Albert Frederick Arthur George. The birth plunged his father into panic about the reaction of his grandmother. The anniversary of the sudden death of the Prince Consort thirty-five years previously, 14 December was a date on which Queen Victoria wallowed in mourning and her family had to follow. Their notions of the seventy-six-year-old Queen's strength knew no bounds – like a malevolent fairy godmother, she could curse a child for life.

The Prince of Wales, grandfather of the baby, was sent to Windsor to break the news. Happily, the Queen was too fond of Princess May to criticise her for being brought to bed on an inopportune date. 'Grandmamma was rather distressed that this happy event should have taken place on a darkly sad anniversary for us,' Edward wrote to his son, 'but I think – as well as most of us in the family here – that it will "break the spell" of this most unlucky date.' He most of all wished to see his mother come to view the death of the Prince Consort with equanimity, for she blamed him for Albert's decline.

The Queen surprised everyone by receiving the news calmly. 'I have a feeling it may be a blessing for the dear little boy,' she wrote of the date. She was most gratified by the olive branch of the name Albert and promptly sent a bust of her lamented husband to the child as a christening present.

Young Bertie was born into the last days of unassailable greatness for the British royal family. He was related to every one of the twenty reigning monarchs of Europe through blood or marriage. His great-grandmother, two years short of her Diamond Jubilee, ruled a quarter of the world's population and was the most powerful individual in her time. Her ministers and soldiers had subjugated peoples across the world, genuinely believing that the other nations benefited from and were strengthened by governance from Britain. Those who wished to please them agreed. Prince . Lerothodi of Basutoland, whose father had appealed to the British for protection from the Boers, declared of Victoria's Golden Jubilee in 1887:

> We hear that Her Majesty's subjects are an immense multitude, numbering more than 300 millions of people, that the sun never goes down on her empire, and that all glory in being her subjects.

At the time of Albert's birth the entire royal family, with the Queen at its apex, believed in their excellence and right to rule. The family had palaces across the country and private estates at Balmoral, Osborne and Sandringham, a collection of jewels rivalled only by those of the Russian royal family, priceless works of art, a royal yacht, staunch courtiers and phalanxes of servants. They were truly, as George VI later dubbed them, a 'family firm'. But their power was already waning. In 1895, Leander Starr Jameson, a British colonist, launched a raid against Paul Kruger's Boer Transvaal republic. His aim was to inspire the British expatriate workers to rise up and fight against the authorities, thus allowing Britain to seize the republic. They did not, and Kruger received messages of support, including one from Kaiser Wilhelm II. It was the beginning of the crumbling of the Empire. But still the Diamond Jubilee, for which little Bertie was only two, thrilled the nation. On a Jubilee Mug the Queen's 'Notable Achievements' were listed: 'Railways 1837', 'Imperial Institute 1897', 'Afghan War 1839'. The Labour leader, Keir

Hardie, wrote in the *New Statesman* that 'future historians' would look back on the Jubilee celebrations with much interest. 'To the visitor from Mars two things might seem incontrovertible, first that the world was at peace, second that the thrones of the world were firmly embedded in the hearts of a loyal and grateful people.' But, as he put it rather hopefully, the people would turn out for the installation of a president, the troops were compelled to be there and the statesmen cheered because 'Empire means trade and trade means profit, and profit means power over the common people'.

In 1897 Queen Victoria was exhausted, lame and increasingly weary of leading the Jubilee razzmatazz. Happiest when surrounded by her tokens and memorabilia of the dead, she tyrannised her family. 'In our position, which is quite different from other people's, one ought not to be left alone, without a child or a near Relation.' Her family, to her, existed to predict and fulfil her practical and emotional needs – and when they did not, she shifted her preference to her servants.

The Prince of Wales and future Edward VII loomed large in the lives of his six children and grandchildren. Pure Hanoverian, he was greedy, domineering, lascivious and ruled by the awful 'Hanoverian spleen'. It was fortunate that his wife, Alexandra, was rather deaf. The Prince was also, like his ancestors, convinced of the right of kings to rule and the superiority of the royal family. He brought up his children to be bad-tempered and narrow-minded.

'I was frightened of my father and I'm damn well going to see that my children are frightened of me,' Prince George declared of Edward VII. He and May had six children – Princess Mary arrived in 1897, with three further sons, Henry, George and John, in 1900, 1902 and 1905. Prince

John, an epileptic, was sadly treated, sent to a secluded villa away from the family until his death in 1919. The rest of the family lived in York Cottage in the grounds of Sandringham.

Crammed into the ugly, dark and poky York Cottage, tempers ran high. Both George and May found it difficult to express love – their early courtship was marked by letters in which they apologised to each other for seeming stiff and shy. Terrified of his sons becoming dissipated royals as his dead brother had been, George was excessively stern, and bullied and criticised his sons. Even as adults, his children were not allowed to speak in his presence unless he spoke to them first. Margot Asquith told him his harsh treatment would drive the children to drink, but he ignored her.

Princess May was so concerned about bringing up properly virtuous children that she too was overly strict and, once she became Queen, so devoted to assisting her husband that she was offhand with her children. After suffering from paroxysms of shame as a girl, thanks to her parents' lack of decorum, she grew up always believing people were laughing at her. As a consequence she developed what Lady Airlie, her lady-in-waiting, called a 'hard crust of inhibition'. She never embarrassed her children, but they did not feel loved by her. May busied herself collecting together old Christmas cards and reading about royal genealogy, while her husband shut himself into his study, smoking and inspecting his stamp collection.

Even worse, the royal couple hired cruel staff. The nanny of the infant Princes Edward and George attempted to make herself indispensable by pinching them before presenting them to their parents, ensuring that they cried terribly and it appeared as if they were content only with her. The children grew up miserable: Prince Edward was painfully obsessed with staying thin and Albert suffered from a nervous stammer and vicious rages. Before his marriage to the chic and gentle-natured Princess Marina of Greece, Prince George had been a rapacious bisexual with a penchant for cocaine and dubious nightspots, while Prince Henry grew up to be as dishonest and greedy as the sons of George III. The elder two were the best of the lot.

As a child Elizabeth's father, Prince Albert, always felt second best. Lacking the easy charm of his elder brother, he was physically unprepossessing and forced to wear painful splints for knock-knees. His tutors made him write with his right hand when he naturally favoured his left. 'Like his brother, he cannot get on without a "bit of a shove",' the family tutor wrote in his final report, before Bertie left the schoolroom for the Royal Naval College at Osborne. The tutor was hopeful: his charge was a 'straight and honourable boy, very kind-hearted and generous; he is sure to be popular with the other boys'. Unfortunately, at Osborne the thirteen-year-old Albert struggled with lessons, had little clue how to play team sports like cricket and football, and his stammer meant he hesitated to answer questions – giving the impression he was slow (as, indeed, he often was). He was badly bullied. One cadet remembered coming out of the mess hall after breakfast to find Bertie tied up in a hammock in a gangway, calling out for help after being bundled in by his classmates.

Prince Albert was at Osborne when his grandfather, Edward VII, died on 6 May 1910 at the age of sixty-eight. Princess Alexandra allowed her husband's mistress, Mrs Keppel, to visit the deathbed. Bertie's father was now King George V. The family moved into Buckingham Palace and Princess May became Queen Mary. David, now heir apparent, was created Prince of Wales in the following year. Even more than ever, poor Bertie felt like second best to his glamorous brother. Handsome and blond, clever and outgoing, David absorbed all the attention. As Bertie later told Mrs Stanley Baldwin, he had, as a boy, 'felt envious that eighteen months should make so much difference'. In the autumn of 1911 David went to Magdalen, Oxford – a course of study Bertie could never contemplate. He graduated sixty-first out of sixty-seven from Dartmouth Naval College, then transferred to begin work as a midshipman. Although he was eager to serve, he was initially posted to a desk job at the Admiralty.

To Bertie and his family the world was a place ruled by their relatives. Kaiser Wilhelm II of Germany and Nicholas of Russia were his cousins. But the world was changing. In 1912 King Victor Emmanuel of Italy narrowly escaped an assassination attempt and King George of Greece, brother of Princess Alexandra, was shot in the following year. At the same time Germany's power was resurgent and the behemoths, Russia, Germany and the Austro-Hungarian Empire, were in dispute over the Balkan states, namely Romania, Bulgaria, Serbia and Greece. Russia was snapping at the borders of the Austro-Hungarian Empire, and the ministers and people were in belligerent mood. The British, so fond of their ideology that populations were better off governed together, could not comprehend that other countries might wish for their own empires as well. By 1914 every country in Europe wanted their own set of people to rule.

'Terrible shock for the dear old Emperor,' recorded the King in his journal on 28 June. On that day Bertie was on board his ship when Archduke Franz Ferdinand of Austria, the heir to the throne of the Austro-Hungarian Empire, was touring Sarajevo with his wife. Six Serbian nationalists lay in wait along his route. His motorcade was bombed, but he survived, only to be shot a little later on his way to visit the wounded. The Austro-Hungarian Empire suspected a national plot against their heir. Bertie noted in his diary only that there had been a visit from fifty Roedean schoolgirls to his ship, with dancing before tea.

'I expect it has caused rather a stir in Germany,' the Prince of Wales remarked of the assassination, rather more presciently than his brother. On 28 July the Austro-Hungarian Empire declared war on Serbia, and Germany, eager to crush Russia and invade France, allied with them.

Although Queen Victoria had fretted about German nationalism since unification, the royal family saw Germany as a friend and the sudden aggression was shocking. 'The way they have behaved will go down to history as about the worst and most infamous action of any govt!! Don't you agree?' wrote David to Bertie. Like everyone, he was convinced of Britain's invincibility: 'serve them right too if they are absolutely crushed, as I can but think they will be.'

Britain declared war on Germany on 4 August 1914. The crowds cheered outside Buckingham Palace on the announcement of war until the King and Queen appeared with the Prince of Wales, and the crowds sang patriotic songs and waved Union Jacks throughout the night. 'The streets were full of people shouting, roaring, yelling their heads off,' wrote Elizabeth Bowes-Lyon, the future Queen, who was in London at the time. It was all rather jolly.

The King saw the war as a slight inconvenience to his summer sports, because it forced him to postpone his trip to Cowes. 'I shall indeed be disappointed if we are unable to go,' he wrote to Bertie. 'I had hoped to have raced in the "Britannia" four times next week.'

'Let it be admitted without shame that a thrill of horror quickened every pulse,' wrote David Lloyd George later in his memoirs of the announcement of war. Young men hurried to sign up and the government was besieged with volunteers. As *The Times* reported, so many men had arrived at the London recruiting office that mounted police arrived 'to hold them in check'. Within four days of the outbreak, men were signing up at the rate of one hundred per hour. How could Britain fail? A short, sharp shock would put Germany in its place. Men across England hurried to be a part of the certain victory. Factories worked around the clock supplying munitions, women signed up to work in those factories and 80,000 served as non-fighting members of the three British women's forces. Prince Bertie's senior officer was sanguine, noting that he didn't mind his leave being cancelled, because he would be able to take it in autumn – at an ideal time for partridge shooting.

Bertie did not cover himself in glory. Three weeks after the war began he fell ill with appendicitis. It was the beginning of a long convalescence and the end of his opportunity of active service. As thousands of men were sent to grimy trenches, the second in line to the throne began working at a desk job at the Admiralty. The Prince of Wales, by contrast, received a 'wonderful and joyous surprise' when he was told he could go to France as an officer of the Grenadier Guards, even though he would be rather shorter than the others. In France, however, he found he was kept away from the action. He begged Lord Kitchener to allow him to fight, but the response came that it was not his death that was of concern but the risk that he might be captured. Still, to his brother and the world, David was playing the hero while Bertie was retired from the action. 'Nothing to do as usual,' the second son wrote in his journal.

By 1915 it became clear that victory would be slow in coming. Despite the efforts of the authorities to keep the reports from the newspapers, and the practice of returning wounded soldiers to stations late at night, people became aware of the terrible casualties. Zeppelins ballooned in the sky over their houses as the Germans bombed London and the coasts. Britain was heavily dependent on imports for food and when enemy submarines began sinking merchant ships the food supply dropped. In 1916 there was only enough wheat to last six weeks – so bread was rationed, along with coal. Later butter, meat, sugar, cheese and margarine were similarly restricted. The King responded to the national emergency by declaring he would give up alcohol. The point was partly restraint, but also intended to aid industry by setting an example to the workers: Lloyd George in particular worried that factory output could be much higher if the workers did not drink. It was not just the working classes who were supposed to be devoting themselves to work. With the outbreak of the war came the end of the royal functions: Ascot, court balls, levées and the presentation of debutantes. The move was just as well: there were fewer aristocrats to participate.

Monarchs around him were falling and the King was conscious of the need to preserve his family's rule above all. The anti-German hysteria was so intense that he himself was accused of being a spy. Lord Kitchener had to swear to the Cabinet that the lights seen flashing over Sandringham during a recent air sortie were 'caused by the car of the rector returning home from dinner'. The First Sea Lord, Louis

Mountbatten, was also seen as too German and had to stand down, even though, as George V wrote of him, 'there is no more loyal man in the country.'

At a meeting of the Privy Council in July 1917 George V had decreed that all male descendants of Queen Victoria should bear the name of Windsor, rather than Saxe-Coburg. The Kaiser mocked his relative's initiative, declaring he was looking forward to seeing 'The Merry Wives of Saxe-Coburg Gotha' (one of his few recorded jokes), but the move was popular with the British public. 'Ours is by far the most solid,' the Prince of Wales wrote to his father about the British monarchy, 'tho' of course it must be kept so and I more than realise that this can only be done by keeping in the closest possible touch with the people.'

Not all of George's relatives were so shrewd. The King's beloved cousin, Tsar Nicholas, had made the poor decision to depart from Russia personally to direct the war effort, leaving his wife, Tsarina Alexandra, as regent. Anti-establishment feeling swelled, fuelled by anger at the privations of war as millions went hungry and the people became obsessed by the mystic Grigoriy Rasputin, the Tsarina's self-styled adviser. After a severe winter at the beginning of 1917, strikes were convulsing the cities and the Tsar could not continue. He begged his cousin, King George, to give his family shelter. The British government was sympathetic, but although George was fond of Nicholas and also cousin to the Tsarina, he refused. He believed that harbouring the Tsar would damage his own position, even though Britain and Russia were allies. The King was afraid of appearing too foreign. All the networks of influence, created by Victoria's project of marrying her children into the royal families of Europe, were coming to seem more of a burden than a joy.

Nicholas and his family were later executed on the orders of Lenin. The collapse of the Russian Empire undermined British morale. By 1917, both sides in the conflict were suffering: the casualties had been great and trench positions had made no significant movement since 1915. The Germans and the Allies were fighting a war of attrition.

Bertie finally escaped the sickbay to witness the Battle of Jutland from his ship as a midshipman and subsequently joined the Royal Naval Air Force, but the war ended before he could see active service. The entry of the United States into the conflict on the side of the Allies proved decisive. The exhausted German forces could not compete. The Allied and American soldiers drove back the enemy positions and, on 29 September, the German Supreme Command informed the Kaiser and his ministers that the military operations had failed – and the joint head of the German war effort declared that he did not think the front could hold for another twenty-four hours. Germany requested a ceasefire and soldiers began to withdraw from the Western Front. On 9 November the Kaiser agreed to abdicate and fled Berlin for Holland. The Armistice was signed between the Allies and Germany on 11 November in a railway carriage in Compiègne Forest. The King addressed Parliament in stirring tones. 'May the morning star of peace, which is now rising over a war-worn world, be here and everywhere the herald of a better day,' he announced. So many were dead that there was not enough space to carve all the names on the plaques and memorial stones being erected across the counry.

With the war finally over, Bertie was sent to train to fly – a rather symbolic gesture. As he took his flight exam in July 1919, the Allies were debating the terms of the new Treaty of Versailles, signed exactly five years after the assassination of

Archduke Franz Ferdinand. The huge Empires of Germany, Russia, Austro-Hungary and the Ottomans were replaced by a host of much smaller states, their boundaries created according to notions of self-determination and guaranteed by the formation of the League of Nations. Germany, the old friend of the Hanoverian kings and their hunting ground for properly Protestant spouses, was to be much reduced: the country lost territory, the army was limited to 10,000 and they were set reparations of billions of pounds (the final payment was made in 2010). The King's 'better day' harked back to an old world, when Germany was a mass of princely states and Britain had the power. The new Germany was much reduced, but not vanquished.

After spending the war in the sickroom, Bertie was enjoying his new life in 1919. As well as learning to fly, he busied himself with social visits and then began a short spell of education at Trinity College, Cambridge. The rest of Britain and Europe were suffering. Three-quarters of a million Britons had been killed and millions more were dead across Europe, or had been so severely wounded that normal life was impossible. Over nine million soldiers died, eight million were declared missing and more than twenty million were wounded. Many of those who survived fell prey to influenza, which spread its merciless way across Europe. Economies had entirely collapsed. 'We are at the low season of our fortunes,' wrote John Maynard Keynes. The population of young men in Britain had been so decimated that even Cambridge was haunted with absence.

Many of Bertie's compatriots at Osborne were dead and, like those who had survived, he threw himself into entertaining amusements. In 1919, he and David became Freemasons in two different lodges, following a family tradition; Edward

VII had been a devoted member before his accession. Bertie declared the attraction lay in the charity work, but he was also fascinated by the secrecy and the complicated rituals of dress and performance. For a man who had been excluded from much of the action, the clandestine world of Masonry was very appealing.

Bertie, like his father and grandfather, was obsessive about dress. Edward VII had famously upbraided his Prime Minister, the Marquess of Salisbury, for appearing untidy at a drawing room at Buckingham Palace. 'Europe in a turmoil,' he cried, 'twenty ambassadors and ministers looking on – what will they think – what *can* they think of a premier who can't put on his clothes.' Britain's royal men have been traditionally much more interested in dress than the women and the young Prince could become quite fanatical about the colour of a button or the positioning of a collar. The Masonic attention to dress only added to its interest.

Few could dress with enough attention to please Bertie. One of the few was David, in his sharp suits and plus-fours. The Prince of Wales could do no wrong in the eyes of his brother. Bertie looked up to him with an intense reverence and whatever time they had together could never be enough. 'There is a dreadful blank in my life directly you leave on one of your tours,' Bertie said mournfully to David.

When David went away, Bertie pined for him and carried out the duties of a prince at home. The royal family aimed to be shown as engaging with the widespread unemployment and unrest caused by the depression, and Bertie was appointed President of the Industrial Welfare Association, which aimed to improve the lot of workers through canteens, social programmes and safety improvements. Bertie was in his element meeting workers and shaking hands, but the notion that the economy could be assisted by such measures seems wildly naive. By early 1921 unemployment had doubled. When the government proposed nationalisation of the mines, the miners announced they would strike, and transport and railway workers declared they would join the action. The government instituted plans for distributing food, but the strike was called off on 15 April. In such dramatic times, it was thought, Bertie's role should be stepped up. He instituted a series of summer camps, in which young boys from public schools and factories would come together for a week of games and activities. It was a fun experience for a few lucky boys, but had little impact on the wider problems of unrest and inequality.

At the same July 1917 meeting of the Privy Council in which George V had decreed that the family's name would be Windsor, the King said he had decided that his children should be allowed to take British spouses. The Princes and Princesses were not obliged, as their parents had been, to marry members of the Protestant royal families of Europe. The war had changed even the outlook of the King. Previously, a bride to the second son would be expected to be of royal blood. Not only did such a bride ensure properly royal heirs, but it was thought that only those brought up in the confines of overseas royalty could comprehend the duties and constrictions of life at a palace. Princess Louise, daughter of Queen Victoria, had pleased her subjects by marrying the Marquess of Lorne, though the marriage had been a failure. But the King's act was a necessity: no British royal could take a German bride, now they were the great enemy, and there were few other Protestant royals still in existence.

Bertie, thus, could look anywhere for a wife. In this he followed, as he often did, his beloved elder brother. The

Prince of Wales was his model in everything and David loved attached married women. He was in love with the petite, vivacious Freda Dudley Ward, the daughter of a Nottingham lace manufacturer, a splendid golf and tennis player, and unhappily married to an MP sixteen years her senior. Not long after the war Albert met and became infatuated with Sheila, Lady Loughborough, who was also married. George V was deeply concerned at the friendships of both his sons. He offered to create Bertie Duke of York in June 1920 and a condition was that he gave up Lady Loughborough. Bertie agreed, delighted by the dukedom and the independent household it brought – but pining for Sheila.

In the aftermath of the war the social life based at the palace had begun once more, with Royal Ascot, levées and balls. Still, Bertie complained that it was all too dreary and, as he told Lady Airlie, his mother's lady-in-waiting, 'no new blood ever introduced'. He would have to find the 'new blood' for himself.

In summer 1920 the Duke met the nineteen-year-old Lady Elizabeth Bowes-Lyon at a ball. Small, with dark hair and bright blue eyes, she had entranced dozens of men already with her innocent vivacity and enthusiasm for life – particularly cocktails, sweet foods and hats. Unlike Bertie, Lady Elizabeth, the ninth child of the Earl and Countess of Strathmore, was bubbling with fun and vitality, a noted mimic and brimming with the confident knowledge that she had been a much loved child. Her father had inherited his title when she was just four, along with the great Glamis Castle, and Elizabeth lived a highly privileged life between the castle and her family's other properties – Streatlam Castle in County Durham, a spacious town house in St James's Square and her principal home, St Paul's Walden Bury in

Hertfordshire, a Georgian red-brick house. 'I have nothing but wonderfully happy memories of childhood days at home,' she would say. Lord Strathmore was a kindly man, a good landlord and all was right in the world if he lunched on plum pudding, and Lady Strathmore was easygoing and loving with her children. Glamis was a gigantic and atmospheric house, with ghosts round every corner. 'No electric light here,' one governess reported to her mother, 'all nooks & corners & stairs & down long passages.' On one occasion a visitor saw water pouring down a wall in St Paul's Walden Bury. 'Oh dear, we'll have to move the sofa again,' sighed Lady Strathmore.

Her mother's favourite, Elizabeth spent her days in outdoor sports and games with her host of brothers, dressing up in costumes at the castles and dancing. She was rather too fond of the tea table and had a terrible sweet tooth – her brothers filled in her diary to tease her with long details about 'Cream, honey, jam, buns, & tea. Eat too much'. There was little time for lessons around all the fun, but the Earl and Countess were unconcerned, believing it more important for girls to develop excellent manners and confident sociability than knowledge of history or geography. 'I'm afraid I'm uneducated on the whole,' Elizabeth confessed.

The Great War had broken out on Elizabeth's fourteenth birthday and it forced her to become an adult. Glamis, which had once rung with the shouts of her brothers racing around the grounds, became a convalescent hospital for soldiers. Too young at fifteen to train as a nurse like her sister Rose, Elizabeth busied herself running errands around the hospital and walked to the village shop to buy the men cigarettes. Four of her brothers went to fight. Fergus was killed at the battle of Loos. Michael was imprisoned in a German prisoner-of-war camp for officers and did not return until early 1919.

In the aftermath of the war there were two million surplus women, painfully denied the future of marriage for which they had been intended. Most girls of Lady Elizabeth's age were desperately seeking husbands. She, pretty, rich, well-connected, was spared such concerns. 'I danced with Prince Albert, who I hadn't known before, he is quite a nice youth,' Lady Elizabeth wrote in 1920. She could afford to be cool because she was surrounded by admirers. 'I fell *madly* in love,' recalled one young man. 'They all did.' Bertie was captivated by Lady Elizabeth. She had the confidence and vivacity he lacked, and he was entranced by her carefree and playful nature. Most of all, unlike Sheila, she was just the type of girl to please his parents.

Elizabeth grew weary of the second-in-line to the throne. 'Prince Albert is coming to stay here on Saturday. Ghastly!' she wrote to a friend. Bertie was entranced by the hearty informality of a Glamis weekend. The jokes and games, warm-hearted family teasing and eager spontaneity were very unlike the chilly dignity that prevailed at the palace. Elizabeth's utter lack of enthusiasm only fired his ardent desire to win her.

George V was pleased by the cheery Scottish aristocrat. 'You'll be a lucky fellow if she accepts you,' he said to his son. Elizabeth was just the type of traditional girl he liked. 'The things that my father found wrong with the "Brave New World" would have made a long list,' the Prince of Wales later remarked. 'He disapproved of Soviet Russia, painted fingernails, women who smoked in public, cocktails, frivolous hats, American jazz and the growing habit of going away for weekends.' Although fond of a cocktail or two,

Lady Elizabeth was very unlike the modern 'flapper' girls with shingled hair and short skirts that the poor King found so terrifying.

Emboldened by his family's affection for her, Bertie proposed in early 1921 – and was turned down. 'We can be good friends, can't we?' she wrote anxiously to him. 'Please do look on me as one.' Elizabeth was all too aware of the burden of royalty and unsure that she wished to spend her life in the public eye. She was also fond of a family friend, James Stuart, son of Lord Moray, who had become equerry to Bertie in 1920. The Strathmores themselves were not ecstatic at the prospect of a marriage. Lord Strathmore had always been adamant that none of his children should be a courtier and the prospect of being drawn into royal circles held no particular appeal. Lady Strathmore once remarked that 'some people have to be fed royalty like sealions fish'. At times, the Strathmores were even grander than the royals, and, although they liked Bertie, they thought he was weak. 'He is a man who will be made or marred by his wife,' Lady Strathmore wrote of him. Elizabeth had the strength to take him in hand but she had no desire to do so.

Bertie refused to be dissuaded and he roped in his family to his cause. When Princess Mary became engaged to Viscount Lascelles in 1921, she invited Lady Elizabeth to be her bridesmaid as a favour to her brother. Lady Elizabeth took her duties seriously, writing to Bertie about how difficult it was to walk up the aisle in Westminster Abbey in high heels. Weddings showed royalty at their best and Bertie hoped Lady Elizabeth might be dazzled by the glamour, rather than weary under the heavy lace of her gown. In the spring of 1922 he proposed again. She refused. The relationship was at an end.

Finally, in early 1923, Bertie rekindled the friendship and made one last stab at his ambition. 'This is the last time I'm going to propose to her,' he told the Duchess of Devonshire. By happy coincidence, James Stuart had left his service as an equerry for America. The Duke tried another proposal and, to his great delight, Lady Elizabeth accepted. Bertie was elated. He dispatched an immediate telegram to his parents, declaring the engagement 'my dream which has at last been realised'. The King decreed that the 'arrangements must be of as simple a character as possible', although the planned venue of Westminster Abbey was hardly an inexpensive location. Still, the wedding of Bertie was seen by the nation as a rehearsal for the most important ceremony of all – the marriage of the Prince of Wales to his future queen.

The news was announced and Lady Elizabeth was besieged. 'Telegrams poured in all day, letters & reporters tumbling over each other.' It was all rather exhausting. 'I am so tired already – I think I shall probably die long before I get married.'

The title of the future Duchess of York caused some uncertainty – and was, as the Press Association reported, 'a matter for the King's decision. Recent times supply no precedent.' The problem was that most royal wives had already been princesses by birth when they married. Would Elizabeth be a princess after her wedding? The Home Office suggested that she definitely would, which was fortunate. Mrs Windsor hardly had much cachet.

Lady Elizabeth and her future husband travelled to visit the McVitie & Price factory in Edinburgh, which would supply the giant, nine-foot, 800 lb wedding cake. Elizabeth was fitted for her simple, rather unflattering wedding dress of ivory chiffon moiré. The British Broadcasting Company, only a year old, asked if they might transmit the service on the radio but the Chapter of Westminster decided against it. It could simply not be guaranteed that the audience would listen with due respect and some of them might even do so 'sitting in public houses with their hats on'.

On Thursday 26 April Lady Elizabeth woke at her family home in 17 Bruton Street to the shouts of well-wishers outside and terrible rain. After travelling to the Abbey, the bride paused on her way towards the altar to lay her bouquet on to the grave of the Unknown Warrior – a gesture that has been repeated by every royal bride since. As *The Lady* noted, at the altar the clouds cleared, the sun broke out and 'it was wonderful and dramatic and unforgettable'. The new Duchess of York was quite satisfied. 'Did not feel very nervous,' she wrote in her diary that evening. 'Bertie smiled at me when I got up to him – & it all went off very well.' She was, she concluded, 'very tired and happy'.

'I do wish he was not Royalty,' wrote Lady Strathmore rather sadly. The young couple set off on a five-week honeymoon, first to Polesdon Lacey in Surrey, then to Glamis Castle. Elizabeth fell ill. 'So unromantic to catch whooping cough on your honeymoon,' Bertie wrote to Queen Mary. He was so in love with his new wife that he could not bear anything that separated him from her, even whooping cough.

On their return from honeymoon the young couple occupied White Lodge in Richmond Park, the house chosen for them by the King and Queen. They found it uncomfortable, dilapidated, and too far from London, and spent much of their time at the houses of friends or 17 Bruton Street, where the Duchess had stayed the night before her wedding. It was a pleasant way to pass the early years of their marriage.

'What a fate for a daughter of Glamis,' sighed the chaplain

of the castle chapel to the Archbishop of Canterbury some years later. But against the expectations of many, the marriage was very contented. Elizabeth's freshness and refusal to be daunted by royalty stood her well in strait-laced regal circles. The King, in particular, was devotedly fond of his daughter-in-law. Usually an obsessive stickler for punctuality, he was gentle with her. 'You are not late, my dear,' he would say to her, much to the amazement of his children. 'We must have sat down two minutes early.' The couple's only remaining desire was for a child. In August 1925, finally, the doctors confirmed that Elizabeth was pregnant.

# 2
# 'Such a nice name'

*The Duke and Duchess of York with Princess Elizabeth, 1927*

THE DUCHESS HAD SUCH bad morning sickness that she declared she had even stopped drinking wine, which, for her, was something of a deprivation. As the pregnancy advanced, the doctors became concerned that the baby was too large for her pelvis and the decision was taken that a 'certain line of treatment' or a Caesarean section might be necessary. Such an operation in those days was dangerous and thought to damage the mother's future chances of having children. But the Duchess was not the Princess of Wales and her children were not the heirs to the throne, so the procedure was agreed on without too much discussion. As royals did not attend hospitals, an operating theatre was set up in Bruton Street. The labour did not proceed quickly, so the operation was performed and the baby born at 2.40 a.m. on 21 April 1926, with the Home Secretary waiting in the next room to assent to the legitimacy of the child.

Royals are only private in the womb, as the Princess's governess later pointed out. Crowds soon took up position in Bruton Street, hoping to see the baby Princess – and the King and Queen who arrived to see their first female grandchild. 'Such a relief and joy,' wrote Queen Mary in her journal. Just a month before her birth the first transatlantic phone call had been put through from London to New

York. Elizabeth was the first royal child to be born into the age of communications.

The fires at 17 Bruton Street roared to welcome the new baby – but coal was an ever more expensive commodity. Britain's coal industry was not as powerful as it had been. Coal seams were increasingly depleted, and in the Great War the country had exported less coal and other countries had grown in power as exporters. The 1925 Dawes plan allowed Germany to export coal free to France and Italy. Still worse, Winston Churchill, as Chancellor of the Exchequer, had made the disastrous decision to pin the pound to the gold standard in 1925, at the pre-war exchange rate with the dollar. The currency was so strong that demand for British coal fell.

In an attempt to improve their profits, mine owners lowered wages and increased working hours. The Miners' Union threatened action and, after a governmental Royal Commission sided with the mine owners, the TUC called a general strike for 3 May 1926. Other key workers would strike, including railwaymen, dockers, printers and ironworkers. Less than a fortnight after Elizabeth's birth the General Strike began, with bluster, propaganda and hopes for the future. Stanley Baldwin described it as 'the road to anarchy'. The terrified upper and middle classes feared the beginning of all-out class revolution. The young Elizabeth Alexandra Mary might soon be a commoner, apprenticed to a carpenter as children of French aristocrats had been after 1789.

The government played hard: replacing key workers with volunteers and calling forth the middle classes to transport food between cities. After five days had passed, some of the less enthusiastic strikers began to talk of returning to work. Finally, on 12 May, the TUC called off the strike. Those miners who could return to work found much crueller conditions. 'Our old country can well be proud of itself,' pondered the King, 'not a shot has been fired and no one killed. It shows what a wonderful people we are.' In 1927 the severe Trades Union Act made another General Strike impossible by outlawing sympathetic strikes and strikes intended to coerce the government.

Two weeks after the end of the General Strike Princess Elizabeth was christened in the chapel of Buckingham Palace by the Archbishop of York with water from the River Jordan. She wore the robe of white satin and lace in which every royal child had been christened since Queen Victoria had commissioned it for her eldest child, Princess Vicky, in 1841. Elizabeth had illustrious godparents: the King and Queen; her aunt, the Princess Royal; the Duke of Connaught, last surviving child of Queen Victoria; her maternal aunt, Lady Elphinstone; and her grandmother, Lady Strathmore. The little girl wept loudly, unawed by the grandeur of her surroundings. The party returned for a christening tea at 17 Bruton Street and a cake bearing a single candle.

Elizabeth was born into a world of high privilege but, even though she was much cherished, she was not equal to her cousins, George and Gerald, the sons of the Princess Royal. Women had gained the vote in 1918, but only those aged thirty and above. The fact that women were so dominant in post-war society, in numbers alone, and they had gained more rights: they were permitted to enter the legal profession and accountancy in 1920, the same year that Oxford consented to women taking full degrees; grounds for divorce had only been made the same for women and men in 1923, and finally in 1929 the Privy Council decided that women could become persons in their own right (after an appeal by a group of Canadian women who noted that women could not join the Canadian senate because they were not decreed 'persons'). Life was comfortable, if one was married to a kindly, wealthy, slightly weak husband like Bertie, but for every woman as content as Elizabeth Bowes-Lyon, there were thousands angry at how they were still, essentially, subsumed into the identity of their husbands.

Baby Elizabeth was quickly, as one newspaper dubbed her, 'the World's Best Known Baby'. Her arrival thrust the issue of class war from the newspaper pages. Frustratingly for the strikers, instead of debate about class inequality, the reporters engaged in fervid discussion about how best to raise a modern princess. There was much approval of the news that the Princess's clothes had been stitched personally by Queen Mary, Lady Strathmore and the Duchess, and the most patriotic commentators declared that poor gentlewomen had profited 'by the Duchess's order for fine lawn and muslin frocks, little bonnets and jackets'. The notion that the rich created industry for the poor prevailed.

Almost immediately after her birth, Elizabeth was committed to the care of her nanny. Clara Knight, or 'Allah' (pronounced 'Ah-la'), had been born near St Paul's Walden Bury and was taken on in 1900 to look after the month-old Elizabeth Bowes-Lyon. The middle-aged, respectable spinster daughter of a tenant farmer, dark-haired, strong-featured Allah was an energetic nanny of the oldest breed: a lifelong spinster utterly devoted to her charge. She was the type of nanny sent across the Empire, to work for foreign royalty, whose very presence would ensure order, discipline and that the nursery tea was never late. Baby was to be petted and disciplined, and nanny's spare time was to be spent knitting or on the crossword before bed.

Miss Knight kept the Princess to an exacting timetable of feeding and sleeping. Twice a day, Elizabeth was taken in her shiny perambulator for an airing, and before bed she visited her parents for an hour or so. Otherwise the little girl remained in her spotless nursery and played, very strictly, with one toy at a time. Unlike today's babies, the young Elizabeth II would never have played with a crackling piece of shiny paper, with bubbles floating over her head to an accompaniment of nursery rhymes. Custard play, jelly play, singing songs or putting bare feet on pine cones would have been impossible. The aim was to foster a sense of duty and self-restraint rather than individual creativity or a competitive instinct. Elizabeth thrived under Allah's regulated, unimaginative regime.

A quiet, observant baby, Elizabeth became a particular darling of the Queen. The King was also smitten. Stern and dismissive of his own children, and impatient with his two grandsons by the Princess Royal, he played with baby Elizabeth for hours, allowing her to pull his beard and call him 'Big Ears'. One visitor to Sandringham recalled that the Princess, then twenty-one months, perched on a small chair next to the King and entertained the whole party.

> The King gave her biscuits to eat and to feed his little dog with, the King chortling with little jokes with her – she just struggling with a few words, 'Grandpa' and 'Granny' and to everyone's amusement has just achieved addressing the very grand-looking Countess of Airlie as 'Airlie'.

Unbowed by the burden of being judged as a future queen, she could be everybody's favourite. The child resembled her mother in appearance, although she did not share her habit of unpunctuality, penchant for spending and addiction to sugary treats. For the King and Queen, the infant Elizabeth was Bertie's great success.

'I felt very much leaving on Thursday,' wrote the Duchess of York, 'and the baby was so sweet playing with the buttons on Bertie's uniform it quite broke me up.' Elizabeth was nine months old when her parents embarked on a six-month tour of Australia and New Zealand. The Duke was due to open the Commonwealth Parliament in Canberra. No suggestion was made that 'the baby' should go too. Keeping a child to her routine was the way to ensure that she grew up happy and well-balanced; not touting her about on tours. Moreover, even if taking a royal baby were customary, her father would not have wished for her there. He wanted his wife's attention to himself, for the tour loomed up ahead of him in dreadful Technicolor, with its meetings with various dignitaries and endless speeches. In November 1926, suffering intensely with his stammer, he had paid a rather desperate visit to an Australian speech therapist, Lionel Logue, a calm and talented man who had previously assisted soldiers struggling to speak after the Great War. Logue's sensible programme of breathing and exercises, along with his gentle encouragement, proved a success. Bertie prepared for the tour feeling hopeful. 'Logue's teaching has really done wonders for me as I now know how to prevent & get over any difficulty,' he wrote to his father.

The Yorks departed in early January 1927 and arrived nearly seven weeks later to tumultuous welcomes. As the Prince of Wales had declared, 'Princing' was much easier abroad. The Duchess was delighted by the reception of the New Zealanders in particular, and very pleased when she heard that teachers had to take 'stupendous' oaths of loyalty to the Crown before they were allowed to the classroom. 'Considering that the Crown keeps the Empire together, I think it is a pity they are not more particular about teachers at home.'

Everyone they met, it seemed, had a present for the infant Elizabeth, or 'Princess Betty' as they often called her. 'I am four and a half years old and I should like a photograph of Princess Betty' was a typical letter. The Melbourne Arts and Crafts Society gave a special Australian Noah's Ark, with wallabies and kangaroos, and the Brownies of Auckland clubbed together to offer a large doll. The children of New South Wales sent a gold and silver tea set.

In the spring the Princess and Clara Knight went to stay with the King and Queen at Windsor. The doting grandparents were quite delighted by Lilibet. Every afternoon Clara would bring her to the reception rooms and the Queen would cry, 'Here comes the bambino!' The King and Queen sent regular reports to the Yorks. 'She has 4 teeth now which is quite good at eleven months, she is very happy and drives in a carriage every afternoon,' the King told the Duchess. 'I miss her quite terribly,' the Duchess wrote. Queen Mary assured her that the little Princess was content and had been delighted with 'the parrot Charlotte this morning at breakfast & watched the bird eating pips with an air of absorption'. Clara and the Princess then went to St Paul's Walden Bury – where the little girl learned to utter 'Mummy', even though there was no Mummy there.

The Yorks returned in triumph, loaded with two tons of toys for their daughter. Then, in the Grand Hall in Buckingham Palace, in the presence of both sets of grandparents and the household staff, they met their little girl again. Elizabeth was no longer a baby but a pretty child, with

43

blonde curls, blue eyes and a pink-and-white complexion. The Duchess was enchanted by her daughter, kissing her repeatedly and crying, 'Oh, you little darling!'

'I trust yr sweet little baby begins to know her parents once more & likes them,' the King wrote. The Yorks spent the summer in Scotland, where Elizabeth took her first steps. On their return they took a new house, 145 Piccadilly, a grand, grey-stone, five-storey Georgian town house near Hyde Park with twenty-five bedrooms. As an advertisement of the time solemnly noted, there was a 'principal staircase hall, a secondary staircase with electric passenger lift, a drawing room, dining room, ballroom, study, library'. The house had languished unoccupied for two years, perhaps because the rent was too high for anyone but royalty in post-war England. Certainly, the Yorks needed an extensive staff: a butler, an under-butler, a telephonist, two footmen, a valet, a dresser, a cook, two kitchen maids, a nightwatchman and an RAF orderly. Their neighbours were London's richest: landowners, aristocrats and very successful businessmen. The Yorks quickly put their mark on the house, the Duchess swathing the rooms with her favoured colours of misty blue, fawn and pink. Her bedroom was a sugary concoction of pale-blue carpets and covers, and white wardrobes that lit up inside when opened. The Duke, by contrast, kept a room sparsely furnished with one bookshelf and a dressing table, so extraordinarily neat that it looked like a room on a ship. For many Britons 145 Piccadilly would have been practically a palace – but the Yorks felt they were living in a very homely, restrained fashion.

Elizabeth and Clara Knight occupied the top floor, along with the new nursery maid, Margaret Macdonald or 'Bobo', the twenty-two-year-old daughter of a railway worker from

Inverness. Elizabeth was a disciplined, tidy child. Indeed, Lady Airlie gave her a dustpan and brush for Christmas. Everyone's pet, she was encouraged to be much more expressive than her father had been. At a Christmas party at Sandringham for the estate workers she cheerfully threw crackers at the guests, much to the amusement of the royal family. Since the Duchess still was not pregnant, Elizabeth was the focus of everyone's attentions, not yet unseated by a younger brother.

The King was so tickled by the child's attempt to pronounce 'Elizabeth', managing only 'Lilibet', that he decided it should be her name within the family. The Princess called him 'Grandpa England', which was reported with much amusement in the newspapers. He liked her to sit by him at family meals and fostered in her a lifelong love of horses, taking her to see his best animals on Sunday afternoons at Sandringham and even playing horsey with her. The Archbishop of Canterbury was somewhat surprised on one occasion to see the king pretending to be a horse, 'shuffling on hands and knees along the floor, while the little Princess led him by the beard'. For her fourth birthday the King gave the Princess her first pony, a Shetland named Peggy.

The Princess was one of the few people in the country unafraid of the King. Indeed, she once ordered him after a disagreement to 'come back and shut the door'. But although not intimidated by the man, she was always in awe of his office. Even when she was barely walking, she was able to curtsey to him, and after wishing him goodnight she would toddle backwards out of the room. Even a child could not turn her back on George V.

At the end of 1928 the King fell seriously ill with a bronchial infection and became so frail that his life was in danger.

Churches across Britain were kept open all night long so people could pray for his health. In early 1929 a final last-ditch operation improved the King's health and he travelled to the seaside at Bognor to recuperate. In the middle of March the two-year-old Princess Elizabeth came down to spend the mornings with him. 'She is looking forward wildly to digging in the sand, and talks knowingly of pails and spades,' the Duchess wrote. The Princess had never seen the sea before and she became an enthusiast for sandcastles, making a grand tower with the gardener and sandpies with the stately Queen Mary. According to the *Sunday Dispatch*, the child also entertained the King with 'the most amusing and original comments on people and events'.

The Prince of Wales was seemingly the only person in the country unmoved by the King's fragile health. Holidaying in Kenya when he received the news in 1928, he had been very unwilling to cut short his stay. 'I don't believe a word of it,' he said to Sir Alan 'Tommy' Lascelles, the courtier accompanying him. 'It's just some election dodge of old Baldwin's.' Lascelles, ever calm, lost patience.

> 'Sir,' I said, 'the King of England is dying; and if that means nothing to you, it means a great deal to us.' He looked at me, went out without a word, and spent the remainder of the evening in the successful seduction of a Mrs Barnes, wife of the local Commissioner. He told me so himself next morning.

When the Prince did return, he was shocked by the change in George V. 'You know I have never got on with my father,' he told a friend of Queen Mary, 'but when, on getting back, I found him a little, shrunken old man with a white beard, the shock was so great that I cried.' Still, however, he could not see the need to settle to the lifestyle expected of a king and continued with his house parties and mistresses. The Prince was not as confident as he appeared: without inner resources, he needed constant adulation to stave off low spirits. 'I feel quite ready to commit suicide and would if I didn't think it unfair to Papa,' he had written a few years earlier.

The King's relationship with his eldest son was not easy. He was growing increasingly impatient with David's playboy lifestyle and refusal to marry. Moreover, the King was very envious of his son's popularity with the people – which seemed to come so easily. According to one observer, Lady Elcho, he was 'very jealous of the Prince' and was constantly criticising his eldest son. Like most kings, he could hardly bear the thought of his successor being more loved than he had been without expounding the same effort.

The King's fragile health concentrated attention on the succession. The Duke of York was most amused, as he told his brother, that there had been rumours declaring 'in the event of anything happening to Papa I am going to bag the throne in your absence!!! Just like the Middle Ages!' It was all a joke: no one expected that the Prince would not finally find a bride and produce an heir. In the meantime the Court and the public devoted themselves to Princess Elizabeth. The press peered through the railings at 145 Piccadilly, trying to catch a glimpse of the Princess, and her daily routine was the subject of constant speculation.

The Duke and Duchess often found themselves second best. The Palace had agreed that the Princess should not participate in public ceremonies, but the crowds were still most disappointed if the Yorks arrived without their daughter. 'The only thing I regret is that we have not got Lilibet here,' wrote the Duchess to Queen Mary from Edinburgh in 1929. The Duke had been appointed Lord High Commissioner to the General Assembly of Scotland. The people only wanted the Princess. 'It almost frightens me that the people should love her so much. I suppose that it is a good thing and hope she will be worthy of it, poor little darling!'

Elizabeth wrote her mother a letter, perhaps with some assistance from Miss Knight. 'Darling Mummy. Do come here and see the soldiers and the band I am very well and very busy. Love from Lilibet XXOO.'

# 3
# 'All the equipment a lady needs'

*Elizabeth and Margaret with their governess, Crawfie, in the 1930s*

'I ALWAYS FEEL AS if I am working, not for the King of England, but for the son of the latest American millionaire,' declared Alan Lascelles. By the late 1920s the Prince of Wales was the glittering peak of London society. He danced every night at the Embassy Club in Mayfair and frequented house parties across the country. David flew across the Channel in his private plane piloted by his own pilot, took yachts on the Riviera and was a favourite in the nightclubs of the South of France. 'It's hard to keep out of casinos,' he sighed to a lover. Few others outside his set had money to burn. After the stock market crash in America, a result of the house price bubble, American banks called in their loans from Europe and businesses collapsed across the world.

'I don't think there would be so much discontent if people were only housed properly,' wrote the Queen. Housing everyone properly was not easy in a country suffering, as stock markets and banks collapsed across the world. The industrial north of Britain was particularly badly hit as the industries of mining, shipbuilding and steelworking faltered. 'One really does have to see the conditions of housing, squalor and distress which exist to have any idea of what they have been "sticking",' wrote the Prince of Wales to the government, after a visit to Durham and Northumberland. By the end of

1930 twenty per cent of those defined as able to work were unemployed.

'He is clearly asking himself what the future has in store for the royal family and on the whole he is fairly confident,' wrote the Lord Privy Seal of George V just after the war. 'Why should our people have a revolution? We are the victors.' But victory had soured into economic failure and the people who had cheered in the streets were now hungry and furious with their government. After a split in Cabinet over whether to introduce tariffs or cut unemployment benefit, Ramsay MacDonald's government resigned on 24 August 1931. Faced with the imminent failure of the financial system and government, the leaders of the Conservative and Liberal Parties joined with MacDonald to create a new National Government. They took the drastic measure of removing the pound from the gold standard and the value of the pound dropped by a quarter overnight. It was the beginning of a recovery – but it did not seem so at the time. The Hunger Marches began across Britain as furious people protested their misery. In late 1932, 3,000 people left Glasgow, progressed through Britain and were met by 100,000 supporters in Hyde Park, and nearly 70,000 policemen.

The King decided the royal family had to participate in the suffering of the nation. He cut the Civil List, or moneys taken from the state to support the royal family, by £50,000. The Prince of Wales was telephoned while at a nightclub in Bayonne and told he would lose £10,000 a year – much to his despair. The Duke of York had to give up hunting and sell his six horses. 'The parting with them will be terrible,' he mourned. His wife suggested they adopt a regime of less food and 'weaker cocktails'.

The Duchess thought that the answer to the overall economic problems was to force women to give their jobs to men. Women, she thought, could be happily idle and live on buns all day, whereas men needed to work and had a basic requirement for meat. Such a notion hardly reflected the reality of the royal family, in which Queen Mary was never 'idle' while the Prince of Wales seldom rose before eleven. It was difficult for the Yorks to comprehend the poverty endured by many in Britain. Even though the Duke and Duchess saw themselves as living in straitened, even ordinary, circumstances, they lived in a world largely untroubled by money: clothes, staff, food and animals simply appeared. Like the rest of the royals, they often hardly seemed to comprehend that others did not live with similar ease.

The Yorks were, however, highly symbolic of a new popular domesticity. If the Prince of Wales was the man of the carefree 1920s, the post-war flush of gaiety, the Yorks and their Princess Elizabeth suited the demands of a new, less confident nation. The economy tends to be driven forward by the expenses of marriage, setting up home and childbearing – no expenditure of a single person can rival it, however excessive (indeed, theories of the Great Depression link the fall in consumer demand with a decline of marriage in the 1920s). Divorce rates peaked in 1928, then tumbled by nearly half by 1933. The Yorks, and the encouragement of home life that they stood for, played an important propaganda part.

The King rewarded Bertie for his act of giving up his horses with the present of Royal Lodge in Windsor Great Park. 'I think it will suit us admirably,' said Bertie. Set in ninety acres of Windsor parkland, Royal Lodge was a dilapidated retreat, set around a forty-eight-foot-long Grand

Saloon. George IV had commissioned John Nash and later Thomas Wyatville to rebuild the existing building, creating a handsome large cottage with thatched roofs, a conservatory and verandas. William IV demolished most of it and the house was then used for accommodating members of the royal household until George V decided to give it to his son. The Grand Saloon had been divided into five makeshift rooms and most of the rest was unsuitable for living. The Yorks restored the Grand Saloon, painted it green and hung a portrait of George IV, and designed a large family wing for themselves with ground-floor principal bedrooms. Modern kitchens and bathrooms were installed, the front was washed over in the Duchess's favourite rose pink and the result was a two-storey mansion that more than compensated the Duke for the sale of his horses.

The Lodge was convenient for the King and Queen, and also the Prince of Wales. In the previous year David had taken Fort Belvedere, on the edge of the park, an eighteenth-century folly complete with turrets, battlements, cannon and cannonballs. The King was baffled by his son's interest in 'that queer old place', but David, who flew the flag of the Duchy of Cornwall from the tower, was captivated by a child's fort for a grown-up man. The Prince and his mistress, Freda Dudley Ward, subjected the fort to a comprehensive redecoration and installed a swimming pool. He promptly set its eccentric castellated turrets echoing to the sounds of glamorous swimming parties with married women. The Yorks attended, but without the Princess. A photograph of a pool party remains in which the Prince and his friends are all wearing bathing suits, while the Duchess of York is fully dressed, complete with hat. The pool parties were a great contrast with the wholesome family life of the Yorks.

Elizabeth felt very at home in the Park and her big pink house. As the children of Queen Victoria had been, she was given her own plot of land, but she preferred helping her father to weed and plant his garden. Other children of the time were pristine in white dresses and gloves, but Lilibet was never happier than when covered in mud, preferably with an animal to hand.

The Duchess finally fell pregnant at the end of 1929. The Yorks, assuming that it was their last chance to have a child, were hoping for a boy. In the summer the heavily pregnant Duchess travelled up to Glamis Castle with the Duke and Elizabeth and on 5 August John R. Clynes, the new Home Secretary, went to stay at nearby Airlie Castle to be present to confirm the child's legitimacy. He had some time to wait and amused himself admiring the countryside. 'I feel sorry for Mr Clynes being here so long,' remarked the Duke, wishing he would leave. Finally, on 21 August, Mr Clynes was called to the castle. As storm clouds rolled overhead and thunder began to break, villagers gathered around the North Gate. The Duchess's labour was long and her obstetricians considered another operation, but the baby was finally born at 9.22 p.m. without the need for intervention, weighing a healthy 6lb 11oz, but a girl. The people were elated at the news of a new baby despite her sex. Flares lit up the sky and church bells rang for the first time since the Great War, and over the course of the night 4,000 people packed into the village square. The family's nurse, Mrs Beevers, trotted off with the baby to her cot, but found she had a battle to prevent her from sucking her thumb. Elizabeth, wrote a relative of the Bowes-Lyons, was 'very excited & thought first of all that it was a wonderful Dolly & then discovered that it was alive'.

'I have got a new baby sister,' the four-year-old Lilibet proudly told one of her father's tenants. 'She is so lovely, and I am very, very happy to have her.' Three days after his daughter's birth the Duke retired to Balmoral, leaving his wife and daughters at Glamis. He returned six days later with his parents. 'The baby is a darling,' recorded the Queen. Plump-cheeked and cheerful, the new child was charming, but lacking a name. The Duke and Duchess had hoped for the name of Ann, but the King refused and the little girl was named Margaret, after the eleventh-century Margaret of Scotland. She was christened Margaret Rose in October and her mother was quite satisfied. 'Daughter no. 2 is really very nice, and I am glad to say that she has got large blue eyes and a will of iron, which is all the equipment a lady needs!'

The family returned to 145 Piccadilly and Margaret settled into the pastel nursery, the new pet of Clara Knight, while Bobo Macdonald took care of Elizabeth. Baby Margaret did indeed have a will of iron and she was determined on her own way, just as she had been insistent on sucking her thumb in the hours after her birth. In the classic mould of younger and older siblings, Elizabeth was conscientious, reserved, eager to please and dutiful, while Margaret was capricious, spontaneous and playful.

'She was warm and demonstrative, made to be cuddled and played with,' wrote her governess. As she grew up, Margaret, with her plump cheeks and springing curls, was an imaginative and excitable child who was spiritedly naughty and disobedient. 'Of the two children, Lilibet had the more temper, but it was under control,' recalled the governess. 'Margaret was often naughty but she had a gay, bouncing way with her which was hard to deal with. She would often defy me with a sidelong look.' Most amusingly, Margaret later invented a 'Cousin Halifax', an imaginary friend who was to blame for any naughtiness. 'I was busy with Cousin Halifax,' when she was chastised for being late, and, 'It wasn't me, it was Cousin Halifax,' when told off for spilling milk or untidiness.

Until Margaret's birth, Elizabeth had been sliding into being something of a dull stick – dry and too well-behaved. Margaret brought out her spirit. 'Stop her, Mummy. Oh please stop her!' Elizabeth would cry, as her sister teased her mercilessly. Margaret also became a vital mental prop for the Princess. Throughout their childhood, every time Elizabeth was suffering from fear or trepidation, she would make a point of saying that the family must take care of Margaret. Her sister might fidget at the Coronation service, she thought, or be afraid of bombs during the Blitz. Expressing concern for Margaret was a way of showing her feelings without breaking her reserve. Elizabeth's protectiveness was sometimes excessive: when she was five and Margaret eighteen months the chaplain of the Chapel of All Saints at Royal Lodge paid a call on the Yorks. Lilibet stared at him throughout the meeting, fixated on his buck teeth. 'May I see your little sister?' the Chaplain asked the Princess. The Princess looked at him and shook her head. 'No,' she said with great seriousness. 'I think your teeth might frighten her.'

Margaret's birth gave the Duke his whole family – 'We Four' or 'Us Four' as he would often call them. The family was his beloved refuge. Even though he was second in line to the throne, his public duties were a great deal lighter than they would be today and the Duchess had very little in the way of charity work. Lacking much employment, the Duke and Duchess kept up their social life, enjoyed outdoor pursuits and spent a great deal of time with their children. 'Margaret brought delight into his life,' wrote Marion Crawford, the later royal governess. As a toddler, she would bolt her own lunch, trot to the dining room where her parents were eating and, having poked her 'small fat face' round the door, scramble on to her father's knee to drink his soda or 'windy water' as she called it and eat a few sugar crystals, chatting excitedly about the 'hooshmi', as the Duke of York called spoon-food, of meat, vegetables and gravy, which was her favourite thing. She was indulged and, as one friend said, 'never admonished, and that really can't be a good thing for any child'. Margaret was very good at getting her own way and her infectious smile meant that she was always forgiven, even when she threw tantrums. She was just like the little girl in the nursery rhyme who had a little curl in the middle of her forehead and when she was 'good, she was very very good, but when she was bad, she was horrid'.

The Duke was determined that Margaret should not feel secondary to her sister, as he had done to the Prince of Wales. He decreed that they should always be dressed the same. Identical dress, for the sartorially obsessed Duke, was all one needed to ensure similar treatment. Yet he consciously emphasised the difference by remarking on Lilibet's conscientious nature and indulging Margaret when she played the clown. Their roles in the family were set early on and it was almost impossible for either of them to escape. 'You don't look very angelic, Margaret!' said the Duchess to her second daughter, costumed as an angel for a fancy dress party. 'That's all right,' came the cheery reply. 'I'll go as a Holy Terror.' Elizabeth would never have said such a thing – and if she had, she would not have been petted for it.

For Elizabeth, perfection did not lie in challenging

herself to expand her boundaries but in maintaining method and order. After lunch her parents would often give her a few of her beloved coffee crystals as a treat. She would not allow herself to eat them until she had laid out the crystals in order of size. Much to the fascination of the staff, she became preoccupied by trying to place her shoes exactly parallel under her bed at night, with her clothes folded above them. She often jumped out of bed to adjust their position – unable to sleep unless everything was rigidly arranged. Nowadays such preoccupation with neatness might be questioned or even discouraged, but in the 1930s it was praised, further evidence of a dutiful nature. 'May I say I hope you won't spoil her when she gets older,' her father had written to George V when she was born. But Elizabeth was a hard child to spoil, always striving to achieve goals of her own making.

Elizabeth liked to tidy her clothes, but she was uninterested in what she wore. She was fond of a cherry-red coat and complained about having to put on a long, dreary mackintosh, but otherwise she could not bear the trouble of frills and preferred practical items that allowed her to play outside with the dogs. Even moving towards adulthood, Lilibet did not much care about clothes. Luckily, the young designer Mr Norman Hartnell was sent to her in 1934 to fit her bridesmaid's dress for the wedding of her aunt Marina. It was the beginning of a long and fruitful relationship, in which he would assist her with the quandary that one of the world's most scrutinised and photographed women had little interest in her appearance.

Fashion was Margaret's domain. The younger Princess was teased that the first thing she had done when she was old enough to sit up was to tie a bow in her hair. She followed the fashions of the most stylish visitors to the house and longed to dress like an adult. But there would be no chance to do so. Elizabeth and Margaret were costumed like any upper-class girls at the time and like their Piccadilly neighbours, in stout coats and shoes and practical berets. For parties, they both had a necklace of coral and pearls, made from a string of their mother's that had been broken for them – of which they were terribly proud. Otherwise they only had toy brooches and necklaces. It was no preparation for women who would one day own a collection of jewels that would only be rivalled by those of the Russian royal family.

The Prince of Wales was a regular visitor to 145 Piccadilly to take tea with the family, and play Snap and Happy Families with the girls. But, like the King, he preferred the elder sister and was, according to Crawfie, 'devoted to Lilibet'. He gave her presents and brought her copies of A. A. Milne's novels. He was an enchanting companion for a child because he simply had no respect for the dreary rituals of adulthood and was in many ways rather like a child himself. The Princess's favourite poem was 'Changing the Guard at Buckingham Palace', which they recited endlessly. Churchill, the Prince of Wales, Queen Mary, the King and Crawfie – all were focused on Lilibet. Margaret was the amusing sideshow. As Margaret said later, with much bitterness, 'I detested Queen Mary. She was rude to all of us, except Lilibet.'

Lilibet, tidy, pragmatic and reserved, fitted so well with her grandparents' notions of good character that Margaret could not compete. Her dramatic expressiveness and eagerness for mirth were repeatedly misinterpreted and, as the years passed, her high spirits hardened into wilfulness. 'Her Majesty is rather sorry to hear that Princess Margaret is so spoilt, though perhaps it is hardly surprising,' wrote Queen Mary's lady-in-waiting to the governess. 'I dare say, too, she has a more complicated and difficult character, and one that will require a great deal of skill and insight in dealing with.'

Margaret's birth focused attention anew on Elizabeth. In seven years of marriage the Yorks had produced only two children, and the Duke was thirty-five, the Duchess thirty. The Prince of Wales was thirty-six and showed no sign of giving up his playboy lifestyle. It was growing increasingly possible that Elizabeth might be the heir to the throne. Osbert Sitwell reported a conversation in which the Duke mentioned his elder daughter, alluded to Queen Victoria and said, 'From the first moment of talking, she showed so much character that it was impossible not to wonder whether history would repeat itself.'

Britain's queens – such as Victoria and Elizabeth – had not had younger sisters. There were debates that there was no law that an older sister should take precedence over a younger. The King ordered an investigation and the conclusion was that the first right to the throne would be Elizabeth's. But it all seemed like an academic exercise. The Prince of Wales would, surely, soon settle and marry.

Miss Marion Crawford, a twenty-two-year-old Scotswoman, who had trained at the Moray House College in Edinburgh and planned to specialise in the education of underprivileged children became Elizabeth's new governess in 1933. Her eventual ambition was to be a child psychologist. But during her studies the Countess of Elgin asked her to come as governess to her daughter and also took on the daughter of the Duchess of York's sister, Lady Rose Leveson-Gower, who remembered her as a 'lovely country girl who was a good teacher, except when it came to mathematics'. Lady Rose mentioned her to her sister and the Yorks purloined her immediately. Miss Crawford was asked to come for a month's trial.

Miss Crawford, or 'Crawfie' as she became known, travelled down from Scotland expecting a 'couple of very spoiled and difficult little people'. It was evening and Crawfie arrived in the Princess's fawn-and-pink bedroom to see a 'small figure with a mop of curls' sitting up in bed in a nightdress decorated with pink roses. She had tied the cords of her dressing gown to the bed knobs and 'was busy driving her team'.

'Why have you no hair?' the little girl demanded.

I pulled off my hat to show her. 'I have enough to go on with,' I said. 'It's an Eton crop.'

Miss Crawford asked if Elizabeth always drove in bed.

'I mostly go once or twice round the park before I go to sleep, you know,' she said. 'It exercises my horses.' She navigated a dangerous and difficult corner and went on, 'Are you going to stay with us?'

Crawfie was captivated by her new family. 'The Duke and Duchess were so young and so in love,' she wrote. 'They took great delight in each other and in their children.' She was rather more surprised at how lightly she was expected to teach Elizabeth. 'No one ever had employers who interfered so little,' she wrote. She very soon decided that she wished to stay at Piccadilly, but time continued past her allotted month and no mention was made of further employment. She raised the question with the Duchess – who was greatly surprised. 'But of course you must stay,' she said, as if the whole matter had been settled long ago. The Duchess seemed somewhat confused when Crawfie gently pointed out that she must return to Scotland to collect more belongings. Perhaps, Crawfie thought, 'it is having people always on hand to attend to detail that engenders this rather vague frame of mind among royalty'.

Crawfie remained until her marriage in 1947, and looked set to continue as a favoured old friend of the royal family in a grace and favour cottage in Kensington Palace. In 1950, however, she published a bombshell: an intimate account of her life with the household, *The Little Princesses*.

Miss Crawford's book was a sensation. Royal commentators and historians have often suggested that it could only please, with its saccharine tone and admiration for the royal family. But sharp pen portraits lurk under all the sugar. The Duke of York is often distant; the Duchess is vague to the degree of thoughtlessness and often unaware of others; Elizabeth is cool; and Margaret is plump and babyish. Elizabeth is portrayed as demanding 'Who is that woman' of Wallis Simpson (this was removed in the US and later UK editions) when the royal family would rather have pretended they did not know. No monarch before – and possibly none in the future – will ever be written about in such intimate detail – we learn everything from the colour of her nightdress through her disinclination to undress and sleep in a tent with others at Guide camp to the progress of her relationship with Philip. Miss Crawford often expresses displeasure about the sad effect of press attention on the sisters – she complains that Margaret was cruelly misrepresented by the press and Elizabeth unfairly hounded during her romance with Philip. Yet she herself breached the confidence of the Princesses more intensely than any journalist.

Miss Crawford was very inexperienced to receive such a

plum role as the governess of two princesses. But the Duke
had miserable memories of crusty old tutors intent on dates
and grammar, and he saw study as a torment he wished his
girls to avoid. He was himself lacking in intellectual capacity
(as King, some of his ministers would find him unbearably
dull-witted) and did not want bluestocking daughters who
were cleverer than he was. He chose a youthful, engaging
woman, eager to play games in the nursery, who would not
trouble his girls with much academic endeavour. He and his
wife, as Crawfie remarked, 'wanted most for them a really
happy childhood, with lots of pleasant memories, stored
up against the days that might come out and, later, happy
marriages'.

The Duchess saw education as necessary only for those
women who would have to earn their own living. Her own
brief spell at a London day school had been unhappy and
she saw no point in forcing children to learn. King George
demanded only that the Princesses could write legibly. 'For
goodness sake, teach Margaret and Lilibet a decent hand,
that's all I ask of you,' he declared to their governess. 'None
of my children could write properly.' The King himself
was a ponderous writer and could not spell ('business' was
always a headache). Margaret and Elizabeth did indeed
develop fine and legible handwriting – an important attrib-
ute for a queen.

At 145 Piccadilly the two Princesses would begin their
day with 'high jinks' for a quarter of an hour or so in their
parents' bedroom. Then Miss Crawford gave Elizabeth half-
hour lessons from 9.30 until 11 in the schoolroom, a small
chamber adjacent to the Duchess's bedroom. After lessons
came orange juice and games in the garden. At twelve, the
Princess was sent to lie down for half an hour, followed by

an hour in which Crawfie read to her. Elizabeth took lunch with her parents and spent the afternoon in outdoor exercise, dancing or singing, followed by an hour with the Duchess before supper, and card games before bath and bedtime. The Duke and Duchess came along to play with the girls at bath time and would go downstairs, arm in arm, 'rather damp and dishevelled'. Allah and the nursery maids would take the girls to bed as they called out 'Goodnight Mummy', 'Goodnight Papa' down the stairs.

Lessons took up a very small part of the Princesses' day. The Duchess often popped over to the schoolroom and Miss Crawford complained that dentists, tailors and hairdressers tended to visit in the morning, further compromising her plans for their education. She was also constantly at war with Allah Knight, who she thought was always trying to whisk the girls away and keep them awake too late so that they were not alert in class.

For a child of seven, an hour and a half of lessons a day was glaringly insufficient. It was difficult for the Princess to submit to the necessary boredom of learning and she found rote learning dull. One day, frustrated by a French class of writing out endless verbs, she was pushed to violence, snatched up a large ornamental silver inkpot and upended it on her head. Mademoiselle stood staring in horror as Elizabeth sat there with ink trickling over her face and hair. Miss Crawford attempted to communicate the pleasure of learning by telling stories rather than listing dates, and presenting her student's ancestors and ministers as 'a lot of dusty lay figures of the past – of real people with all their problems and bothers'. Certainly the Princess was fonder of history than of other disciplines – they were her family she learned of, after all. When her aged cousin Princess Marie-Louise apologised for telling a lengthy story, the teenage Princess would not hear a word of it. 'But Cousin Louise,' she said, '*history* is so thrilling.'

Princess Elizabeth had much more aptitude for lessons than her parents had done and many thought her education should be more stringent. Elizabeth I could read Latin at the age of three and Victoria was kept to a strict timetable of learning. Queen Mary believed that the children should be taught history and geography to allow them to understand the importance of Empire, and thought that Lilibet in particular should comprehend the dominions and India. The Queen thought mathematics should be squeezed out of the timetable, and more history and genealogy inserted instead. After all, she said, the girls would never need to compile their own accounts and what other use for mathematics could there be? (For the Princess's fourth birthday the Queen had given her a present of wooden building blocks made from fifty different woods from across the Empire.) She was also displeased that lessons stopped in holidays. 'When I was a girl, I kept up my French and German, and had a certain amount of holiday work,' she declared sternly. Until the Abdication, however, her ambitions had little effect. The girls hurtled out of their lessons to play in the small park behind 145 Piccadilly, dashing around playing Cowboys and Indians, or huddling in the trees and shrubs for Hide and Seek. When they played Tag and Sardines, the statue of Lord Byron in the centre of the gardens was the 'base'. The Duke often joined in and was particularly adept at Hopscotch.

Margaret was babied by Allah, who kept her in the pram and fed her by hand when she was itching to run around and eat independently. She was not allowed to join the schoolroom until she was seven.

The Yorks' emphasis on a light education was short-sighted. The inner resources and introversion that a more meticulous schooling might foster were perhaps not too useful to a queen whose role was to shake hands, open hospitals, host receptions – and never express a political opinion. Lilibet was already serious and needed no schoolroom discipline to learn to apply herself. Margaret, however, with her short attention span and quick intelligence, would have been well served by a more scrupulous education.

In the post-Depression world, independence and intellect were associated with the selfish youth who had remained single. Domesticity was prized. In April 1932 the people of Wales celebrated the sixth birthday of Princess Elizabeth by giving her a thatched cottage, built entirely from Welsh materials. In a period of economic suffering for Wales, the cottage was an advertisement for the nation's craftsmanship. The little house was two-thirds normal size and every effort had been expended on its interior, which sparkled with electric lights. There was a fully working kitchen with gas cooker and fridge, pots, pans, brooms and packets of flour and baking powder, all to scale, as well as hot water on demand from the taps. Sweet blue chintz curtains decorated the windows and there was a miniature oak dresser displaying buttercup-yellow china, as well as linen embroidered with the initial 'E' and a crown. Welsh thatchers regularly came to attend to the roof.

After being shown at the Ideal Home Exhibition in Olympia, 'Y Bwthyn Bach' or 'The Little Cottage' was transferred to Windsor Great Park. Both Princesses happily set about tidying, dusting and polishing their little house. They played in it for hours and adults – who had to crouch to enter – were admitted strictly by invitation only. They enthusiastically packed up the linen and put dust sheets over the furniture whenever they left the house for a period to live in London. It was an excellent domestic training for two girls who would never have to make a cup of tea.

The Princess declared that she wished to marry a farmer, for then she could surely have lots of 'cows, horses and dogs'. She was happiest when riding or running about outside Royal Lodge with her father's dogs. In 1933 the Duke bought a Pembrokeshire corgi, 'Dookie'. Bad-tempered and rather ugly, he terrorised the household and made a habit of biting visitors and courtiers, although he loved the Duchess and Lilibet. The Duke soon purchased another and called her Jane. In 1936 the bestselling picture book, *The Princesses and their Dogs*, was published by the photographer Lisa Sheridan. The family were portrayed at 145 Piccadilly, outside Royal Lodge and Y Bwthyn Bach with Jane and Dookie, three yellow Labradors, Mimsy and her puppies Stiffy and Scrummy, a black cocker spaniel called Ben, a long-haired Tibetan Lion Dog, Choo-Choo, and Judy the Golden Retriever. The Princess loved them all.

Elizabeth viewed horses with her grandfather and began riding lessons at five with Owen, the Lodge groom. Even her family wearied of her devotion to Owen. 'Don't ask me, ask Owen,' her father once said in reply to her question about horses. 'Who am I to make suggestions?'

The Princess had little time for imaginative games or stories unless they involved horses. She and her cousin, Margaret Elphinstone, would pretend to be horses drawing Princess Margaret in a cart. Sometimes she would tie up Crawfie with red reins, a bridle and a nosebag, and perch on her, pretending to be a grocer's driver, delivering goods to various hungry customers, engaging in lengthy conversations with them about the quality of the products. Sometimes she would pretend to be the horse and Crawfie the grocer, 'sidling up to me, nosing in my pockets for sugar, making convincing little whinnying noises'. The highlight of the Princess's year was her visit to the Olympia horse trials and she pored over the catalogue for hours before she went, marking up her favourite horses. She had thirty or so toy horses, each a foot high on wheels, and kept the bridles and saddles perfectly polished, with the assistance of Margaret. Every night all the horses were divested of their saddles, fed and watered, and lined up in neat rows outside the nursery.

When taking their summer holidays at Glamis, the girls' favourite occupation was to take the pony down to the station, where they would shut him up in the waiting room and sit on the platform waiting for the Aberdeen Fish Express to rush past. Sometimes they would wait for hours at the station for the next train, with little to do other than putting pins into chewing gum, sticking them on the lines, and waiting for the tracks to move for the next train and distend the gum into shapes. It was a slow childhood for a woman who would later find every hour fully occupied.

The intellectual pursuits of the Princesses were very much those of their contemporaries. Elizabeth was fond of *Black Beauty*, *Dr Dolittle*, and A. A. Milne, but found *Alice in Wonderland* strange. It was simply too imaginative for her (and there were no horses). Her future husband, Prince Philip, was so fond of the book that he knew it off by heart. Margaret naughtily stole a battered penny dreadful about murderous pirates from Glamis Castle and reread it many times, but illicit reading held no appeal for Elizabeth. High art and classical music had, likewise, little place in the curriculum or the interests of her parents – in contrast to the rackety but cultured upbringing experienced by Prince Philip. The girls had lessons in voice and piano but it was the popular songs of the day that they learned such as 'The Merry Wives of Windsor'. Their cousin, Margaret Elphinstone, claimed they had only one gramophone record, 'Land of Hope and Glory', on their Scottish holidays – and they played it incessantly.

The ideal domesticity of the Yorks was a secular one. Queen Mary despaired over the lack of bible reading on the curriculum and there was no custom of family prayers, as in the palace. In Birkhall, a property bought by Prince Albert near Balmoral where the family sometimes visited for summer, the King had left a sign declaring the old homily that 'Cleanliness was next to godliness'. It was true: virtue for the Yorks inhered in orderliness, good manners and thoughtfulness rather than spirituality. Margaret and Elizabeth were trained to be ideal English wives: practical, cheerful girls with, as one insider put it, the cultural 'tastes of the many rather than the few'.

The hearty fondness for the outdoors of the Yorks suited Elizabeth more than her sister. Margaret was much less fond of dogs and horses (later she would refuse to become a patron of the Canine Defence League). The younger Princess might have made an excellent actress in musical theatre, for she was fond of music, a good pianist, a talented mimic and very expressive. Elizabeth's dreams were about horses and her favourite stories always starred a dog or a horse, while Margaret's were more wildly imaginative. 'I *must* tell you an amazing dream I had last night,' she would say, and Crawfie and Elizabeth would listen 'enthralled as the account of green horses, wild-elephant stampedes, talking cats and other remarkable manifestations went into two or three instalments'.

Neither Princess was particularly enamoured of the domestic arts, despite their reported fondness for dusting Y Bwythyn Bach. The Duke had once made a set of needle-point chair covers and Queen Mary was an excellent knitter. Allah, who was always clicking her needles in her spare time, tried to teach her charges to knit but Margaret was impatient and Elizabeth, like Queen Victoria before her, found embroidery dull. 'I am afraid I am not getting on very well with my needlework,' she confessed. In their free time the girls far preferred to play in the gardens or walk around Hyde Park with Crawfie, watching people swimming and rowing on the Serpentine, and wander to the pond in Kensington Gardens where children sailed toy yachts.

'Normality' only went so far. On one occasion Elizabeth told Crawfie that she thought it must be 'fun' to travel on the London Underground. The governess arranged for a private visit to the headquarters of the YWCA in Russell Square and the girls, smart in tweed coats and berets, set off to Hyde Park Corner station to catch the tube to Tottenham Court Road. There, they paid a visit to the canteen for tea. Elizabeth, forgetting that she would have to serve herself, left the teapot behind at the kiosk and was promptly shouted back in no uncertain terms by the cashier. 'If you want it, you must come and fetch it,' the woman shouted, much to the consternation of the Princess. Soon a crowd began to gather and a limousine had to be summoned quickly from 145 Piccadilly to whisk them home.

Everything the Princesses did was avidly followed – and any outfit they wore was immediately sold out. Despite the depression, the 1930s saw the spread of the department store. Selfridges set up displays from Suzanne Lenglen, six-times

Wimbledon champion, on a specially constructed indoor court, Bentalls employed a Swedish diver to plunge sixty-three feet down the escalator hall into a tank twice a week and, in 1930, Kennards hired three baby elephants to trundle through their 'Jumbo Sale'. Nothing, however, sent clothes, toys, gifts, china, books and furniture through the tills as fast as a suggestion that the Princesses might own something similar.

Elizabeth and Margaret escaped London to summer in Scotland and spend Christmas at Sandringham. The passion of Queen Victoria and Prince Albert for a Germanic celebration with a tree, presents and holly garlands set the fashion for the country in the 1850s and royal Christmases in Elizabeth's childhood were large family gatherings with plenty of Norfolk turkey, even at the height of the Depression. Elizabeth was given a shilling pocket money every week until the age of fifteen and saved much of it for Christmas presents. Just as now, the royal family preferred to exchange modest presents. Like thousands of children trotting to their favourite department store (where, joyously, the goods were laid out in trays to handle rather than behind a counter), the girls went to Woolworths with Miss Crawford for china ornaments, sweets and stickers for the family – and coloured bath salts for Bobo. The Duchess took them to Harrods for larger gifts. They then busied themselves wrapping up their haul and writing long confiding letters to Santa, asking for simple presents. A favourite pastime was helping Cook stir the Christmas pudding. On Christmas Eve the family opened their presents and the Princesses received piles of books, dolls, chocolates and toy horses. One year, two brooches shaped like ladybirds from Bobo were a great hit.

Elizabeth kept neat lists of what she and Margaret had

been given, to ensure that she would send the correct thank-you letters. After Christmas Elizabeth would collect up the wrapping paper and ribbons, and smooth them out to be saved. Wrapping paper, one of the most unwieldy and extravagant items in daily life, was conquered by the extreme neatness of the Princess. In this she was rather like her grand-mother, Queen Mary, who busied herself every year col-lecting up the family Christmas cards and sticking them into scrapbooks.

Like any children, the Princesses fought over toys, disa-greed over what to do and teased each other. Elizabeth could fly into tempers and she would hit out with a sturdy punch, while Margaret tended to bite, and they battled crying, 'You Beast!' Lilibet, Crawfie thought, took more time to recover and bore grudges for longer but 'always had the more dignity of the two'. Elizabeth had less passion overall: she only solic-ited a cuddle from Crawfie on one occasion – at the news of the death of her grandfather Strathmore.

In her memoirs Crawfie presented the girls as isolated and rather lonely:

> Other children always had an enormous fascination, like mystic beings from a distant world, and the little girls used to smile shyly at those they liked the look of. They would so have loved to speak to them and make friends, but this was never encouraged.

Miss Crawford exaggerated. During their time at 145 Piccadilly the Princesses attended the birthday parties of prop-erly suitable little daughters of neighbours and courtiers, such as Sonia Graham Hodgson, daughter of a radiologist who specialised in caring for the royal family. Nicky Beaumont, younger son of Lord Allendale, was their neighbour at 144

Piccadilly and chased around the gardens with them, and they often saw their cousins, George and Gerald, the sons of Princess Mary, only a few years their senior, as well as Patricia and Pamela, Lord Mountbatten's two girls, and Elizabeth Cavendish, daughter of the 10th Duke of Devonshire, who later became lady-in-waiting to Princess Margaret. Every summer holiday, they played with their cousins Jean and Margaret Ephinstone in Scotland, and had competitions over who could eat the most slices of brown bread and golden syrup and played at being circus horses. Really, the Princesses were simply not in the business of 'making friends' with ordinary children. They were royal and they were set apart – and that was that.

The Princesses were never in any doubt of their status. As Elizabeth said to her cousin, Margaret Elphinstone, when they were squabbling over a wooden seat, 'I'm the biggest "P" for Princess'. The sisters received curtseys and obeisance from courtiers and those they encountered. At the theatre, managers slipped chocolates into the royal box, especially for them.

It was a strange anomaly to be a child royal in the 1930s. Children were, on one hand, lesser citizens, not seen as worthy of any particular interest, judged by their obedience and encouraged to silence, yet royals possessed, it seemed, a secret brilliance and grandeur, set apart, special and unlike the ordinary people, taught to regard themselves as of a higher creation. One member of the circle told Harold Nicolson that he believed royals saw the rest of society as an undistinguishable mass – with little real difference between the Duke of Devonshire and any commoner.

'Good morning, little lady,' the Lord Chamberlain said, encountering the Princess in the corridors.

'I'm not a little lady,' she replied imperiously. 'I'm Princess Elizabeth.'

Later that day Queen Mary arrived in his rooms with Lilibet, announcing, 'This is *Princess* Elizabeth who hopes one day to be a *lady*.'

It was a conundrum for adult visitors: the Princess was at once their inferior and superior. Many dealt with the anomaly by investing her with a premature adulthood. Churchill met the little girl at two and a half, and judged she had an 'air of authority and reflectiveness astonishing in an infant'. Miss Crawford declared she had met many children but 'never one with so much character at such a young age'.

The girls found it hard to distinguish between the adults they met, on one occasion demanding why they were forbidden from biting their nails when the Prime Minister, Mr Chamberlain, was openly doing so at official functions. In Princess Elizabeth a typical childish repugnance towards unknown adults was married with a certain royal imperiousness. Aged about eight she went to a Royal Tournament with the King and watched a tableau about the Duke of Wellington.

'Who is that funny old man with the beaky nose, Grandpapa?' she asked with disdain.

'That's the Iron Duke – the Duke of Wellington, you know. You mustn't call him a funny old man. He was a very great general and a fine gentleman.'

'*I* know. He made all those battles in the Peninsular War and I can't ever remember the names of them. Well he *is* ugly, anyhow!'

Queen Mary's plans for history lessons might have failed to hit their mark, but her granddaughter had inherited her habit of grandeur.

The dominion to which Elizabeth was third in line was contracting. Queen Victoria and Edward VII had seen themselves as great rulers of an Empire, but in 1931 the Statute of Westminster gave autonomy to Canada, Australia, New Zealand, South Africa, Newfoundland and the Irish Free State. The Statute declared the 'Crown the symbol of the free association of the members of the British Commonwealth of Nations'. The great Imperial mission was fizzling out: the Empire had become the Commonwealth and George V was the King of the autonomous dominions. Not only was the political mood one of self-determination, it also seemed increasingly outlandish that Britain, battered by the economic depression, should rule other larger, richer countries.

But although Britain's power was diminished, the monarchy's appeal only grew. In the aftermath of the war there were fewer monarchies to admire and most of those that remained were much reduced. The royal family, and the Yorks in particular, were still gold dust for the editors of picture magazines. At the age of three the young Princess Elizabeth was on the cover of *Time* magazine. There was a wax model of her on her pony at Madame Tussaud's and Princess Elizabeth Land in Antarctica was named for her.

The Princesses, however, were largely hidden from public view. At the wedding of Prince George to Princess Marina of Kent in 1934, Elizabeth attracted the admiring attention of the crowds in the blue velvet bridesmaid's dress created by Mr Hartnell. Margaret, however, was not so fortunate, for a rumour had been intensifying that she was hardly seen because she was deaf and dumb. After the wedding, at the balcony appearance, the King swooped down to the three-year-old Margaret and held her up so she could be seen by the crowds. The child was terrified at being suspended over the balcony, but his act did the trick. If the King was not ashamed of his granddaughter, the thinking went, she could not be deaf and dumb.

As George V grew frailer, the question of who would govern his realm became more important. The King thought his eldest frivolous, untrustworthy and too used to admiration – and there was still no sign of a marriage. In 1929 the Prince had met the beautiful Thelma Furness, the wife of Marmaduke, Viscount Furness, and twin sister of Gloria Vanderbilt. He loved glamorous American women who did not demand too much of his intellect – and Thelma was perfect. They spent Thursdays at the Embassy Club and weekends at the Fort. Life at Belvedere was light and enjoyable. 'Our talk was mainly about people we knew or had known, and about places we knew and liked,' Thelma recalled.

In 1935 King George V celebrated his Silver Jubilee. On 6 May, the anniversary, the royal family drove in open carriages to St Paul's to celebrate. The two Princesses were dressed identically in pale-pink dresses and pink bonnets. As one onlooker recorded, the Duchess of York appeared most gracious, 'the baby princesses much interested in proceedings'. When the Princesses waved out to the crowd, the people roared with delight. That evening the King broadcast to the nation a speech written by the Archbishop of Canterbury concluding, 'I dedicate myself anew to your service for all the years that may still be given me.'

The King and Queen went to the balcony, to be cheered by a crowd of 100,000 people. The same scenes were repeated every night that week. The King, who had been the second son, never intended to rule, was frequently surprised by the adulation. 'I am beginning to think they must really like me for myself,' he said to his hospital nurse. 'I cannot understand it,' he once said to the Archbishop of Canterbury, ' I'm really quite an ordinary sort of chap.'

'Yes, Sir, that is precisely it,' replied the Archbishop, with honesty if not tact.

# 4
# 'Queen, Empress of India, the whole bag of tricks'

*Princess Elizabeth in 1936*

From his childhood this boy will be surrounded by sycophants and flatterers by the score and will be taught to believe himself as of a superior creation. A line will be drawn between him and the people he is to be called upon some day to reign over. In due course, following the precedent which has already been set, he will be sent on a tour round the world, and probably rumours of a morganatic marriage will follow and the end of it all will be the country will be called upon to pay the bill.

SUCH WERE THE PROPHETIC words of the Labour leader, Keir Hardie, soon after the birth of Prince Edward, in 1894.

In January 1934 Thelma Furness was called away to America. Aware of her lover's need for constant entertainment, she asked her friend, Mrs Ernest Simpson, to divert him while she was away. The Prince had met Mrs Simpson before and she had visited the Fort as a friend of Thelma. But, devoted to his 'Toodles', he did not notice her rake-thin friend. Mrs Simpson was rather on the sidelines of the social scene in London, for she was seen as plain and angular, and although she and her husband kept up respectable appearances in their flat in Bryanston Square, he had suffered great losses in the Depression.

Perhaps Thelma Furness thought that Wallis was a safe bet, a woman with whom she could leave the Prince. He liked wealthy, petite ladies and he tended to choose mistresses who would flutter around him and mother him, as Mrs Furness had done. Wallis was not rich, she was skinny rather than elfin, and her sharp sense of humour meant that some found her rude. David, however, was always desperately dependent and he needed constant female attention, otherwise he languished into depression. He suffered from dark moods. 'If only the British public really knew what a weak, powerless misery their press-made national hero was, they would have a nasty shock,' he said. He was, moreover, wearying of the charm of 'Princing'. 'I'm getting too old now for all that silly artificial nonsense,' he confessed to Thelma.

David had been deeply moved by his father's illness and he was particularly vulnerable, now he had passed what was to him the dreadful milestone of forty. Mrs Simpson, who wisecracked and teased, refused to be stunned by his glamour and kept up a flow of witty repartee, was an entrancing companion. Thelma Furness returned from America and visited Belvedere, to find the Prince and Mrs Simpson giggling over private jokes. Her friend turned and gave her a cool look and then, as Thelma recorded, 'That one cold, defiant glance told me the whole story.'

Bessie Wallis Warfield claimed she was born in Pennsylvania in June 1896, although it was possible she was born a year earlier, before her parents married. Her father died soon after her birth and her mother depended on the charity of her dead husband's brother, and found herself running a boarding house in Baltimore. Bessie attended the most elite girls' school in Maryland, thanks to her uncle, and began to befriend girls of high families. In 1916 she married

Earl Winfield Spencer, a pilot in the navy, but the relationship quickly deteriorated. He drank and Wallis began affairs with other men during a posting in China. She lived there independently after separating from her husband. The marriage was dissolved in 1927, enabling her to wed Ernest Simpson, an Anglo-American shipping executive, who had divorced his wife for the bewitching Wallis. The Simpsons set up home in Mayfair, and Wallis befriended prosperous Americans in London and became part of Thelma Furness's set – until Thelma's fateful voyage home.

David found Wallis exciting, chic and daring, and was fascinated by her travels and experiences abroad, and was attracted by her refusal to be daunted by royalty. Where her predecessors, Freda and Thelma, had pandered and soft-soaped, Wallis criticised and commanded. She seized the carving knife from him at dinner when he was too slow, berated him until he cried and flurried to please her. His days with Thelma had passed in cosy, domestic style, but life with Wallis was intoxicating and dangerous. Finally, his nervous personality had fulfilment. As Winston Churchill remarked, with her he was 'a completed being rather than a sick and harassed soul'. As the Prince himself said, 'If she agreed with some point under discussion, she never failed to advance her own views with vigour and spirit. That side of her enchanted me. A man in my position seldom encountered that trait in other people.'

The affair moved fast. The Prince took his mistress on a cruise to Biarritz and bought her jewels at every opportunity. Ernest played the complaisant husband. In November 1934, Mr and Mrs Simpson attended the reception at Buckingham Palace in honour of the wedding of Prince George to Princess Marina of Greece. Everyone behaved politely to Wallis and she was triumphant, telling her aunt about 'the excitement of the Prince bringing the Queen up to Ernest and self in front of all the cold, jealous English eyes'. The eight-year-old Elizabeth was a bridesmaid along with her cousin, Lady Mary Cambridge, but the ceremony bored the Prince. At the Greek Orthodox service that preceded the wedding at Westminster Abbey he caused a stir by taking out a cigarette and lighting it on a candle. Among the guests was the thirteen-year-old Prince Philip of Greece. Mr and Mrs Simpson sat close to the action, in excellent seats.

The King and Queen were furious that Mrs Simpson had been invited. The King stormed to his private secretary that his son had 'smuggled Mrs Simpson into the palace'. She was brash and American and his mistress, but worst of all she and her husband were both divorced. Divorcees were not permitted at Court, at balls, or into the Royal Enclosure at Ascot. They were really never meant to appear in the presence of the King at all. 'That woman in my own house!' cried the King.

Ernest was accompanying his wife less frequently, and in the following February Wallis and the Prince went skiing together for a month in Austria. 'Aren't I doing splendidly, Wallis?' he called out to her over the mountain, as she stood nearby, wobbling in outlandish high heels. The American press printed stories about the Prince, his mistress – and her fabulous collection of jewels. The stones were so huge that the diarist Mrs Belloc Lowndes thought them costume jewellery, and was amusedly told that the Prince had given Wallis fifty thousand pounds' worth at Christmas, with another sixty thousand pounds' worth at New Year a week later. This was a staggering sum. A guest at Fort Belvedere remarked that Wallis was 'glittering, and dripped in jewels and clothes'.

The royal family grew afraid. If stories about the Prince became widely known across the Empire, the reputation of the Crown would be severely undermined. By 1935, Wallis and Ernest were under surveillance by Special Branch and the police had suggested that she had at least one other lover. The Prince was resolute. 'My private life is my own affair,' he tended to say. When the King challenged him directly he declared he had never had immoral relations with his dear friend. Just before the Silver Jubilee the King's private secretary had visited the Prince and made it clear to him that the country would not tolerate him spending his time with a married woman, however innocent the friendship might be. The Prince refused to listen and the King responded by decreeing that Mrs Simpson should be forbidden to be present at any of the Silver Jubilee functions.

The Prince of Wales begged a favour of Helen Hardinge, wife of his father's assistant private secretary. He wondered if she might be able to find space for one or two scullery maids to watch the procession from her St James apartment, since his home at York House did not overlook the route. Lady Hardinge agreed – only to find that the two maids were in fact Mrs Wallis Simpson and a friend, both of whom had no doubt relished the opportunity to pretend to be maids. Mrs Simpson was invited to the Jubilee ball, where she decided the King gave her a penetrating stare 'filled with an icy menace for one such as me'. The King could glare all he wished, but there was little to be done. The Prince gave Wallis a pair of expensive diamond earrings to celebrate their success.

The Princesses were neglected. Once the favourites of Uncle David, he made plans to see them, then forgot, and when he did visit he always seemed distracted. He was totally obsessed. 'Mrs Simpson has complete control. He never leaves her and she can make him do anything and talk to anyone,' declared a friend. The Prince loved assuming the submissive role – one friend reported seeing them act out a ritual in which he knelt, put up his hands and begged like a dog for a light for his cigarette. It was only a joke but it reflected the truth of the relationship: Wallis issued orders and the Prince scurried to fill them, glorying in self-abasement, inviting her to berate him, pleading for more. 'I love you more and more every minute and NO difficulties or complications can prevent our ultimate happiness,' he wrote a little later. Uncle David had become a devoted slave of someone other than Princess Elizabeth.

The Silver Jubilee marked the beginning of the aged King's decline. He struggled to make his Christmas broadcast and could hardly walk to look at his stables. On Saturday 18 January 1936 the first bulletin about his health was released. On Monday he held a last meeting of the Privy Council in his bedchamber and authorised them to set up a Council of State on his behalf. He signed the documents with a very shaky GR. The family and courtiers planned the funeral and his physician, Lord Dawson, sent the news that the King was dying to the BBC for the evening broadcast. 'The King's life is moving peacefully to a close,' the nation was told at intervals throughout the evening.

The funeral and proclamation were planned. Dawson instructed his wife to advise *The Times* to wait before printing for the news of the King's death. Yet the sturdy King refused to die. Lord Dawson judged that his state of 'stupor and coma' could last all night, and resolved to act to speed matters. The royal family wished the news to be broken in *The Times* and other morning newspapers, rather than the 'less appropriate evening journals'. The King had regarded almost all papers except *The Times* as 'filthy rags of newspapers' and the family could not bear the idea that the death might be broken by the vulgar pages of the *Evening Standard* or the *Evening News*. The Queen and her children exited the room, leaving only the King's nurse, Sister Catherine Black, who was highly disapproving of the doctor's course of action. Dawson 'decided to determine the end and injected ... morphia gr. ¾ & shortly afterwards cocaine gr. 1 into the distended jugular vein'. His efforts were successful: 'In about ¼ of an hour – breathing quieter – appearance more placid – physical struggle gone.'

The royal family returned to watch the King expire. As Dawson put it, 'intervals between respirations lengthened, and life passed so quietly and gently that it was difficult to determine the actual moment.' The King's death was recorded as occurring at 11.55 p.m. Queen Mary watched her husband die, then turned to her son and kissed his hand. The new King wept aloud. 'I hope I will make good as he made good,' he said.

The BBC broadcast the news of the King's demise at quarter past midnight. The people grieved deeply and churches across the land filled with mourners. Crawfie hurried to Royal Lodge from Scotland, where she had been holidaying with her family. The Duke and Duchess had left her a note: 'Don't let all this depress them more than is absolutely necessary, Crawfie. They are so young.' Margaret was too little to understand properly, but Elizabeth, at nine, took it hard. She stopped in the middle of grooming one of her horses. 'Ought we to play?' she said. The Yorks took her to see the King lying in state at Westminster Hall. Clutching the hand of her mother, dressed in a black coat and beret, she observed how the people stood silently around the coffin. Uncle David stood entirely still, she noted. 'Not even an eyelid. It was wonderful. And everyone was so quiet. As if the King was asleep.'

Margaret spent the funeral playing in the nursery. Crawfie took Elizabeth to see the gun carriage bearing the King's body to Paddington station to embark on a train for burial. They arrived early to a station full of weeping people and a stationmaster put them in his private room where they played Noughts and Crosses on railway stationery. On the concourse, when the bands began playing and the coffin covered in the Union Jack came into view, her resolve quivered. She was soon diverted: a sailor fainted and his fellow chaps simply closed around him and held him up, marching along – a military efficiency that amused her and took her mind from her sadness. As Crawfie rather practically put it, 'She did not like all this, but she meant to go through with it, making no fuss.' The principle of 'going along' and 'making no fuss' served Elizabeth well in 1935. The same attitude, over sixty years later in 1997, would severely compromise her reign.

'I miss him dreadfully,' wrote the Duchess of York about her father-in-law. She was, she admitted, 'suffering from the effects of a family break-up – which always happens when the head of a family goes. Though outwardly, one's life goes on the same, yet everything is different – especially spiritually and mentally.' Lilibet had lost her beloved grandfather and she was now the niece of the King – and, if he did not have children, the heir to the throne. But for the first time the Yorks were overshadowed. The Prince of Wales was now King and the people cheered him wildly. As the Home Secretary, Sir John Simon, put it, 'he was the man born to be

King' and 'the most widely known and universally popular personality in the world'.

The new King made his first broadcast to his people on 1 May: 'Although I now speak to you as King, I am still that same man who has had the experience and whose constant effort it will be to promote the well-being of his fellow men.' David was now King Edward VIII, the ruler of a nation and Emperor of India. He thought only of Wallis. He was incensed when his father's will was read and he found that he had been given a life interest in Sandringham and Balmoral, but no money, whereas his siblings had received bequests of three-quarters of a million each. He wanted money to lavish on his Mrs Simpson. In the first months after he became King he gave her jewellery worth £16,000 (about £450,000 in today's money) and a bracelet inscribed 'Hold tight'. As Wallis told her aunt, 'He is very rich now.'

The King had told his friend and adviser, Walter Monckton, that he would 'be available for public business but his private life would be his own'. Utterly blind to how his people expected the royals to set an example, and wilfully ignoring his role as Supreme Head of the Church of England, he continued much as he had previously, visiting Bryanston Court and taking Wallis to Fort Belvedere. Until the seventeenth century, monarchs traditionally lived at the Tower of London during the period between accession and coronation, to ensure their safety at such a vulnerable time. It would perhaps have been better had David done so. Instead, he simply relished his freedom from the disapproval of his father. When finally persuaded to tour the gardens and glasshouses at Windsor, he followed the gardener into the peach house where a wonderful mass of flowers promised an excellent crop of peaches. The gardener was justly proud of his achievement. The new King's only response was to tell the gardener to cut the blooms and send them to lady friends, chiefly Mrs Simpson.

Wallis was his de-facto queen, and received the homage of London society. No Queen Mary, she joked about the Court mourning, saying 'she had not worn black stockings since she gave up the Can Can'. The heiress Emerald Cunard acted as Wallis's social secretary and praised Mrs Simpson to everyone who would listen. 'The King is Mrs Simpson's absolute slave, and will go nowhere she is not invited, and she, clever woman, with her high-pitched voice, her chic clothes, moles and sense of humour, is behaving well.'

One afternoon at Belvedere the King was admiring his new car, an American station wagon. 'Let's drive over to Royal Lodge,' he said to Wallis. 'I want to show Bertie the car.' Wallis agreed and they set off to visit the Yorks. Bertie was unconvinced by the car, but the King was in his element, pointing out how it worked. They then went in for tea with the ten-year-old Princess Elizabeth and Margaret, nearly six. Mrs Simpson thought the Princesses 'both so blonde, so beautifully mannered, so brightly scrubbed, that they might have stepped straight from the pages of a picture book'. Crawfie thought her a 'smart, attractive woman with that immediate friendliness American women have'. Wallis recalled that it had been 'a pleasant hour, but I left with the distinct impression that while the Duke of York was sold on the American station wagon, the Duchess was not sold on David's other American interest'. She was being disingenuous: she and the Duchess of York detested each other. Wallis was contemptuous of the Duchess, whom she called 'Cookie', on account of her looking like a fat household cook (and, the inference was, not behaving unlike one either), and the Duchess thought her an adventuress and tried her best to avoid her.

According to Crawfie, the meeting was not mentioned again. 'The general hope,' wrote Crawfie, 'was that if nothing was said, the whole business would blow over.' Burying the head in the sand was a common royal strategy. The Yorks, aware of the King's frivolous nature, assumed he might change his mind and attach himself to someone else.

Unfortunately, King was growing ever more dependent on Wallis. He loved the trappings of royalty and the awe he inspired, but was less enthused by the business of kingship. He had little time for dreary receptions and no interest in his role as Supreme Head of the Church of England. He decreed state papers 'mostly full of bunk' and refused to have regular hours, scuttling off to Belvedere, which was out of the reach of his courtiers from Thursday to Tuesday. His lover berated him for not reading his papers properly and expecting them to be read to him. 'Wallis is quite right,' he said mournfully. 'I shall learn it quite soon'. But he was so lax with his duties that Stanley Baldwin, who had succeeded Ramsay MacDonald as Prime Minister just after the Silver Jubilee, suspected that documents were not read and dispatch boxes were left open and unattended. Shocked that some of the boxes returned bearing the stains of cocktail glasses, he began to omit secret documents.

Baldwin's secret documents were of the highest importance. Outside the gay life of Belvedere and the schoolroom at 145 Piccadilly, Europe was changing. A chastened, suffering Germany, struggling with high inflation, had gathered to the furious, charismatic call of Adolf Hitler.

'Humanity cries out for peace and the assurance of peace, and you will find in peace opportunities of duty and service as noble as any,' the King announced to troops in Hyde Park in 1936. Churchill had assisted him to draft the speech, even though he believed that Britain should strengthen its army in response to German belligerence. In 1930 Hitler's National Socialist Party had won a great majority in the Reichstag, and in 1933 Hitler declared Nazism the only government, preached Aryan supremacy and introduced conscription.

'London is seething with excitement about Mrs S. War is never mentioned at all,' the wife of Canada's Governor General had written to her husband. While the eyes of the government had been trained on Wallis's tiny form and her jewels, German nationalism was soaring. In March 1936 Hitler, emboldened by Mussolini's invasion of Abyssinia, marched on the Rhineland, in direct contravention of the Treaty of Versailles. Baldwin's Cabinet pondered military action. But war had very little support in public opinion, even from the industrialists. The King spoke for many of his people when he expressed his terror of 'the appalling conse-quences of another world war and its futility'. Another war in Europe, he thought, 'would utterly destroy civilisation'.

The King was of the opinion that Britain should make overtures of friendship to Germany. At the end of January 1936 he told his cousin, the Duke of Saxe-Coburg, who was a member of the Nazi Party, 'Who is King here? Baldwin or I? I myself wish to talk to Hitler and will do so either here or in Germany.' The King's attempt to find understanding with Germany marked him and his circle down as possible traitors. 'Many people here suspected that Mrs Simpson was actually in German pay,' the American Ambassador told Roosevelt. Although he thought this 'unlikely', he did suspect she was a tool of German policy.

The King seriously believed that the Germans did not wish for war, and that conciliation could dissuade Hitler and

Mussolini from undue aggression. When Anthony Eden, the Foreign Secretary, suggested that Emperor Haile Selassie, who had been driven from Abyssinia by the Italians, should be allowed to come to Britain and that it would be popular if he were received at the palace, the King was outraged. 'Popular with whom?' he demanded. 'Certainly not with the Italians!'

The Court spent their summer at Balmoral, a tradition instigated by Queen Victoria. Edward, however, chose to spend his first summer holiday as King in 1936 cruising the Dalmatian coast with Wallis. Before embarking he had asked that all books be removed from the ship's library. The King then travelled to Balmoral, but Queen Mary's hope that the customs of the family would be re-established was in vain: Mrs Simpson came too and enthusiastically tried to introduce three-decker toasted sandwiches to the Balmoral menu.

Queen Mary had thought that a spell at Balmoral would remind her son of his duty; instead, the King was even more devoted to Wallis than ever. Dreary old Balmoral only rendered Mrs Simpson more exotic.

The international press discussed the scandalous cruise and Mrs Simpson, but the home newspapers kept quiet, fearing an outcry from a still loyal people. The King was much idolised and editors were afraid that readers would be so distressed that they would reject the paper. As even Kingsley Martin, the anti-monarchist editor of the *New Statesman*, observed, 'It would no doubt have sold for the moment but would have led to a storm of protest from readers.' Others, royalists themselves, wished that the affair of Mrs Simpson would blow over. They hoped in vain. By the end of summer the King persuaded his lover to begin steps towards a divorce.

If Wallis Simpson had married twice before but been wid-owed, rather than divorced, the marriage probably would have gone ahead, with a few raised eyebrows at the King choosing such an experienced woman. She would have had her moment in Westminster Abbey, and Britain an American Queen Consort and part-American royal family. But David would not have been attracted to a widow. As he had writ-ten a few months earlier, he was 'just going mad at the mere thought ... that you are alone there with Ernest'. Jealousy piqued his interest and made him fall in love. And thus the King set himself on a collision course with his friends, his fam-ily, the Church of England, his Parliament and his country.

In late October Wallis filed for divorce. Stanley Baldwin, sixty-nine and looking forward to retirement, had not expected to be thrown into such a trying situation. He visited the King on 20 October to beg him to prevent the divorce. The King would not be dissuaded. Seven days later Wallis obtained her decree nisi (on the basis of Ernest Simpson's adultery in a hotel in Bray with one Buttercup Kennedy) and within a week the US newspapers exploded into a flurry of headlines about Mrs Simpson. There was gossip about lovers and talk that she was not even properly divorced from her first husband, since it had not been approved on the grounds of adultery, the only acceptable reason for divorce under English law.

The King simply did not understand the catastrophic implications of his actions. Lady Londonderry, a supporter of the King, collared Wallis at a party and told her that 'if the King had any idea of marrying her, he ought to be quickly disabused of the notion, since the English people would never stand for a Queen or a King's consort who had been twice divorced and whose previous husbands were still living'.

Baldwin and his government were resolved to prevent it. He had seen his last government fail thanks to the General Strike and he was well aware that his Labour opponents had their eye on exploiting any dissatisfaction. The terrible Hunger Marches were only three years in the past and the nation was still poor. The King was loved by his people and they welcomed him delightedly, even in the most deprived areas. As Malcolm Muggeridge said, he was 'idolised as few men outside of the Orient have ever been'. Throughout the hard years of the Great War and the subsequent depression, one constant had been the monarchy. Without it, what was holding the country together? If the King could give up so easily on his responsibilities, might not the nation?

Ten-year-old Elizabeth understood that there were difficulties afoot. 'It was plain to everyone that there was a sudden shadow over the house,' recalled Crawfie. It would have been impossible not to understand that there were serious matters being debated. Their home at 145 Piccadilly had become a place of business and the Yorks had no more time for the 'high jinks' at bedtime. Stanley Baldwin, various ministers and bishops and archbishops were frequent visitors. Her father was worried and miserable, while her mother fell ill with the anxiety.

To distract the girls, Miss Crawford and Allah took the Princesses to swimming lessons at the local Bath Club, equipped with chocolates and toiletries supplied by Allah. Taught by the charming young swimming teacher, Miss Amy Daly, the sisters learned how to swim by first making motions while lying on a wooden bench. Margaret, plumper, clumsier and younger than her sister, was at a disadvantage. 'You look like an aeroplane about to conk out,' her sister shouted. When the time came to approach the water, Margaret hung by its sides and Elizabeth was sharp, calling out, 'Don't be a limpet.' In participating in swimming classes, the Princesses were joining with the craze for health and beauty that swept Britain in the 1930s. The first lido, an outdoor pool with a sunbathing terrace and a cafe, was opened at the Serpentine in Hyde Park, and over sixty more lidos were soon built in London alone. Women, too, were active participants in the new drive for health, as in the hugely successful Women's League for Health and Beauty, which put on exercise classes around the country. The Princesses, splashing proudly about the Bath Club, the other girls told firmly to regard them as 'normal', could not have been joining in with an activity more likely to make them very popular with the nation.

If the Duke of York did have to take the throne, the Princesses were his trump cards. The family was charming and engaging, and his daughters were everyone's darlings. One of the more lurid rumours in society was that the Duke would refuse to be king and Queen Mary would act as regent for Princess Elizabeth. Others suggested (a story encouraged by Wallis) that the Duke was too slow to rule. Still, the manufacturers worked on the Coronation souvenirs. In October, the *New York Journal* declared 'The King Will Wed Wally'. The paper arrived in Britain with the sections cut out.

Since the Statute of Westminster, any alteration of the succession required the assent of all the parliaments of the dominions. Even though, by rights, the King still had the privilege of consultation, Baldwin began asking the premiers their opinion. He was leaning towards the option that the King might make a morganatic marriage with Mrs Simpson, so she would be his wife but not his queen. He had himself even suggested that he 'wouldn't mind if she was a respectable whore ... kept out of public view'. The King was prepared to countenance the notion of a morganatic marriage and even suggested giving a public radio address to ask his people if they agreed. The problem was that such a move would be tricky to sell to the Empire and the middle classes. The idea was equally unpopular with Queen Mary. The sixty-nine-year-old dowager Queen had been made unhappy by the morganatic marriage of her parents and she saw it as fatally undermining the dignity of the monarchy. David, in her opinion, was born to be King. The role simply could not be disposed of at will.

On 16 November the King invited Baldwin to Buckingham Palace and told him that he wished to marry Mrs Simpson. If Parliament approved, he would do so and be a better King, but if they did not, he would renounce the throne. Baldwin begged him to reconsider but the King was determined. At dinner time he marched round to his mother at Marlborough House and told her he was in love with Wallis and would abdicate to be with her if he had to do so. Queen Mary was devastated and wrote to 'implore you not to do so for our sake and for the sake of the country'. As she told him,

> I do not think you ever realised the shock, which the attitude you took up, caused your family, and the whole Nation. It seemed inconceivable to those who had made such sacrifices during the war that you, as their King, refused a lesser sacrifice.

The King was playing a bluffing game. As convinced that he had been appointed to rule as any Hanoverian, he thought there would be such an outcry against his abdication that he could marry Wallis and remain on the throne. Throughout his life he had obtained his desires – and he wanted Wallis.

When Prince Paul of Yugoslavia asked him what she would be called, he replied, 'Queen of England, of course.'

'She is going to be Queen?' asked a baffled Prince Paul.

'Yes, and Empress of India, the whole bag of tricks.'

But, if matters came to it, abdication was not unappealing. The Prince found 'Kinging' dull. He thought that if he resigned the throne, he would simply live very much as he had done as Prince of Wales: a royal with few responsibilities, entertaining his friends at Belvedere and travelling on exotic holidays, while Bertie shook hands at receptions and read the papers in dispatch boxes.

Across Britain, manufacturers were preparing for the Coronation. Artists in the potteries were painstakingly painting Edward VIII on commemorative plates and mugs, jewellers created enamelled pins and necklaces of the King, artists copied portraits and thousands of seamstresses sewed Union Jack flags. All the while, the royal family were in despair. On 25 November, Bertie wrote to a courtier, 'If the worst happens & I have to take over you can rest assured that I will do my best to clear up the inevitable mess, if the whole fabric does not crumble under the shock and strain of it all.' Really, he worried he did not have the courage for the role. As he confessed, 'I am very overwrought as to what may befall me'. The Duchess of York wrote secretly to her 'Darling David'.

> Please be kind to Bertie when you see him, because he loves you and minds terribly all that happens to you. I wish that you could realise how loyal and true he is to you, and you have no idea how hard it has been for him lately. I *know* that he is fonder of you than anybody else, and as his wife I must write to tell you this. I am terrified for him – so DO help him, and *for God's*

*sake,* do not tell him I have written. We both uphold you always.

Despite such appeals, David was blasé and his very casualness was even more upsetting. As Bertie wrote to Queen Mary, 'David has been trained for the position he holds and now wants to chuck away'. It was as if the throne was an unwanted bottle of wine.

On 28 November Baldwin sent telegrams to the leaders of the dominions to canvas their opinions officially on three possibilities: the King married Mrs Simpson and she became Queen; he married her but she was not Queen, in a morganatic marriage; he married her and abdicated for the Duke of York.

The Irish Free State replied that it viewed the matter 'with detachment', the New Zealanders were unsure, but the other dominions refused the first two options. Mr Lyons of Australia declared the King should abdicate whether he married Mrs Simpson or not. The Cabinet also rejected the proposal that the pair make a morganatic marriage. Baldwin informed the King of the decisions. David was still desperately convinced of his popularity in England and commented 'there were not many people in Australia'. But the plan for a morganatic marriage had failed. The King would have to give up his throne.

On 30 November, Crystal Palace caught fire, turning the entire sky above London bright orange. The fire could be seen as far away as Brighton. To a reporter on the *Daily Mail* who flew over in a specially hired plane, it looked like 'an iceberg on fire' as thousands of tons of molten steel and glass flooded the hill. People flooded to see the blaze and had to be held back by the police; others hired their own private planes to see. For politicians and some in society, it seemed like an omen; the palace created for Victoria and Albert's Great Exhibition in 1851, the celebration of British greatness, had collapsed into rubble.

On 3 December the British newspapers broke the news. 'The King and his Ministers: Great Constitutional Crisis', the people were told. The royal family were completely exposed as they had never been before.

Crowds arrived at Downing Street crying 'We Want Our King' and women marched outside Buckingham Palace bearing placards crying 'God Save the King from Baldwin'. The postrooms of newspaper offices were swamped with letters, ninety per cent of which, apparently, were in support of the King. Woolworths sold out of Edward VIII Coronation mugs on the spot. All London, wrote Virginia Woolf was 'excited', except for the 'nobs', who say that 'Royalty is in Peril' and 'The Empire is divided.' She thought they were right − and 'the King may keep us all waiting, while he sits, like a naughty boy, in the nursery, trying to make up his mind.'

Baldwin fretted that the King was consulting Winston Churchill and that together they would undermine his position and his government might be forced to resign. A decision would have to be forced. On Sunday, Baldwin told the King he must decide by 5 p.m. The King failed to do so. And then, seized by his own importance, he declared to Baldwin, 'If the Angel Gabriel came through that window and told me not to do this thing, I would still do it.' Finally, on the evening of Monday 7 December, the King called his brother to see him at Belvedere. 'The awful and ghastly suspense of waiting is over,' Bertie wrote in his journal. 'I found him pacing up & down the room, & he told me his decision that he would go.' Bertie was to be propelled into a position he had never planned for and never wanted. He was to be the new King. 'I'm quite unprepared for it,' he told his cousin, Louis Mountbatten, 'David has been trained for this all his life ... I'm only a Naval Officer, it's the only thing I know about.'

When Bertie told Queen Mary, he broke down and wept. 'I don't think we could ever imagine a more incredible tragedy, and the agony of it all has been beyond words,' the Duchess of York lamented. 'And the melancholy fact remains still at the present moment, that he for whom we agonised is the one person it did not touch.' David was delighted at his success, entranced by a vision of himself as Britain's beloved Prince of Wales once more, glamorous and feted. He lied to his brother, Churchill and the government that he had no money of his own and required a large subsidy in order to live. Bertie agreed to give him £25,000 a year.

On 10 December Bertie wrote that 'I was present at the fateful moment which made me D's successor to the throne. Perfectly calm D signed 5 or 6 copies of the Instrument of Abdication & then five copies of his message to Parliament, one for each Dominion Parliament. It was a dreadful moment & one never to be forgotten by those present.' David's reign had lasted only 325 days, the shortest in English history since the nine-day reign of Lady Jane Grey almost four hundred years previously. Drapes, celebratory books, jewels, medals and huge amounts of china were sold off cheaply or thrown into industrial bins, and the painters began hastily sketching out pictures of Bertie's face, garlanded with wreaths. Children dashed around singing their latest playground song: 'Hark the Herald Angels Sing/Mrs Simpson's pinched our King'

The new King chose the name George, the last of his four

Christian names. George would provide a line of continuity with his father, as well as the Hanoverians, and both Albert and Frederick were a little Germanic; Arthur perhaps too daring.

In 145 Piccadilly, on the afternoon of 10 December, Elizabeth wrote up the notes from her swimming lesson as crowds gathered outside. The new King, just two days short of his forty-first birthday, returned to London after dining at Royal Lodge to find people flocking around his gate, his children overexcited and his wife ill in bed. 'I was overwhelmed,' he said. The new Queen, the brave daughter of Glamis, had been staunch through the Great War and Depression, and would later be indomitable in the face of Hitler. But on 10 December, for the first time in her life, she was daunted, sick and fearful at the thought of her shy husband ruling the country. 'We must take what is coming to us and make the best of it,' she said. We Four were now on the throne.

The freshly named George VI knew that he was receiving support because of his strength in stepping up to the new role, rather than his popularity as King. The British were still in love with David. 'I thought we were to have such a king as never was,' said a railway worker about the Prince. Bertie had only ever been the younger brother. Because, as Duke of York, his schedule of public engagements had not been particularly great, the people did not know him well, and their notions of him were dogged by the ill health he had suffered during the war and his unfortunate stammer. 'We would still prefer to cheer Edward but we know we've got to cheer George,' the journalist Kingsley Martin imagined a member of the public saying. 'After all, it's Edward's fault that he's not on the throne and George didn't ask to get there.' It was wisely decided that the new King should be crowned as quickly as possible. Bertie would simply take over Edward's date for the Coronation – less than six months later, on 12 May 1937.

At 10 p.m. on Friday 11 December, the nation huddled round the radio, as the Director General of the BBC, John Reith, broadcasting from Windsor Castle, introduced 'His Royal Highness, Prince Edward'. For seven minutes factory workers put down their drinks, Surrey bankers paused on their crosswords, Norfolk housewives abandoned their sewing and children were shushed. It was the same across the Commonwealth. Farmers in Alice Springs stopped their 7.30 early-morning feeds and Sydney clerks listened at 9 a.m. before they began work. Toronto schoolchildren gathered round the wireless at 5 p.m. and Vancouver shop assistants caught the details on their 2 p.m. lunch break. 'At long last, I am able to say a few words of my own,' the Prince began. His speech had been polished by Churchill, and his ringing tones reached every corner of Britain and across the Empire. He explained his sacrifice. 'I have found it impossible to carry the heavy burden of responsibility and to discharge my duties as King as I would wish to do without the help and support of the woman I love.' He thanked his family and Mr Baldwin for treating him fairly. 'And now we have a new King,' he concluded. 'I wish him, and you, his people, happiness and prosperity with all my heart. God Save the King'.

Across the world, people turned off the radio, in shock that the King had finally uttered the long-dreaded words. Helen Hardinge wept but said that most of the aristocrats and Court set thought it vulgar. The middle and working classes were largely captivated. In pubs and restaurants across the country, men and women openly sobbed and cried out, 'God Save the King.'

Bertie and David had met a few hours earlier to discuss another matter. 'By the way, David,' asked the new King. 'Have you given any thought about what you are going to be called now?' David had not done anything of the kind. 'Why no, as a matter of fact, I haven't.' Bertie, horrified by the suggestion of Lord Reith that he introduce the former King as Mr E. Windsor, had been thinking hard about a properly dignified title. 'I shall create you a Duke,' said Bertie. 'How about the family name of Windsor?' After the broadcast David went to Royal Lodge to bid farewell to his family. 'It isn't possible!' cried the Duke of Kent. 'It isn't happening!' Queen Mary was present, supported by the Princess Royal, but the new Queen was still too ill to attend. The new Duke bowed to his brother. 'It's all right, old man,' he apparently said, 'I must step off with the right foot from the first.' Then he drove away into the foggy night towards Portsmouth to embark on the HMS *Fury* to France, on his way to Austria. He spent the journey drinking heavily and pacing the officers' mess. He had been distressed to learn that every one of his servants refused to accompany him. They too felt betrayed to be no longer working for the King. 'Your name's mud', one told him.

Walter Monckton travelled to Fort Belvedere to sweep it for anything incriminating. He took into his bag a piece of paper bearing Wallis's private telephone number from the Duke's bedside table, and from her room a biography of Mrs Fitzherbert, morganatic wife of George IV – a gentle woman who had gained respect from society with her restrained behaviour, but ultimately lost her lover.

Although the Yorks had been in Scotland at the same time as David and Wallis in September, relations had been frosty. The last time the two Princesses had properly seen their Uncle David had been the afternoon at Royal Lodge when the King had motored up in his new American car. In his speech, David had praised his brother's advantages, remarking that the King was not only possessed of 'fine qualities' and a 'long training in the public affairs of this country', he had 'one matchless blessing, enjoyed by many of you and not bestowed on me – a happy home with his wife and children'. But the 'happy home' of 145 Piccadilly, where he had once visited to play Snap with the girls, would have to be broken apart for ever.

The country mourned its King Edward. When the Archbishop of Canterbury gave a BBC address criticising the former King's interest in 'vulgar society' and his 'craving for private happiness', he received 250 letters, many of which were furiously abusive. The golden Prince, charismatic and beloved, had abdicated his throne, chosen love over duty and turned his back on the country. It was a harsh rejection. Victoria, as Britain's longest-reigning ruler, had secured the monarchy and ensured its popularity, rescuing the reputation of the throne after the rules of the spendthrift and reactionary George IV and William IV. But success had come at a price: after her, the monarchy was indelibly associated with a virtuous home life. Unlike the Hanoverians before her, Victoria had toured the country, attended receptions and been consistently visible to the people (hence their fury at her attempt to withdraw from public view after the death of Albert). The monarch existed to be seen and to set an example to the people. Edward VII was forgiven his excesses thanks to lingering affection for his mother and high esteem for his gentle and beautiful wife, Queen Alexandra. But George V had rigidly maintained the appearance of duty and dignity, to the detriment of his relationships with his children. By the end of his reign, the bar by which the monarchy was judged had been set high. David, as rebellious as George IV but lacking the rage that kept that King feared, at least, could not live up to the standards his father had set.

In his final speech David had claimed that he had abdicated so that he could be with the woman he loved – but it was not so simple. He was in love with Wallis, of course, but she also provided a convenient exit from a job that he found dismayingly dreary. The Duke had always loved the trappings of royalty – the money, deference and irresistible effect of HRH on women – but the idea of living like his father repelled him. His beloved life of cocktails, house parties, fast women and fashion simply did not square with the round of official functions, royal visits and meetings with ministers. He saw his best self as most alive in nightclubs, rather than opening hospitals in Basildon. Moreover unlike Bertie, who picked in Elizabeth Bowes-Lyon a wife as willing to subjugate pleasure to duty as Queen Mary, David had been attracted to women who were hopelessly unsuited to the role of queen consort, even if they had been unmarried. Ironically, of all the women the Prince had squired, Mrs Simpson had the personality most suitable for the life of a queen, for she was habituated to hiding her feelings and maintaining a gracious smile.

The people of Britain, the Commonwealth and the Empire had to accept it: he had been born Prince of Wales, but he was not up to the job. To many still suffering the fallout from the Depression, the sight of David living for pleasure with wealthy Americans was deeply affronting. The belief that the royals were somehow more excellent than their subjects was crumbling. Bertie would pay for his brother's excesses as the monarchy became more subject to gossip and judgement, and, most of all, increasingly disempowered. Politicians were braver about refusing to listen to the suggestions of kings and princes. The development of the purely symbolic British monarchy began with the abdication of Edward VIII.

The new King was still infatuated with his brother. Even at the dinner at Fort Belvedere after David had decided to relinquish the throne on 8 December, he was fascinated. 'Isn't my brother wonderful, isn't he wonderful,' he said to the party, awed by David's ability to charm his guests in the midst of crisis. But within a year the brothers were no longer on speaking terms. The Duke's demands began almost immediately after he left. He asked for money, complained that £25,000 was insufficient and fussed over royal possessions – including the stamp collection of George V. Most of all, he wanted Wallis to bear the title HRH. He was, as Lord Mountbatten told Harold Nicolson, 'unable to comprehend why it is that everybody, including Queen Mary, did not welcome Mrs Simpson'. The lady herself was no less deluded. Convinced that she had behaved honourably, she wanted her lover to push the King 'not to treat you as an outcast and to do something for me so that we have a dignified and correct position'. She wanted to be a princess, even if she could not be 'Empress of India and the whole bag of tricks'.

The King, grappling with the strains of his new position, found his brother's lengthy discontented phone calls very wearing. When he discovered that his brother was not penniless, as he had claimed, but in possession of a fortune of nearly a million pounds (the equivalent of over forty million pounds today), he was furious.

Bertie's very suitability as King made the politicians, Queen Mary and the people more amenable to the Abdication. Had the second son been irresponsible and womanising, Edward VIII might have been put under pressure to remain. But Bertie had proved himself with the Australia tour, he was quiet and responsible, and, most of all, he had the perfect home life for a king. As Queen Mary said in her address to the nation of the Duchess of York: 'I know that you have already taken her children to your hearts.' Not only was the nation receiving a new, superior King, but they could also look forward to their beloved Princess Elizabeth as Queen.

There had been a brief discussion about the possibility that Edward should abdicate for the youngest brother, George, Duke of Kent, because he had a son, but this had been discounted surprisingly quickly. Girls, in 1936, were really intended to be men's helpmates and domestic servants. They were not allowed to be ministers in the Church of England or borrow money, they could not receive full degrees from Cambridge or sit in the House of Lords, few occupied the professions or earned significant sums, and those who did work were expected to cease on marriage. But in the wake of Victoria women were seen as good rulers (and certainly, unlike the male royals, tended not to get into trouble with the opposite sex). 'The English like Queens,' Princess Victoria's maternal grandmother had said at her birth. Society had come some way since Prince Albert had written to his brother, Ernest, on the birth of his daughter, Vicky, in 1841, 'Albert, father of a daughter, you will laugh at me.' It was almost as if the monarchy, traditionally seen as a reactionary institution, was one of the most forward thinking of all in terms of women's roles.

The Princess, of course, was not heir apparent, but heir presumptive. If her father had a son, her claim to the throne would recede. The Queen was thirty-six and healthy, and another child was possible. Thus, although it had already been established that Elizabeth would have precedence over Margaret, she would not be appointed Princess of Wales. The title was still reserved for the wife of the Prince of Wales.

On 12 December, the day of the Proclamation, the girls gave their father a hug goodbye as he departed from Royal Lodge for the Privy Council, nervous and pale and dressed as an Admiral of the Fleet. It would be the last time they did not have to curtsey to him. On the new King's return his two girls curtseyed in his presence, just as they had done to the old King. It was the clearest possible indication that everything had changed. Shy, nervous Bertie was now the King of Great Britain and its dominions. Ten-year-old Elizabeth was heir to the throne – unless her father had a son.

# 5
## 'Great changes'

*The Royal Family on Coronation Day, 12 May 1937*

'I AM AFRAID THERE ARE going to be great changes in our lives,' said the Duchess – now the Queen. Elizabeth and Margaret were baffled by the news that they would have to live in Buckingham Palace. 'You mean for ever?' said Lilibet.

Lady Strathmore, her grandmother, claimed that the Princess was ardently praying for a brother, but for Elizabeth, like most children, adulthood seemed so far away as to be irrelevant. She was more concerned about the immediate changes to their lives. Mummy and Papa were now always to be referred to in company as the King and Queen, there would be no more family fun in the mornings and evening – and they would have to leave her beloved 145 Piccadilly. Although they had visited the palace frequently to play and pay calls on the King and Queen, they had always returned to their cosy home. Now they must live in the giant, forbidding and rather chilly palace, and her mother and father would be engaged for much of the day. 'But I have only just learned to write York,' said the six-year-old Margaret sadly, when she understood that her father was King. 'I used to be Margaret of York and now I'm nothing.'

The Princesses busied themselves preparing their toy horses for the journey, saddling them and packing up their grooming brushes and cloths into a basket. The staff worried over what they might wear to attend their employers in such an august situation. Crawfie fretted that she would find herself spending the bulk of her salary on clothes (indeed, she found herself adapting old curtains into evening gowns).

The King and Queen took occupation of Buckingham Palace within weeks of George's ascension to the throne. As the servants packed up the furniture at 145 Piccadilly, Elizabeth and Margaret were brought over on regular visits to accustom them to the palace. The King and Queen occupied the pink-and-gold Belgian suite, and new rooms overlooking the Mall were chosen and painted in cheerful hues for the Princesses. Elizabeth would share with Bobo and Margaret with Allah. For the schoolroom the King chose the bright room overlooking the Mall that Elizabeth had used when visiting her grandparents. The outdoor schoolroom was the summer house that had been used by the old King, left just as it had been when he was alive, complete with pens and inkpot.

Felix Mendelssohn declared Buckingham Palace was the only house in England that was properly comfortable. Many disagreed. Huge, grey and looming, with long frosty corridors and cavernous underpassages, it was at once without intimacy or grandeur. Prince Albert had railed against the leaking drains and dirty windows in 1841, and matters had improved only slightly. The electric lights had recently been installed, the furniture was old, and the walls were damp and cracked. The only really comfortable inhabitants were the copious mice, who dashed about the rooms, eluding the efforts of the Vermin Man and his traps bearing tempting lumps of aniseed. The chimneys were draughty and the coal fires were simply inadequate at heating rooms with such high ceilings. As in many of the great houses at the time, serving properly hot food at meals was nigh on impossible, for the kitchens were nearly half an hour away from the rooms where the family ate. As Lilibet said, 'People here need bicycles.'

'Life in a palace rather resembles camping in a museum,' commented Crawfie. The Princesses were also living in a large company headquarters. With over ninety offices for the business of monarchy, nearly eighty bathrooms and fifty-two guest and royal bedrooms, the palace was a huge operation. It had its own post office and postmen trotted up and down the corridors. At 145 Piccadilly they had had a staff of under twenty, whereas the palace was serviced by fleets of char-ladies scrubbing the basements, housemaids attending to the rooms, footmen, butlers, pages, cooks, chefs and porters. A table decker came every day to renew the palace flowers and the clock winder arrived weekly. The Queen had two dress-ers and the King employed two valets. As well as secretaries, dozens of clerks, attendants and ladies-in-waiting, there were some strange and archaic occupations. There was a Yeoman of the Gold Pantry and a Yeoman of the Silver Pantry, who spent their days caring for the plate. During the day, minis-ters and courtiers flocked in and out of the King's rooms, and dignitaries lined up in the state rooms for evening receptions. Their earlier home had been a warm bubble, a place visited by friends and family. In Buckingham Palace it was almost impossible to be private.

The family were now followed everywhere by two detec-tives, always co-ordinating with the local police on any trips. Dookie the corgi grew even crosser at the palace, and bit the visitors, often obeying only the Queen. The politician Lord Lothian received a rather hard bite and bled copiously, declaring with fortitude that he did not feel anything. Lothian had aided the *Washington Post* in publishing the scoop about Mrs Simpson. Perhaps, as dogs are wont to do, Dookie had imbibed the Queen's dislike.

The palace was the grandest and most impersonal house ever lived in by two English children, but there were compensations. In Hamilton Gardens, the Princesses had been stared at by eager onlookers and their games were interrupted (one friend of a neighbour overturned a pram of full of leaves that Princess Margaret had been carefully amassing). At the palace they had forty acres of gardens to themselves, and could row on the lake looking for ducks' nests, hide in the hillocks and the bushes, and run up to the perimeter wall to watch the cars and the passers-by. The two girls dashed up and down the corridors, Margaret crying out, 'Wait for me, Lilibet, wait for *me*' and much amusement could be derived from the hundreds of servants. Margaret, fond of practical jokes, would hide wheelbarrows from gardeners and put sticky lime balls in the pockets of equerries. Elizabeth discovered that every time she walked in front of a sentry he would present arms – and she began merrily walking past over and over to see the trick repeated.

Crawfie was still in charge of the nursery, for the King and Queen wished to maintain a continuity for their daughters. But in the Buckingham Palace schoolroom, nursery meals were served by two liveried footmen.

The cheerful routine of 145 Piccadilly was a memory. The King spent the morning in his study in discussion with ministers and ambassadors, while the Queen saw dressmakers and replied to her correspondence, attended by her lady-in-waiting. The family usually took lunch together, but it was a formal affair. The King and Queen then normally proceeded to a function or reception and the Prime Minister or other official would often attend around teatime. Although the royal couple still tried to see their children in the morning, the Piccadilly habit of fun around bath time was no longer possible because receptions and performances took up the evenings. There was no more time for playing Happy Families or making chairs out of needlepoint.

The family tried to recapture some of the old intimacy by returning to Royal Lodge at weekends and shorter holidays to ride horses and picnic in the grounds. But the fun was over by teatime for the King, as then the dispatch boxes full of papers arrived for him to review. The Princesses busied themselves riding large rocking horses outside the door, thumping away on their steeds while their father ploughed, slowly and diligently, through the long words and complicated concepts he found so difficult.

The King did not begin work immediately. His first official engagement was a visit to the East End in February, which Edward VIII had been scheduled to undertake in December. The Lord Chamberlain told him to make the visit in the hope of quelling the 'growing impression that the last King was "pushed out" because of the interest he took in the poor'. Even ensconced in France, David cast a long shadow over his brother.

The Queen quickly recovered from her low spirits at the end of 1936 and rose to the demands of public appearances. Swathed in pastel crêpe and huge pearls, propped up on high heels to add to her height, the Queen had a much more friendly mien than that of her mother-in-law. Unlike royals before her, she smiled at the crowds and developed a manner of friendly interest with 'study, planning and tremendous concentration' – an endeavour that led, inevitably to 'some artificiality'. 'Wave, Bertie,' she would often hiss at the King, smiling sweetly all the while. She was soon content in her new role.

'Little Elizabeth Lyon, the future Duchess of York *I don't think*,' the Duke of Windsor had written dismissively when he had heard Bertie was courting her. But now 'little Elizabeth Lyon' was Queen and Empress of India, feeding the 'sealions' of the people with fish, as her mother might have said. Mrs Simpson and others who had laughed at her as plump and provincial had been sidelined, and she was Queen. No one would compare her again to a fat Scottish cook. She was certain that she was fulfilling her new role with more grace and aplomb than Wallis could ever have done. 'The pleased expression on the Duchess of York's face is funny to see,' fumed Wallis. 'How she is loving it all.' She could never bring herself to refer to her sister-in-law as Queen Elizabeth.

The King, by contrast, was unhappy, out of his depth and still worried by his childhood feelings of inferiority to his golden-haired brother. Every communication with his brother made him nervous and he was still convinced the people preferred David. He looked to the Coronation with dread. He knew that the politicians, courtiers and the royal family, particularly Queen Mary, were intent on a great ceremony. The dignity of the monarchy was due to be restored. Britain had to be shown to its Empire and the rest of the world as infallible, its magnificence and pomp intact. A resurgent and aggressive Germany and Italy were threatening Europe. Great Britain had to display its power.

Queen Mary understood her son's discomfort and took an active role in attempting to assuage it. She volunteered to accompany him to the Coronation, the first Queen Dowager to do so. For a royal as preoccupied by protocol as Queen Mary it was a truly significant gesture. The King knew that the ceremony was his chance to prove that he was up to the task – and that some doubted his ability to do so. *Time* magazine reported that he had considered issuing a denial of rumours circulating on the stock exchange that he had been suffering from epileptic fits. It was, as *Time* reported, 'a matter of utmost interest to British businessmen in view of the approaching Coronation in which they have many millions at stake'. There were suggestions that the King was so nervous and fragile that the entire ceremony would have to be shortened to the absolute minimum. The government, sure that the answer to a problem was to throw money at it, planned a huge celebration – it would cost the staggering sum of £524,000, over £20 million pounds in today's money and more than two and a half times the sum spent on George V's investiture as king.

The new heiress presumptive had to be prepared for the Coronation. She was the first in modern history to watch the crowning of her predecessor. Queen Victoria was twelve when her uncle had been crowned William IV, but her mother refused to allow her to attend. By contrast, the new King gave Elizabeth a specially bound edition of the service to read.

Elizabeth was eager to embrace the ceremony. After avidly reading Queen Victoria's account of her Coronation, she preoccupied herself by worrying over Margaret, then not quite seven. 'I do hope she won't disgrace us by falling asleep in the middle,' she fretted to Crawfie. 'After all, she is *very* young for a coronation.'

The Abbey, closed to the public from the beginning of the year, was a hive of activity. The canons' rooms became dressing rooms with tables and mirrors, and sandwiches were laid out in a side room to fortify the royal family and their attendants (at Queen Victoria's coronation the arch-bishop had turned over two pages rather than one, thus she was sent away early and hurried straight to the food table). The Princesses were fitted with lace frocks with gold bows down the front, ermine cloaks and specially made coronets. Margaret complained vociferously that Elizabeth had a train, whereas young ladies of the time would wear gowns no longer than ankle length before they became debutantes and thus near to 'coming out'. Thrillingly, the Princesses were allowed to wear properly long gowns, painstakingly designed by Mr Norman Hartnell, as well as elbow-length gloves and their first strings of pearls.

Elsewhere, manufacturers were frantically churning out Coronation goods, hoteliers debated putting up their prices and restaurateurs worried about employing sufficient staff. On 30 April, 26,000 London busmen went out on strike, demanding better working hours and conditions, and refused to resume work. All those who wanted to come to London for the Coronation would have to find a way other than by bus. Still, people covered the streets in bunting, banners and enough gold to sink a ship, photos of the King were displayed in every window, and houses were decorated with flags. Selfridges department store was the *piece de resistance* of London, covered in the most incredible facade of, in the words of the *New Statesman*, 'huge half reliefs of gilt and sil-vered plaster, enormous gilt lions, swollen tassels, fussy and over-decorated hangings of every kind'. Erected at a cost of thousands, the Selfridges front attracted nightly crowds, eager to goggle at all the gilt, and the whole lot was finally bought by an Indian rajah who shipped the entirety home to decorate his palace in Rajasthan. In the East End, they hung out banners declaring 'God Bless the King and Queen – and the Duke of Windsor'. A thousand special trains were laid on to bring people from across the country to London and hundreds bedded down on the streets, despite the drizzle.

At 5 a.m. on 12 May, Elizabeth woke to the sound of the Royal Marines striking up outside her window. Wrapped in an eiderdown, she looked out at the crowds with Bobo and then failed to eat much at breakfast because she was too excited. The King and Queen were already awake, roused by the 3 a.m. testing of loudspeakers on Constitution Hill. As the King recalled, he too could not eat and 'had a sinking feeling inside'. Wearing their white gowns and velvet capes, the Princesses trotted to their parents' room to find the Queen dressing and the King in his breeches and stockings, with a crimson coat as if he were at the Court of George IV. The Princesses descended to the Irish State Coach, accompanied by Queen Mary, who was, Elizabeth thought, 'too beautiful in a gold dress patterned with golden flowers'. The carriage was 'very jolty but we got used to it'. Margaret perched up on a seat built especially high to allow her to see out. At the Abbey, in the Royal Gallery, Elizabeth settled herself next to Queen Mary and paid great attention to the proceedings.

> *The Coronation*
> *12th May, 1937*
> *To Mummy and Papa*
> *In Memory of Their Coronation*
> *From Lilibet*
> *By Herself*
> *An Account of the Coronation*

Elizabeth's account of the Coronation, written in pencil on lined paper and bound with pink ribbon, was dedicated to her parents and remains in the Royal Archives today. 'I thought it all <u>very</u>, <u>very</u> wonderful and I expect the Abbey did, too,' she wrote. 'The arches and the beams at the top were covered with a sort of haze of wonder as Papa was crowned, at least I thought so.' To her, the white-gloved arms of the peeresses when they put on their coronets 'looked like swans'.

Elizabeth was entranced by the spectacle. 'What struck me as being rather odd was that Grannie did not remember much of her own Coronation,' she wrote. 'I should have thought that it would have stayed in her mind forever.' She did, however, admit that the service became 'rather boring as it was all prayers'. She and Queen Mary turned forward in the prayer book to find out how much longer they would have to wait. At the end of the ceremony she permitted Princess Margaret to whisper to her as they left the Abbey.

'They looked too sweet in their lace dresses & robes, especially when they put on their coronets,' recalled Princess Mary. Elizabeth was quite satisfied with her sister's behaviour. 'I only had to nudge her once or twice when she played with the prayer books too loudly,' she reported to Crawfie. In fact, Margaret had at times been very confused about what was happening, but had managed to sit patiently through the service. The King had found that matters had gone rather less to plan. He knelt at the altar to read the Oath, but his supporters, the Bishops of Durham and Bath and Wells, could not find the right page. The quick-thinking Archbishop lowered his book for the King to see – but his thumb obscured the necessary words. The Marquess of Salisbury got his garter chains caught up in the cushion on which he was carrying the King's crown to be taken by the Archbishop.

After they departed the Abbey, the new royal family set off to tour London from the Embankment to Hyde Park and up to the palace along Constitution Hill. The official photographs were taken and they did not sit down for tea until six. That evening they waved from the balcony at, according to Elizabeth, 'millions of people', all shouting 'We Want the King' and 'We want George'. 'The King wants his dinner,' the King grumbled good-humouredly. It was the beginning of a great surge in popular affection for the King and his Queen. 'A wonderful day,' Queen Mary wrote with relief. Elizabeth fell asleep almost as soon as she climbed into bed. (Afterwards, the stools in the Abbey were sold off for twenty-five shillings each.)

Thousands of people had listened to the Coronation on the wireless. One was the Duke of Windsor. In the home of a friendly businessman, the Château de Condé, in the Loire Valley, David sat in an ornate armchair, knitting a blue jumper for his beloved Wallis while the room resounded to the cries of loyalty to his brother.

Wallis's divorce was granted on 3 May, but she suggested they wait to marry until after the Coronation, so that crowning would not steal any of their thunder. She and David wished for a royal ceremony, conducted by a bishop. But the family refused to attend and forbade relations such as Lord Mountbatten to go. In turn, the Duke chose the date of 3 June, the anniversary of the birthday of George V, leaving Queen Mary 'enraged' at the thought of her son's 'revenge'. The family wrote that Wallis would not bear the title HRH and the Duke was distraught. 'Why in God's name would they do this to me at this time?' he cried.

On 3 June 1937, in the salon at the Château de Condé, the wedding took place, conducted by a vicar from Darlington who had agreed after others had turned it down (he had an eye for a chance to make money). The bride was elegant in a long pale blue dress and diamonds and the Duke wept with emotion at the end of the ceremony. Two hundred journalists waited outside. As they left the chateau on the following day, the grateful Duchess threw red roses into the crowds. (Among the gifts was an inscribed gold box from Adolf Hitler.)

The officiating minister promptly set off on a tour of the United States, enthralling audiences with stories about the wedding. In Britain, by contrast, the marriage was part of the regular news bulletin, in a piece just over fifty words long. 'Alas!' wrote Queen Mary in her diary, 'the wedding day of David and Mrs Warfield ... We all telegraphed to him.' Really, the royal family wished for him to be forgotten. 'We are thinking of you with great affection on your wedding day and send you every wish for future happiness,' wrote the new King and Queen. It was, they hoped, a final communication.

The new King and Queen could not countenance the Duke and Duchess living in London, attracting all the attention. Although the Duke did not wish to make his permanent residence in England (no longer King, he would have to pay income tax), he had expected to spend long periods of time there, meeting friends, drinking in his London clubs and entertaining at his beloved Fort Belvedere. The King and Queen desired him to stay away as long as possible, suggested at least a five-year absence and decreed that he must request permission before he did arrive. Bertie, nervously trying to stabilise 'this rocking throne', as he put it, worried over David's great popularity with the people and particularly the working classes. George VI genuinely feared his brother's power to lead a revolt of the working man against him. The Duke and Duchess took up residence in a grand Louis XVI mansion near the Bois du Boulogne in Paris, complete with large saloon and marble staircases. It was ideal for entertaining. But when the King and Queen arrived in Paris on an official visit in July 1938, they refused to meet the Duke and Duchess or invite them to a reception.

There was another reason for the royal family not to give David too much thought: the sticky problem of his heirs. In his abdication statement, he had vowed to 'renounce the throne for myself and my descendants', but it was not clear that any child of the marriage would not have qualified as an heir to the throne. The ceremony could not be dismissed as morganatic, since the King had agreed to it – although it perhaps could be defined as illegal, since Wallis's first divorce had not been on the grounds of adultery. Fortunately for the King and Lilibet, David's marriage remained childless.

Elizabeth had been very fond of her favourite uncle, but she quickly learned to forget him. Valuing duty and order above all else, she could not forgive him for falling short. She was very influenced by her mother and the Queen was fiercely protective of her husband, and had come to detest the Duke for selfishly giving up the throne and then hounding her husband with pleas for money.

At Buckingham Palace David was never mentioned – in the hope that his existence might be forgotten. Writing of the death in wartime of George VI's younger brother, the Duke of Kent, Crawfie declared, 'It was the second uncle they had lost completely, for though the first, Uncle David, was not dead, they did not see him any more.'

After the Coronation, the new King seemed to grow in stature. Buoyed up by the success of the ceremony and the sight of the cheering, he felt less like an imposter-King and he was grateful for the support of his wife. On a day to day level, he greatly enjoyed the chance to indulge his obsession with clothes. Life as a monarch involved interminable engagement with the questions of outfits and crowns – which suited him entirely. The household was invited to come to see the King and Queen ready to go out, occasions the King particularly enjoyed. 'Don't you think the Queen's hat is just a little too much up?' he might say, or ask about the exact positioning of a collar. It was just as well he found dress so fascinating. In the burgeoning age of photography and mass media, the tilt of the Queen's hat could be significant.

Queen Mary finally achieved her ambition of teaching the girls more history. In the Coronation year alone she took her granddaughters to the Tower, Hampton Court, Kew, Greenwich Palace and what was for Margaret far too many museums and galleries. 'When I grew up,' the younger Princess remembered, 'I decided my children should never be allowed to see more than three great pictures at a time so that they would actually plead for 'just one more', instead of dropping with fatigue and longing to go home.'

The old Queen also got her way over Elizabeth's history lessons. In 1938, Elizabeth was sent to Eton twice a week to learn constitutional history from the Vice-Provost Henry Marten, the co-author of the successful school textbook *The Groundwork of British History*. In his room, piled high with shaky towers of books, Miss Crawford unobtrusively read P. G. Wodehouse novels while Sir Henry instructed the Princess about the history of the monarchy and the court-yard below rang to the sound of the pupils of the school scurrying between lessons. One would sometimes enter with a message or a book, bow politely to the heir to the throne and leave the room. Absent-minded Marten occasionally addressed Elizabeth as 'Gentlemen', as he would his boys, but he was acutely aware that he had a chance to form the mind of the future sovereign. He told his eager pupil that the secret of the British monarchy was its adaptability and encouraged her to think about the importance of the 1931 Statute of Westminster as founding the basis of the modern British Commonwealth. Marten laid a particular emphasis on broadcasting, telling her that it encouraged loyalty among the nation and the Commonwealth by allowing the family to talk directly to their subjects. It was a proposal the Princess was initially reluctant to put into practice as Queen. But as her reign progressed, she became too keen to do so, authorising both the sensational television documentary *The Royal Family* in 1969 and the joke game show *It's a Royal Knockout* in 1987. Marten thought the Princess a shy girl who depended heavily on Miss Crawford. This was exactly how Miss Crawford wished matters to be.

Even if Elizabeth had not been confirmed as heir to the throne, it seems surprising in retrospect that her academic timetable was not expanded and enhanced with a further governess when she reached the age to attend senior school. As heiress, indeed, she surely required a more thorough grounding than that offered by a nursery governess, however capable. Princess Victoria had received the Duchess of Northumberland for formal occasions when it became clear that Uncle William would not have children. Princess Charlotte, heir to the throne before her untimely death in 1817, was taught by various tutors. One might have expected the royal family to appoint a lady with more academic qualifications. But the King and Queen were as hesitant about education as ever and Crawfie remained in charge. Indeed, Elizabeth received slightly less attention because Margaret joined them in the schoolroom – rather late at the age of seven.

The schoolroom timetable was revised to add more history, in accordance with Queen Mary's suggestions, but there was even less time for study at the palace than there had been at 145 Piccadilly. As well as the dentist, who had to check the braces on Lilibet's teeth, dressmakers and hairdressers visited much more frequently, usually in the morning. There were also occasional receptions to attend, and the King and Queen would often pop in to the schoolroom and take the Princesses to greet a relative or see something interesting. Elizabeth and Margaret naturally much preferred visits to learning dates or practising subtraction, and took every opportunity to be Princesses rather than schoolgirls.

In the minds of the courtiers, constantly aware of how Elizabeth was presented, there was a difficult balance to strike: the Princess must be educated to understand her position and her responsibilities, but she must not be too learned. The public would not like to think their adored young Princess was a bluestocking. Reports were put out that she was learning to cook in the kitchens of Royal Lodge, baked cakes in her little Welsh cottage to be sent to children in hospitals, and was perfecting her housewifery skills of scrubbing, much to the pleasure of Queen Mary (in reality her grandmother was much more exercised that she learn constitutional history).

The Palace and indeed the government were most concerned that the Princess was not too isolated. The future leader of Empire needed to practise how to rule. Her aunt, Princess Mary, was the Honorary President of the Girl Guides and it was mooted that a Guide company should be started for Princess Elizabeth. Miss Violet Synge, later the national Guide Commissioner, was consulted. 'How could it ever answer?' she said in shock. 'Guides must treat each other like sisters.' The answer was, of course, that the girls invited to join the company would be relatives and the daughters of high courtiers. The plans for the pack went ahead and Princess Margaret, too young to be a Guide, was attached as a Brownie. The King's only stricture was that they should not wear black stockings – as preoccupied by dress as ever, he complained they reminded him unfortunately of his youth.

Every Wednesday afternoon the Buckingham Palace (1st) pack of twenty Guides congregated in the most famous building in Britain, setting off into the gardens for adventures if the weather was fine. Initially, some of the families sent their daughters in full 'tea at the palace' regalia: gloves, lace dresses, accompanied by nannies and governesses. They had to be firmly told that the point of Guides was that the girls were to go trekking and exploring in the palace grounds. Miss Synge ordered them into three patrols and the Princess was appointed deputy patrol leader to the Kingfishers, with her cousin Patricia Mountbatten in charge. The Princess, at thirteen, was far too young to achieve such an honour as deputy, but it was simply unthinkable that the future Queen would not be in charge of *something*. Patricia decided she was 'very capable and efficient'. The girls engaged in veritable pre-war adventures: cooking sausages over an open fire, trekking the grounds and even practising signalling in the lengthy corridors of Buckingham Palace.

Despite such efforts, Elizabeth was leading a life very unlike that of a normal girl. The public was fascinated by the Princesses. Their every move was reported in the newspapers and it was almost impossible for them to go out without being surrounded by well-wishers. When the royal family were encouraged to visit Eastbourne so that the King could take the air, they borrowed the house of the Duke of Devonshire in the hope of gaining some privacy. People flocked after them at church and stood watching the Princesses as they played on the sands. At the palace garden parties, 3,000 loyal men and women wanted to see the Princesses. 'You must not be in too much of a hurry to get through the crowds to the tea table,' Elizabeth told Margaret firmly, although without a push through it was likely that they would never manage to enjoy any buns at all.

At the palace, the differences in the character of the two girls were growing ever more apparent. Apart from the odd joke played on the sentry, Elizabeth had become much more eager to please her parents and very serious minded. She was more carefully disciplined than her sister. Margaret was allowed many more friends and even to socialise at the age of ten or so, but her elder sister was given less freedom and kept in girlish frocks when she did attend evening parties.

The glitter of palace life was encouraging the Princess to think of being Queen herself. On the nights on which formal Court receptions were thrown for the presentation of debutantes the palace would bustle and sparkle – and the girls were excluded. They would perch up behind the stairs in their dressing gowns to watch the royal procession form to enter the throne room. Margaret sighed over the beautiful gowns. Elizabeth consoled her that one day both of them would be down there, 'sharing all the fun'. She had visions of herself being just as stately as Mummy and Papa. 'I shall have a perfectly *enormous* train, yards long.' Elizabeth was sounding very like a girl who wished to be Queen.

# 6
# 'Who is this Hitler?'

*The Royal Family walking in Sandringham Park, 1943*

THE KING'S PREOCCUPATION WITH his brother did not lessen as the months wore on. In October 1937 the American Ambassador wrote to his wife that 'the King does not yet feel safe on his throne and, up to a point, he is like the medieval monarch who has a hated rival claimant living in exile'. He suffered, just like 'his medieval ancestors – uneasiness as to what is coming next – sensitiveness – suspicion'. The Queen and the courtiers were equally fixated on David as a rallying point, and Conservative politicians still worried about his popularity with the working man.

While the eyes of the royal family and many of their ministers had been trained on Wallis's bejewelled form, German nationalism had been soaring. By late spring 1939 Hitler had ridden roughshod over international principles of diplomacy. After signing pacts with Italy and Japan, he felt unstoppable and, as with so many conquering dictators before him, he proceeded by allaying the fears of his intended victims by signing treaties of restraint, then promptly breaking their terms. In 1938 he marched on Austria. Neville Chamberlain, who had replaced the exhausted Stanley Baldwin as Prime Minister a few weeks after the Coronation, knew the people of Britain were afraid of war. The Church of England, servicemen's organisations and industrialists all supported negotiations for peace. One of the few politicians agitating for an aggressive response was the former Chancellor of the Exchequer, Winston Churchill, but his decision to put the country on the gold standard, followed by his attempt to dissuade Edward VIII from abdicating, had damaged his reputation and many did not take him seriously.

In October 1937 the Duke and Duchess of Windsor had made an ill-advised trip to Germany, encouraged by their host in France, Charles Bertaux, who had business interests in the country. The Duke aimed to promote peace and genuinely wished to make a study of working conditions in other countries, in the hope of being some use in a future role that was yet undefined in his mind. As he had said in his abdication speech, 'If at any time in the future, I can be found of service to His Majesty in a private station, I shall not fail.' But rather than being met with gratitude, the news of the Duke's interest in other countries was greeted by the British government with alarm. As ever, they worried he might call up the working classes to his cause and stage a bid for the throne. That their main concern about the German trip was the possibility that David was strengthening his claim on the British people was a terrible error of thinking. While the King and Queen and their courtiers fretted that David was a 1930s Bonnie Prince Charlie, and the government worried over class war, Hitler was plotting to conquer Europe. His initial aims had been tied to his policy of *Lebensraum* – room for the people – and a desire to unite the German minorities in countries across Eastern Europe. His successes in the 1930s emboldened him to aim higher.

David, so skilled at charming, so little allowed to do so, wished to see his best reflection in the eyes of adoring German crowds, even though he had promised the British government he would not make any formal speeches. He also hoped to give Wallis an experience of a state visit – the newspapers were told to refer to her as Her Royal Highness. On the first night they dined with officials including Himmler, Hess, Ribbentrop and Goebbels, and proceeded to tour factories, mines, housing projects and youth camps. The Duke genuinely wished to assist. 'Peter Pan is determined to help working conditions,' said Wallis.

Hitler had invited the Duke to visit Germany for reasons other than showing off his hospitals. He had plans to invade Britain and put the Duke and Duchess on the throne as his puppet king and queen. The Duke and Duchess met with the Führer at his mountain retreat outside Salzburg. The Duke apparently declared that 'the German and the British races are one, they should always be one'.

The Duke was naive but few in England could understand how aggrieved Germany had been in the wake of the Great War and how bent on revenge. Lord Halifax, President of the Council in Chamberlain's council, made a visit a month after the Duke, and met Hitler and his officers. He found them all rather clownish. Not even Churchill was truly cognisant of the danger. He wrote to the Duke of Windsor after his return: 'I was rather afraid beforehand that your tour in Germany would offend the great number of anti-Nazis in this country, many of whom are your friends and admirers.' He was pleased to see that this had not been the case – 'I am so glad it all passed off with distinction and success.'

After Austria in 1938, Hitler turned his attention to the Sudaten Germans, who had become part of the new Czechoslovak state in 1918. The King suggested he write to Hitler as 'one ex-serviceman to another', begging him to spare the young of Europe another war, but Chamberlain did

not consider it a good idea. The government began preparations for war. Bomb shelters were erected and plans for ARP
wardens laid out, windows were painted black and major
buildings were reinforced with sandbags. From the palace
windows, men could be seen working by the lights of lorries
digging trenches in Green Park, as others were doing in parks
across the country. Anti-aircraft batteries were erected on
Horse Guards parade, the guns pointing to the sky. Families
across the land – including the royals – were advised by leaflet
on the air raid system and how to construct a bomb shelter
in the back garden. Elizabeth and Margaret, like thousands
of children in Britain, were issued with their regulation gas
masks, which had to be carried at all times. They were given
the children's gas masks modelled on Mickey Mouse, with
red and blue noses – and hated them, as did many children
at the time. But at least they were not infants, like their small
cousins, for there were no masks for children under four –
parents were advised to wrap them in a blanket.

'We wait in suspense, watching helplessly while the
nations of Europe slither down into the abyss. Is it possible
that in a week's time there may be bombs raining down from
the sky on half the cities of Europe?' worried Alan Don,
Chaplain to the Archbishop of Canterbury. Chamberlain
agreed to discuss the transfer of the Sudatenland territories, in
the hope that Hitler would make no more demands. Rather
like the King with his offer to write, Chamberlain convinced
himself that if he went over to discuss the matter with Hitler,
the move would win him over – and 'it might be agreeable
to his vanity that the British Prime Minister should take so
unprecedented a step'. Such a statement was more revelatory
of his vanity than the Führer's.

'How horrible, fantastic, incredible it is that we should

be digging trenches and trying on gas masks here because of a quarrel in a faraway country between people of whom we know nothing', Chamberlain said in his speech to the nation on 27 September. Three days later, he returned from a meeting with Hitler with a piece of paper bearing the latter's promise to make no more territorial demands. He declared it was 'Peace in our Time' and went straight to Buckingham Palace, where he waved out from the balcony with the King and Queen to the cheering throng and crowds sang 'For He's a Jolly Good Fellow'. The stock market soared and there were suggestions that pieces of his umbrella should be sold off as souvenirs. 'What a shave', wrote Virginia Woolf.

The 'shave' did not last. Hitler made increasingly aggressive speeches and persecuted the Jewish populations. Despite reviling the horrors, the government retained the tight regulations of immigration and only the wealthy and those with sponsorship from an employer were permitted to enter. In December 1938, the first Kindertransport of Jewish children arrived in Harwich from Vienna. The majority were accommodated in a nearby holiday camp while foster homes were found for them. Nearly 10,000 had arrived by the following year, hurried onto boats by parents who would later die in the concentration camps. On 14 January, the cinemas gave ten per cent of their takings to the Jewish refugees. In the same month, the government began recruiting volunteers to the war effort – ambulance drivers, air wardens and ARP wardens. A list of occupations that would not be subject to the call-up was also published. These included farmers, lighthouse operators, prison warders – and ice-cream makers. Also, but not explicitly noted on the list were the close servants and equerries of the royal family. Factories in Birmingham and other industrial cities moved to further the war effort, making rifles and radar equipment. Factories that had previously made cosmetics turned to aircraft parts.

On 15 March, German tanks arrived in Prague. The peace was shattered. 'Who can hope to appease a boa constrictor?' demanded the *Daily Telegraph*. Chamberlain pushed through bills of rearmament and introduced conscription.

In France, meanwhile, cheered by their success in Germany, the Duke and Duchess of Windsor were pondering a tour to the United States. All eyes of the nation were on war, but the King and Queen were still obsessed with the Duke. No British monarch had visited America since it had gained independence in 1776 and for David to make a tour was a shocking affront, clearly revelatory of his ambitions to seize the throne. They set about planning their own tour to America.

President Roosevelt was keen to entertain the King and Queen, and wrote inviting 'either or both' Princesses: 'I shall try to have one or two Roosevelts of approximately the same age to play with them!' The King thought the tour would be too exhausting for his daughters, so he and his wife set off without them for six weeks in May 1939. The leave-taking at Portsmouth inspired public sympathy for the two Princesses. The notion of We Four as a family unit that could not be broken had taken hold of the imagination. One who was there declared that 'Margaret's face puckered up, Elizabeth looked tearful', while the King and Queen stared after them 'until the two little figures merged into the blue of thronged quays'. The newspapers congratulated the King and Queen for their devotion to duty, nobly separating themselves from their two beloved daughters for the good of transatlantic relations. The Queen's holiday reading was a copy of Hitler's *Mein Kampf*. 'Have you read it, Mama?' she asked Queen Mary.

In Canada the royal couple conducted their first ever transatlantic telephone call to the Princesses, who were staying at St Paul's Walden Bury. The Princesses ended the conversation by pinching cross old Dookie so that he would bark down the phone. Otherwise, the Princesses were left to Crawfie – and the educational plots of Queen Mary. She took the girls to the Bank of England to inspect the gold in the vaults. Elizabeth thought it disappointingly like bricks. The Governor, Montagu Norman, told her that if she could carry it, she could take it away.

Unfortunately for the Queen's plans to introduce the girls to historical monuments, her granddaughters were the two most sought-after children in the country. A visit to London Zoo turned into a press farrago, and Sir Eric Miéville, the courtier responsible for press relations, rued that somehow, 'by some extraordinary means', every time the Princesses were due to visit an institution, 'news always leaks out ahead to certain members of the press'. It seemed impossible to stop the talk. As he remarked: 'One has to remember that in these days such information given to the newspapers is worth money.' When the newspapers were full of doomy predictions and reports from Germany, pictures of the Princesses were welcome light relief. Indeed, while the sisters examined the animals, the Zoo itself was making plans for an invasion: the snakes would be shot, the black widow spiders killed with boiling water, and the elephants were to be evacuated to Whipsnade, the adults walking all the way and staying in barns along the route already picked out because they had ceilings high enough to accommodate them,

The girls received letters from all over America and Canada from ordinary people with news about their parents. Many sent photographs. A stationmaster from a small town wrote to say that he had seen the King and Queen pass through his station and he thought they would be pleased to know that they looked well. Others sent comics and little presents.

Press interest became almost feverish as the royal couple's return date approached. Elizabeth and Margaret, it was reported, were spring cleaning their Welsh cottage in expectation. On 22 June itself the Princesses travelled to Southampton to board a destroyer to carry them to the liner *Empress of Britain*. The press packed out Southampton along with crowds of enthusiastic royal watchers, all looking on avidly as the pair shook hands with the officers on the destroyer before setting sail to meet their parents. The Princesses ate cherries on deck, given to them by the captain, as they waited to descend the barge to reach the *Empress*. They threw themselves into the arms of their parents, then ate with them, the officers and local dignitaries on the ship, in a dining room that had been specially decorated with balloons to please the girls. Among the gifts for them were some small totem poles and frilly American pinafores. Although it had only been six weeks, the sisters had greatly changed. The King's eyes were fixed on Elizabeth. Thirteen-year-old Lilibet was becoming an adult.

The tour had changed the family. The King, feted across the country, had become more confident of his abilities and thus less dependent on his family for approbation. 'This has made us', both the King and Queen avowed. It was fortunate. While the royal couple had been away, Britain had become prepared for war. Men in uniform filled the streets, housewives stocked up on tins, hospitals were cleared for the injured and lorries bearing heavy artillery made the houses shake as they passed.

★

On 22 July 1939 the royal family made a visit to the Royal Naval College in Dartmouth. They stayed on the King's yacht, the *Victoria and Albert*, which had changed little since the days of the old Queen and was decorated in ponderous nineteenth-century style. On the Sunday morning the family were due to attend service at the college, but when the news came that two of the boys had been taken ill with mumps, the King decided that the girls must stay behind. They were taken to the house of the Captain of the College, where the Princesses and Miss Crawford busied themselves playing with a toy train set – perhaps not the toy of choice for many thirteen-year-olds.

After a while a tall, blond cadet with chiselled good looks and a jaunty stride entered the room and greeted Elizabeth. Prince Philip of Greece, then a cadet at the college and second in line to the Greek throne, had been present at the wedding of her Uncle George and at other family gatherings, but she did not know him other than by sight. He knelt beside Lilibet and the two played at trains, and the three ate ginger biscuits and drank lemonade. He soon demanded that they go to the tennis court and 'have some real fun jumping the nets'.

The girls were entranced by the eighteen-year-old Prince's looks, grace and commanding nature. 'How good he is, Crawfie,' Elizabeth said. 'How high he can jump.' Crawfie thought him a show-off but her charge would not be discouraged. She did not take her eyes from him – but he was enjoying teasing Margaret. He had already had some success with women and Elizabeth was just a child with braces on her teeth.

Philip's uncle Lord 'Dickie' Mountbatten was a great friend of George VI. Just as Leopold, King of the Belgians, had pushed Victoria towards his nephew Albert, so Dickie encouraged the meeting and put his nephew on his best behaviour. In the run-up to war, as Mountbatten knew, no young man could be more fascinating to a girl than one training for the services. As the son of the Captain of the College, North Dalrymple-Hamilton, recalled in his memoirs, he was asked to get out his toy trains for the Princesses and then 'Philip came along to assist looking after them – I think Dickie rather fixed it that he should'.

At fourteen, Dickie had suffered greatly when he saw his father, Louis, forced to resign from his position as First Sea Lord because he was German. 'Of course I shall take his place,' he said. Named Louis, he was called Dickie, even though Richard was not one of his names because Queen Victoria, his great-grandmother, had called him Nicky – but then this name became muddled with the Nickys of the Russian royal family. Dickie had originally been very friendly with the Prince of Wales. While accompanying him on a trip to India, he met the glamorous Edwina Ashley, daughter of the Conservative MP Wilfrid Ashley, and married her in 1922. After the Abdication crisis he came down on the side of Bertie and by 1939 was one of the King's confidants. With Philip, he hoped to come to influence the next generation.

After the morning with trains and tennis nets, Philip visited the royal yacht for lunch and joined the party on their visit to the swimming pool. That evening he dined on the yacht, but Elizabeth had been sent to bed early with Margaret. Next day he visited once more for tea. 'Philip came aboard *V & A* for tea and was a great success with the children,' wrote Mountbatten in his diary. Elizabeth was particularly solicitous, asking him eagerly what he would like to eat and gazing at him with fascination as he enjoyed a banana split.

The Princess had been very sheltered. She still spent her time in the nursery and the adults she met were courtiers and dignitaries, some of whom were too awed by royalty to speak. She had few friends her own age other than her cousins and was not particularly familiar with young men. Seeing the Eton boys as they passed through the rooms of Henry Marten hardly counted. When she did attend dances she found it difficult to enjoy herself. 'Could you this year only invite Princess Elizabeth to your party,' Crawfie would ask friends. 'We are trying to separate them a bit because Princess Margaret does draw all the attention and Princess Elizabeth lets her do it.'

Most thirteen-year-old girls would have been impressed by Philip of Greece; indeed, the majority of women fell under his spell. He was successful, sophisticated and handsome. He had already achieved much more success in his training than her stolid father, and would gain the prize for best all-rounder and best cadet after only a year at Dartmouth.

As the royal yacht departed from Dartmouth, the cadets were allowed to take whatever boat they could to follow after the party. Hundreds did so until the King declared that they must be told to turn back – for they were rowing too far out. Most obeyed the signal to retreat, apart from Prince Philip who continued to row hard after them in a little boat. Lilibet watched him keenly through the binoculars. 'The young fool!' shouted the King. 'He must go back!' Officials shouted at Philip through a megaphone until he surrendered and returned.

Elizabeth's interest in Philip put her more than a few steps behind the European newspapers. He had been mooted as a suitor long before the King's Coronation. There simply were not many eligible young men to be considered. The

Great War had ended some bloodlines, other monarchs had been thrust from their thrones. But Germany, the traditional hunting ground for fitly Protestant spouses in the past, was now closed to the royal family. Prince Philip had an impeccable lineage. His grandfather and uncle had been Kings of Greece, both his parents were royal (unlike the Princess). He was fourth cousin once removed to the Princess and his mother, Princess Alice of Battenberg, was sister to Lord Mountbatten, cousin of George VI. He had been schooled in Britain and he was training for the navy. In many ways he was ideal. Yet his family history was unhappy, he was Greek Orthodox (his mother later became a nun) and, worst of all, he was German. His mother had been German, all four of his beloved sisters married Germans and he had spent much of his childhood in the country.

Philip of Greece had been born five years before the Princess on 10 June 1921, on the kitchen table in Villa Mon Repos, the Greek royal residence on Corfu. He was the fifth child and only son of Prince Andrew of Greece and his wife, Princess Alice of Battenberg, and sixth in line to the Greek throne at birth. His grandfather, King George I of Greece, had been born a Danish Prince. He was just eighteen when the newly formed country of Greece offered him the throne, after a long and bitter war for independence with the Ottoman Empire. The Greeks had hoped for Prince Arthur, son of Queen Victoria, but Victoria had refused. Still, the young King George attacked the job in hand with gusto, enthusiastically travelling the country by foot, pausing to practise his Greek by chatting with his subjects. He visited Russia to find a suitably Orthodox bride and proposed to Princess Olga, daughter of the Tsar's youngest brother. They were married not long after her sixteenth birthday and she arrived in Greece with a trunk of dolls and teddy bears.

Prince Andrew, their sixth child, had been premature at birth and so tiny that he had to sleep in a cigar box and be fed with a toothpick. In 1902, at the Coronation of Edward VII, who was his uncle by marriage, he met Princess Alice of Battenberg. The granddaughter of Prince Alexander of Hesse, she was very much a German. In 1913 King George was shot and his son, Andrew's brother, became Constantine I.

During the war King Constantine followed a policy of neutrality. The Allies bombarded Athens and followed it with a blockade. In 1917 the King finally abdicated, in accordance with Allied demands. His second son, Alexander, was deemed sufficiently anti-German to take over the throne, but the rest of the family were sent into exile. After reigning for three years, King Alexander died of blood poisoning in 1920 after being bitten by a monkey, and Constantine returned to resume the throne. Already the Greeks had made an attack on Smyrna (now Izmir) on the western coast of Turkey, a wealthy city with many Greek inhabitants. Constantine intensified the campaign. 'What a triumph if we win!' he declared. Andrew became a commander but as the war progressed, he began to question the wisdom of the military plans, feeling that his men were sometimes required to attack when they had no hope of winning. In the following year Ataturk launched an assault on Greek forces and drove them from Smyrna; 30,000 Greek and Armenian Christians were massacred, and a million Greek refugees fled.

In September of the following year King Constantine I was forced to abdicate again. In December a revolutionary court tried Prince Andrew for refusing an order to attack at the battle of Sakaria, found him guilty and banished him from Greece. George V sent an English warship and the family departed on the day after the trial – Philip bundled in a cot made from a fruit box. They took up occupation at a house at St Cloud on the outskirts of Paris, provided by Philip's aunt. It was to be a sad beginning to his life. His father was bitter and lonely, and Alice fell prey to nervous illness and religious mania. In 1930 she was committed to an asylum for schizophrenia and the couple were deemed separated. Philip began his schooling at an American school in St Cloud, and was then sent to Cheam, an English preparatory school. By the time he was eleven his family had fallen apart: his mother was in an asylum, his father at the Riviera with a mistress, and his four beloved sisters were all married and living abroad. In 1933 he arrived at Salem, in Baden, one of the leading schools in Europe and near to his sister, Theodora, and her German husband. The German boys addressed him simply as 'Greece'. It was 1933, Hitler was rising and the inspirational German-Jewish headmaster, Kurt Hahn, had fled the Nazis for Britain, just before Philip began at the school. After an unhappy year, Philip was sent back to Britain once more and in 1934 began at the new school Hahn had established, Gordonstoun, in Morayshire in Scotland.

Twenty-seven boys attended the school when Philip arrived, but it expanded rapidly and by the time he left there were 150 pupils. At Salem, Hahn had developed an educational philosophy perfectly in tune with 1930s Germany: service, pride in physical excellence and outdoor activities. He had declared the high jump the great way in which a boy could confront his weaknesses, stating that eighty per cent could clear five feet by the time they left. Gordonstoun was founded on the same lines with the motto 'More is in you'. The day started with a cold shower and long run through the damp Scottish gorse, and there were frequent breaks for javelin throwing and running until supper at 6.30, where meat was never on the menu. After a spot of tennis, lights out was at 9.15. Two afternoons a week were taken up with building and steering sailboats off the coast of Hopeman, a nearby village. Spare time was for beating one's demons, such as the dreaded EBM (eating between meals). Hahn believed in service to the community as well as to the school, and boys joined either the school coastguard, fire service or mountain rescue. Philip thrived in the atmosphere of hard work and physical rigour, and took to the seamanship classes with enthusiasm, spending hours helping the boatbuilder, Mr Findlay. His academic record was solidly average, although he leaned more towards the arts than sciences. Made head boy in 1938, he was popular with the other boys and, as the headmaster noted, had inherited from his Danish family the capacity to 'derive great fun from the smallest incidents'. He also, the headmaster thought, took matters very much to heart, whether joy or sorrow, and found it impossible to hide his feelings. Sometimes guilty of recklessness and impatience – he had to be chastised for riding his bicycle with too much abandon around Hopeman – Philip, Hahn reported, was a 'born leader' but needed the 'exacting demands of great service'. He simply was not good at being second best – or following behind.

Philip spent his holidays with his sister Theodora in Germany, his grandmother, who was living in Kensington Palace, and his uncle, the Marquess of Milford Haven. He became expert at charming, fitting in – and keeping up appearances on very little money and depending on the kindness of virtual strangers and distant relatives. In 1938 he accompanied Alexandra, Queen of Yugoslavia, and her family to Venice and she remembered him as a 'huge hungry dog, perhaps a friendly collie, who had never had a basket of his own'. Handsome, witty and vulnerable, he was a great hit with women. Although only seventeen, he charmed various girls while holidaying with Queen Alexandra. 'Philip gallantly and I think quite impartially squired them all,' she recalled. She did not know how he had fallen in love with Cobina Wright, aspiring actress and daughter of a New York socialite. Cobina and Philip wandered the streets together in Venice and later London for a month. He was smitten but she, already under contract to Twentieth Century-Fox and destined for a glittering marriage, had bigger fish to fry than a penniless schoolboy, even if he was a prince.

'I do not think anyone thinks I have a father,' the Prince once said ruefully. 'Most people think that Dickie is my father anyway.' After the death of the Marquess of Milford Haven in 1937, his younger brother 'Dickie' stepped in as Philip's friend and guardian. A naval officer himself, he thought Philip suited to Dartmouth College. Just over two months after beginning at the college Philip was introduced to Elizabeth.

'Who is this Hitler, spoiling everything?' demanded Margaret. Throughout the summer, Germany continued to build its troops and showed no sign of withdrawing from Czechoslovakia. Britain readied itself for invasion. The National Gallery took down its luminous Rembrandts, Rubens, Constables and Turners and packed them onto special freight trains, guarded by men with revolvers, to North Wales (word had it that Goering wanted Poussin's *Rape of the Sabines* for his drawing room). There, the great works were buried in specially built studios in a slate mine near Blaenau Ffestiniog. The British Museum boxed around the Elgin

Marbles to protect them and packed some into the Aldwych branch of the Piccadilly Line, while the Victoria and Albert museum sent tapestries, carpets, watercolours and furnishings to country houses and underground stores. Hitler, with his eye for art and antiques would not get his hands on the treasures of Britain, it was thought. The handsome gold State Coach was removed from the Royal Mews and taken to Mentmore House, in Buckinghamshire.

The royal family mooted cancelling their usual holiday, but decided to retain their normal routine, as if the King holidaying as ever would be sufficient to dim Hitler's ambitions. On 22 August, news came of the signing of the German-Soviet pact. Parliament was recalled and the King returned to London on the overnight train. The Queen followed five days later. 'Why had Mummy and Papa to go back?' begged Margaret. 'Do you think the Germans will get them?'

On 1 September Germany invaded Poland. The British Cabinet threatened Germany that if the troops did not withdraw they would have to go to war. Emergency sittings were convened in a blacked-out Palace of Westminster and at 11.15 on Sunday 3 September Chamberlain broadcast to the nation that war had begun. 'We have a clear conscience, we have done all that any country could do to establish peace,' he said. Housewives preparing Sunday lunch stopped stirring gravy, men came in from their allotments, old women drinking tea after church put down their china cups. Within half an hour of the announcement, the air raid siren wailed out over the country. The King and Queen fled to the shelter in Buckingham Palace and waited for the bombs to fall.

At the time of the announcement of war, the Princesses were at the local church with their cousin, Margaret Elphinstone. They listened to the minister, Dr Lamb, tell his flock that the dreams of peace after the First World War were now over. The King and Queen decided that the girls should remain in Birkhall for as long as possible, with their holiday governess Georgina Guerin. Elizabeth, as always, worried about Margaret. 'I don't think people should talk about battles and things in front of Margaret,' she said. 'We don't want to upset her.' That evening, they listened to their father broadcast to the nation and the Empire. 'In this grave hour, perhaps the most fateful in our history, I send to every household of my peoples, both at home and overseas, this message, spoken with the same depth of feeling for each one of you as if I were able to cross your threshold and speak to you myself.' He announced that the country had been 'forced into a conflict' and for the sake of 'the world's order and peace, it is unthinkable that we should refuse to meet the challenge.' The Queen began training with a pistol in a shooting range laid out in the palace by her husband. 'I shan't go down like the others,' she said, stoutly.

'How difficult to decide where to live with every country quivering,' mused the Duchess of Windsor in Paris. On 2 September the Duke of Windsor wrote to Hitler with 'my entirely personal simple though earnest appeal for your utmost influence towards the peaceful solution of the present problem'. But he too had to flee France and was furious when his family refused to accommodate him. After fussing over a plane journey, he was saved by the ever loyal Churchill who sent a destroyer to Cherbourg to collect him. The Duke was demanding and troublesome, so an effort was made to find him a role back in France. But as the Germans advanced, he and Wallis also fled to Spain and there entered into lengthy debates with the British Embassy, declaring he would not return to Britain unless Wallis was received at the palace and he was compensated for the higher rates of tax for which he would be liable there. Churchill, so long devoted, finally lost patience and in July 1940 the Duke was offered the role of Governor of the Bahamas. Throughout the war he continued to bombard Churchill with requests that Wallis become HRH and expounded his opinions to the newspapers – often unhelpfully.

The King and Queen telephoned Birkhall every evening and on 18 September, the Queeen came to visit for a week. Not long after, Crawfie and the French governess, Madame Montaudon-Smith, arrived to take over from Miss Guerin (who later returned to France and joined the resistance). The governesses were instructed to carry on as normal. Elizabeth wrote her essays for Henry Marten and posted them off for marking. As the rest of the nation reinforced their bomb shelters, frantically sewed blackout drapes and rushed to stay with relatives in the country, Crawfie read the newspapers to the Princesses after tea – even though Elizabeth, at thirteen, was quite old enough to read them herself – editing out the 'horrible details'. Hitler caused all of them to fear. 'I hope he won't come here,' said Elizabeth.

Almost overnight, the great cities of Britain went dark. Theatres and cinemas were closed, and illuminated signs were turned off after sunset and trains and trams masked their lights. In Birkhall, every window had to be blacked out with drapes, the glass taped up for bombs. The King and Queen made visits to the regiments, the Red Cross and the YWCA. The Princesses tuned in avidly to the news on the wireless, although there was little to hear. On 1 September, the BBC radio output had been reduced to a single channel, the Home Service. Along with the 34 million other British listeners, the Princesses heard on the unleavened diet of war announcements sandwiched by dreary recorded music and the BBC Theatre Organ. Fortunately for them and all the other people trapped at home after dusk, programmes proper recommenced at the end of September. Propaganda stations also began to broadcast, most notoriously Radio Hamburg, featuring the so-called Lord Haw-Haw, William Joyce, a naturalised American citizen brought up in Ireland and living in Germany. Haw-Haw, crying out 'Germany calling', accused the upper classes of decadence, ridiculed Churchill, criticised the government's social policy and gave the impression he knew every detail about Britain. By January 1940, nearly a third of the British population were tuning in to Haw-Haw. His broadcasts had a horrid fascination – and for many, relieved the tedium. The Princesses also tuned in and threw books and cushions at the wireless as he made his dire pronouncements.

Elizabeth and Margaret pored over *Jane's Fighting Ships* and became experts on the ships of the Royal Navy. When they heard of the sinking of the battleship *Royal Oak* by a German U-boat on 14 October, with the loss of 800 men, Elizabeth leapt up in anger. 'Crawfie, it can't be! All those nice sailors.' They were particularly eager to do war work and every Thursday afternoon a sewing party was instigated in the Birkhall schoolroom. The wives of the farmers and workers on the Balmoral estate arrived to sew for the troops, fortified by drop scones, jam and fruitcake, for rationing had not yet begun. The Princesses played gramophone records on a machine so large and noisy that they stuffed the horn with six scarves in order to deaden the racket.

Conscientious as ever, Elizabeth practised wearing her gas mask every day and cleaned the eyepiece each evening with ointment. But she and Margaret also put them on to run around the grounds and pretend to be monsters, on one occasion terrifying the local plumber's boy. There seemed little other use for them. The progress of the war was slow, with little action on land, leading it to be dubbed 'the Bore War'. The King and Queen remained in London and life in Scotland was quiet. There was the dentist in Aberdeen for Lilibet's braces, the Girl Guides, sewing and occasional films in the evening, thanks to a villager who owned a projector and a set of Laurel and Hardy and Charlie Chaplin films. In Scotland, the Princesses delighted in taking the pony to visit the new Canadian lumber camp just outside Ballater, where men in bulldozers were busily cutting down the pines. As autumn wore on, men around the estate started to leave for the front, and the gardens appeared depleted and overgrown. Even the farms looked empty.

'We have got hundreds all about from Glasgow,' wrote Elizabeth. Almost immediately after the declaration of war, the movement of evacuees began. Nearly one and a half million children and mothers with infants from the vulnerable inner cities and tenements were hustled onto trains, clutching their gas masks, a few belongings and a stamped addressed postcard to send to their parents on arrival. Unlike English children, who were evacuated with their schools and were often picked off by locals and separated from their siblings, Scottish children went with their mothers and a large group of women and children arrived to live in Craigowan House on the Balmoral estate. The children at Balmoral were billeted in family groups and food was plentiful. But still, they missed home and found the countryside cold and dark. 'The sound of the wind groaning through the trees at night terrified them,' recalled Margaret. They thought it 'the sound of witches and devils'. Like many evacuees, they began drifting back when the bombing raids did not come.

Queen Mary was also evacuated. The King sent his seventy-three-year-old Queen mother off to Badminton, the home of her niece, Mary and her husband, Henry Somerset, 10th Duke of Beaufort. The old Queen wished to stay in London but her son prevailed and she set off for the country-side with sixty-three staff and a fleet of limousines.

The winter of 1939 was the coldest for nearly fifty years. In London, the Thames froze over, milk iced on doorsteps and ice a foot thick covered the emergency tanks. The Princesses huddled around the stove at their sewing circle and listened to a recording of 'Your Tiny Hand is Frozen'. The girls woke in the mornings to find their face flannels had frozen in their bathrooms and their water jugs were full of ice. Across the country, vegetables were scarce because they could not be dug from the petrified ground.

'A long face never won a war,' chivvied *Picture Post* on 10 December. 'There should be no doubt that this is the very year when we should think not less but more about Christmas, not only as an escape from the horrors of war but as a reminder of nobler ideals'. But the toy departments of many shops were subdued, churches cancelled midnight mass because stained glass windows were so hard to black out, and Westminster Abbey did not hold a carol service because all the choristers had been evacuated.

The royal family were keen to celebrate. On 18 December, Elizabeth and Margaret caught the train to London and then to Sandringham, the little ornaments, stickers and costume jewellery they had bought from Aberdeen Woolworths wrapped up carefully in their luggage. On Christmas Eve, their mother gave both girls diaries and exhorted them to write in them every evening – a discipline Elizabeth still continues. The King gave his first Christmas Day broadcast to the nation. 'A new year is at hand,' he announced. 'If it brings continued struggle, we shall be undaunted.'

The people who had besieged the grocers' shops at the outbreak of war had been prescient. In the New Year, despite the lack of action, rationing was introduced. Butter, sugar and bacon were the first to be restricted, with meat, tea, eggs, cheese, lard, milk, jam, biscuits, breakfast cereals and canned fruit to follow. Each person in Britain was allowed 4oz of sugar, 2oz of butter and 2oz of cheese per week. Even unrationed items were often sparse. Fish was rare and fruit became almost impossible to buy for the general population: lemons and bananas were scarce, oranges generally reserved for children and pregnant women, and apples sporadic. The rationed items were not always of high quality: most milk was used to make a rather flavourless 'Government Cheddar'. Sausages were bulked out with bread and so much water that they often exploded under high temperatures – hence the name 'bangers'. The Princesses' beloved chocolates were now quite different: darker and grittier and no longer encased in shining silver paper. Tin foil was needed for the war effort and so they came in wax paper.

The rich found ways around the rationing system. Restaurants were initially not rationed and only after protests were limits brought in, such as just three courses. The Princesses, too, were fortunate. The King declared that the Princesses must follow the rules of rationing, although their diet was supplemented with the copious game from the estate and fruits and vegetables from the garden. Still, their ritual of receiving coffee crystals at lunch continued although rather than taking them from a bowl offered by their father,

they were served by a footman. And at the height of rationing they still worked for their Cook badges at Guides, in the
kitchens of the Windsor Castle housekeeper, sending their
resulting stews and cakes up to the ARP men who guarded
the walls. Windsor Great Park was turned over to agricul-
ture and the Princesses benefitted from the fresh food grown
there. Unlike millions of other children, the princesses did
not have to stand in line for half an hour with their mothers
at the shops and no one at the Lodge had to tune in to *The
Kitchen Front* on the wireless at 8.15 every morning for suggestions on how to use up leftovers or make cakes without
eggs.

In February, the princesses left Sandringham for Royal
Lodge, its pale pink walls now painted green and brown
to disguise it from bombers. The official line was that the
Princesses were staying 'somewhere in the country'. No
journalists tried to break the spell of secrecy. There, in Royal
Lodge, the sisters continued to live tranquilly, following the
King's strictures. With the outbreak of war, thousands of people had taken their dogs, cats and other pets to be put down,
fearing they would be killed (and others were later destroyed
because their owners could not afford to feed them), but the
Princess was still surrounded by her animals and the beloved
corgis, Crackers, Susan and Ching.

Elizabeth began her lessons at Eton with Henry Marten
once more. She and Margaret joined the local Girl Guide
company, along with many of the new evacuees from the
East End, and there were picnics in the woods and long
walks. Matters were rather different from the Buckingham
Palace Girl Guides. There, their companions had been the
daughters of courtiers and eager to cede to the Princesses,

laugh at their jokes, and assume the more difficult chores. The East End children were less eager to play second fiddle, and the Princesses found themselves gathering firewood and scavenging. Crawfie was once amused to see the Princess standing in front of a giant tub of greasy water, less than enthusiastic about submerging her hands to do the washing up. But taking part only went so far: later, when at Windsor Castle, while the Guides camped out in tents the Princess would usually stay in Queen Victoria's summer house in the Windsor grounds. Margaret found sleeping under the stars in sleeping bags with her chums very entertaining, but her sister was more reserved. In any case the camps did not last long – once the bombing raids commenced, the children would go home at nights.

Life in the early months of the war was still privileged: Elizabeth and Margaret had dancing classes every week from Miss Vacani, a celebrated teacher. Other little girls from suitable families in Windsor (not the East End evacuees) came in their party frocks, accompanied by nannies, and the whole party tucked into tea after their exertions.

Everybody was waiting for the Germans. Ministers suggested that the danger was such that the Princesses should travel to Canada, just like many upper-class children of the time. Lord Mountbatten conveyed his wife and sons overseas, Chips Channon sent his son and many of the wealthiest families made private arrangements. After public pressure, the government opened a scheme to send British children overseas, with free passage to Canada, America and other eager host nations. But two weeks after its opening, the programme was closed to applicants. It was simply impossible to find enough battleships to escort the children overseas, or even sufficient passenger ships to carry them in the first place (these were being used to expel enemy aliens). One boat that did embark privately, the SS *City of Benares*, set off from Liverpool on 13 September. After five days, its battleship escort was called away, and on the following day, a 500 lb torpedo shot through the hull of the boat, killing two children instantly. The rest attempted to clamber into lifeboats, but the Atlantic was freezing and lashed with winds, and the few surviving older children desperately tried to hold up the infants and keep them out of the water. Over seventy-seven out of the ninety evacuees died. In the wake of the horror, Churchill decreed that the government would no longer enable the sending of children abroad.

Through it all, the Princesses staying 'somewhere in the country' were used to set an example. Unlike many other wealthy offspring, they would be remaining in Britain, and they would brave an invasion, if it came. As the Queen put it, 'The children will not leave unless I do. I shall not leave unless their father does, and the King will not leave the country under any circumstances whatsoever.'

# 7
# '*Do* let me see what is happening'

*Margaret and Elizabeth in 1945*

THE KING, QUEEN AND their daughters were vital as patriotic symbols. It was up to them to show British power, significance and virtue – and why men fought for 'King and Country'. The strength of the King was metaphoric of the strength of the nation. In the early part of the war the royal family were shown as refusing to change, determined to continue normal life. As the photographer Lisa Sheridan wrote in her memoirs, 'There was a determination on the part of the King and Queen to maintain a simple, united family life, whatever calls there might be to duty.' Although the King and Queen were in London and their children elsewhere, the notion of the unified royal family was very potent.

The 'Bore War' or 'Phoney War' could not last forever. In the spring of 1940, German troops invaded Denmark and Norway. Allied attempts to turn them back were a failure. Chamberlain's authority was dangerously weakened and on 10 May, when Germany launched an attack on Holland, Belgium and nearby France, he was forced to resign. That evening he broadcast to the nation in stirring tones:

And you, and I, must rally behind our new leader, and with our united strength and unshakeable courage, fight and work until this wild beast, which has sprung out of his lair upon us, has finally been disarmed and overthrown.

The Princesses were listening by the wireless in Royal Lodge. Queen Elizabeth wrote to Chamberlain that the Princess had wept at his words. 'I *cried*, Mummy,' she said.

Winston Churchill had long been calling for a policy of ruthless attack on Germany; he now had his way. The wild beast, everyone had realised, could not be tamed or calmed – it had to be tied up, penned, put to death. Germany's attacks were, he announced, 'the first crunch of the war'.

The King was a great supporter of Chamberlain and, if he was to be replaced, desired the Foreign Minister, Lord Halifax, to be Prime Minister. Churchill had supported Edward VIII after all. The Conservative Party also wished for Halifax, but at a meeting with Chamberlain, Halifax did not press his position. Churchill, rough, argumentative, often mistaken but also resolute, determined and a great orator, was the better leader in a time of war. 'You ask, what is our policy?' he demanded in his speech to the House of Commons. 'It is to wage war, by sea, land and air, with all our might and with all the strength that God can give us.'

The King and Queen had chosen Madresfield in Worcestershire as their shelter in the event of an invasion. They would, they agreed, lead the Resistance from there. Buckingham Palace filled up with foreign royals. King Haakon of Norway arrived seeking refuge and Queen Wilhemina of the Netherlands dashed from the Hague at the last minute, to be collected by the King at Liverpool Station.

Two days after the commencement of attack on the Low Countries, the Princesses were sent to Windsor Castle, 'at least for the rest of the week', said the Queen. They would live at the castle for the rest of the war. Windsor had been chosen, not because it was rural but because it was well defended. Plans were made for their safety: a small group of hand-picked soldiers from the Brigade of Guards and the Household Cavalry were on alert to whisk them (and the corgis) away to a safe house in the country.

The castle was dull and gloomy. All the pictures, tapestries and chandeliers had been taken away in case of bombing, the cabinets turned to face the walls and every window draped with heavy blackout curtains. The castle was freezing (fires were only allowed in sitting rooms, not bedrooms) and all the bright light bulbs had been replaced by dimmer versions, to suit the lighting regulations. Every day, the Princesses attended their lessons with Crawfie and in the evening, dined in virtual darkness with their protection officers and courtiers under a single light bulb. Baths were a strict three inches deep and a black line was drawn around the sides to ensure obedience.

Two nights after they arrived, the complicated system of alarm bells jangled through the castle to indicate an air raid had begun. The Princesses and Allah had at first wanted to dress, but they were told to hurry straight to the shelter. Margaret fell asleep on Crawfie's knee and Elizabeth read a book until the all-clear sounded at two in the morning. Next day, Crawfie and Lilibet decided that they should put proper beds into the shelter and also assemble their treasures ready to go, to save time in the next air raid. They packed suitcases that had been given to them by the French government with their favourite toys, brooches, books and their diaries. As the bombs fell more frequently, the Princesses were equipped with siren suits. These were zip-up all-in-one garments that they could leap into quickly with no fuss about dress, but which would keep them warm and protected. Winston Churchill was the most enthusiastic wearer of siren suits, sitting for a portrait in one, and having them made in stylish and handsome red, green and blue velvet. As the bombing intensified, the Princesses took to wearing them every night. Along with the rest of Britain, nightly cycles of broken sleep, fear and relief became a way of life. The sisters were determined, still, to play outside and continue guiding. When the alarm sounded if they were outside, they simply bundled into the trenches.

Three days after the Princesses arrived, there came a company of Grenadier Guards. They provided a much needed injection of gaiety. The sisters watched them marching and digging trenches around the castle for their protection. 'They wouldn't have kept anybody out, but they kept us in', commented Princess Margaret. Princess Margaret and Crawfie amused themselves playing tricks on Elizabeth by pretending to press the button that would summon the whole palace guard. The eldest princess would rush into the castle with the dogs, crying, 'You can't do it. You can't do it!' The guards invited the Princesses to take tea in the guardroom, with a tablecloth specially borrowed from the housekeeper and cakes painstakingly baked by their mothers and sisters back home. Elizabeth was delighted to be asked to be hostess and pour the tea, before they all played a vigorous bout of charades.

The Princesses were not familiar with the castle and they spent hours exploring its corridors and crannies and playing hide and seek in the passages. One day, they were wandering around their new home when the King's Librarian invited them to the underground vaults.

There, in a rather incongruous-looking set of boxes,

wrapped in old newspaper, were the Crown Jewels, cunningly hidden from German invaders. Elizabeth and Margaret had never been so close to the glittering diamonds of the Imperial Crown.

The King and Queen would usually arrive to spend the weekend at Windsor with the children. The Princesses would often walk down to meet them, along with the corgis, Jock, the Shetland pony, and Hans the Norwegian pony. The Queen was full of ideas for how to liven up the gloomy palace and instigated an after-dinner tradition of a game called 'Kick the Can', in which the princesses and the party chased around the house and every visitor had to join in – even stately gentlemen such as the Lord Privy Seal. Otherwise, the evenings were long and dull. Elizabeth, like many people across Britain, took solace in reading (indeed, demand for reading soared, even though there was little paper for printing). She was particularly fond, as always, of books about horses.

In April 1940 the Queen announced that the Princess's birthday cake would be a plain sponge, as an economy. Princess Elizabeth was fourteen – old enough to leave school and work, as so many of her contemporaries were forced to do – but she was still kept in sheltered seclusion. Yet she played a key part in the battle for propaganda. If the men were fighting for King and Country, they were also fighting for the two Princesses. The Ministry of Information put out reports that they were bearing the loneliness of their isolated life in the country with courage – they too made sacrifices for the war effort, as did their people. The Princesses, the people were told, wore their gas masks, obeyed rationing and were given their own vegetable patch to plant carrots, potatoes and vegetables, following the government's exhortation to

'Dig for Victory'. Just as George V had gained respect from the people for giving up alcohol in the First World War, so the reports of the royal family's minor frugalities were enthusiastically received.

'*Do* let me see what is happening,' said Elizabeth, her eyes wide at a bombing. Crawfie often had to shout at her to come away from the window. She wanted to play a greater part, but continued her isolated life in Windsor. The King's unhappy experiences of school and, indeed, work, made him determined not to submit her to the same.

But she had a much more confident personality than her father and her natural conformity, spirit of fair play, eagerness to take part and practical nature made her the ideal type of girl to fit in well at school. Perhaps if war had not intervened, the Princess might have been allowed a spell at school or abroad to widen her horizons. But with the advent of war she was too valuable. She had to remain at home to exemplify what the troops were defending.

At the end of May, the sisters were playing outside the castle when the noise of explosions and gunfire started to tear the air. Aircraft screamed overhead. They could think only of their parents but Crawfie told them the explosions were too far away to be in London. On 31 May, they learned the truth from the BBC: the Germans had invaded France as far as Calais and all British troops were being evacuated. The Princesses had heard the earlier announcements asking everybody in possession of a boat to take it to the authorities (along with a good supply of food), but there was no indication as to why. When the operation began, Churchill told the Commons to expect 'hard and heavy tidings'. The King asked the nation to give a week of prayer to enable the safety of the evacuation. Families of soldiers in France listened to the radio and hoped for good news. The operation was incredibly successful. By 5 June, over 330,000 British and French soldiers had been rescued from Dunkirk harbour in northern France, borne in 850 boats, some of them small fishing boats. Most of their equipment had been left behind. They arrived in England, only to be hurried into cinemas, churches and halls, given food by volunteers, so exhausted after their escape that they often fell asleep where they stood. The British were now exposed to the Germans on all sides – and the war had truly begun.

At the end of Dunkirk, Churchill had announced that 'Britons would defend our island, whatever the cost may be'. That summer, now that they could launch planes from France, German bombing intensified over the south of England and the coast – in preparation for invasion. By the end of the war 300 high-explosive bombs had fallen in the vicinity of Windsor Great Park. The Castle shook on its foundations as bombs dropped and Crawfie and the girls sang, read, and told stories in an attempt to forget what was going on outside. At times the sky over Southern England was almost a carnival of aircraft, fire, and wind as planes were shot down and fell in a mass of flames. The Princesses knew the names of most of the aircraft and became so familiar with the different planes that they could say either 'Ours' or 'Theirs' as they heard them go over.

On 1 July, the Germans entered the Channel Islands, Jersey, Guernsey, Alderney and Sark, nearly every house flying a white flag of surrender. Britons on the south coast armed themselves with pitchforks and shovels, just in case, and watched out for parachutists. The MPs moved from the Houses of Parliament to the nearby Church House, in case of bombing. In factories around the country, work was stepped up, with some men working thirty-six hour stretches. Towns across Britain set up their own 'Spitfire Funds' – the inhabitants collecting rubbish, selling bric-a-brac, or sending in their savings to reach the £5,000 needed to buy a plane.

At lunchtime on 10 July Lady Reading, the head of the Women's Voluntary Service, appealed to the women of Britain to donate their aluminium to be made into aeroplanes. As she said, 'we can all have the tiny thrill of thinking as we hear the news of an epic battle in the air, "Perhaps it was my saucepan that made part of that Hurricane".' Almost immediately, people began donating their pans, baths, kettles, fish slices and even artificial limbs to the WVS centres. A Cardiff housewife gave a set of pans bought in Germany fifteen years before. The Princesses gave their prized set of little teapots and kettles that had come with Y Bwthyn Bach.

George V had been wise to change the family's name for, once more, Germans were at best disliked and at worst under suspicion. In May, all male Germans between sixteen and sixty were rounded up and interned, and women soon followed, apart from those who were heavily pregnant or infirm. In June, after Mussolini's announcement that Italy and Britain were at war, mobs wrecked Italian cafés, ice-cream parlours, hairdressers and grocers and Churchill ordered that all male Italians between sixteen and sixty, resident in Britain for less than twenty years, should also be sent to the camps. Those left behind plastered their shops with declarations they were British and displayed Union Jacks. Unlike in World War I, there was no suggestion that the King was too German nor aspersions cast on Queen Mary – who might, theoretically, have qualified for interning, had she not been too old. Lady Elizabeth Bowes-Lyon and the two heartily English little girls had ensured that no one thought the King an 'enemy alien'.

In September 1940, Hitler changed his policy from attacking British coastal towns to the cities. His planned invasion would be prepared for by assaulting factories, industry, docks and ports. On 7 September, 'Black Saturday', the air siren started at 4.43 p.m. An off-duty fire officer in Dulwich looked up and saw the sky was full of an advance of black dots that he realised were planes in numbers he had never seen before. As another ARP warden recorded, 'The East End was getting it'. Over 300 bombers circled around the docks and the factories on the banks of the Thames. The Tate and Lyle sugar barges blazed and the warehouses on the river flamed solidly for 1,000 yards. The fires could be seen brightly from as far as Brighton. Thousands of people disobeyed the ban on entering the underground and surged into Liverpool Street Station for protection. At 6 p.m. the all-clear sounded, but at 8 p.m., the bombers came back and dropped over 300 tons of explosives. The cheaply built houses collapsed. By the time the second all-clear sounded at 4.30 a.m., 430 people were dead and over 1,600 injured. On the next morning, Winston Churchill came to visit and almost wept at the sight of the Union Jack flags, perched in the piles of rubble that had once been houses. That night, the bombers returned for the City.

Seventy-six nights in a row, Britain, particularly London, was battered by the bombings. The German aircraft came every night, sometimes fewer than fifty, other times three hundred, dropping massive high explosives. The Londoners of the East End were at first stoic, and then resentful, booing the King and Queen on a visit, jeering at the Queen for wearing her furs, and demanding to know why the West of London had escaped so lightly. The royal couple began returning to Windsor Castle at night to avoid the raids. They were wise; on the evening of 9 September, the palace was hit by sticks of bombs and the windows were shattered.

Less than a week later, Buckingham Palace received a direct hit. As the Queen wrote to her mother, she had been trying to remove an eyelash from the King's eye when they heard 'the unmistakeable whirr-whirr of a German plane'. 'It all happened so quickly that we had only time to look foolishly at each other when the scream hurtled past us and exploded with a tremendous crash in the quadrangle.' Another bomb exploded through the royal chapel. It was clearly an attack on the palace. 'I am glad we've been bombed,' said the Queen famously. 'It makes me feel I can look the East End in the face.' Forty journalists arrived to cover the story and the growing hostility to the riches and safety of the royal family was dissipated almost overnight.

Undaunted, the royal couple spent the afternoon touring the East End. 'I felt as if I was walking in a dead city,' she wrote, 'all the houses evacuated, and yet through the broken windows one saw all the poor little possessions, photographs, beds, just as they were left.' In the chaos after the bombing, hundreds of rats ran free over the palace, and so the Queen was able to practise her revolver shooting on moving targets. The palace would be bombed nine times in total and, although servants were injured, there was only one death: PC Steve Robinson, on duty at the palace, was killed by debris in 1941.

'If they hurt the King and Queen or the Princesses, we'd be so mad we'd blast every German out of existence,' declared one woman – a view said to be typical. Simply, the

King and Queen would not give in. When the Queen was at Windsor and the alarm sounded for the bombing raids, she would walk in stately fashion to the shelter, refusing to be hurried by the courtiers. Not even the Nazis would make her run. If the King was with them, he would take his revolver, prepared to fight to the end.

The Blitz, for the Princesses, was a time of great fear. They were given ear plugs to mask the sound of aircraft and they tried to sleep through the raids in the shelters, but like the rest of the country, they were fearful. The bombing was seemingly incessant. On 17 September, 350 tons of bombs were dropped on London, more than the total dropped on Britain during the previous war. Many other cities were also attacked, including Liverpool, Hull, Cardiff, Plymouth and Warrington. By the end of the month, over 5,700 people were dead and 10,000 injured.

The Blitz changed everyone's minds about the idea of the Princess broadcasting. Henry Marten had taught Princess Elizabeth the importance of the radio, but the Palace had taken a dim view of their precious heir presumptive appearing on such a vulgar medium. In 1938 a request for Princess Elizabeth to broadcast to the United States, in order to open National Children's Week, was firmly turned down. The British Ambassador decried the use of the Princess for 'stunts' and the Palace was of the same mind, replying, 'There is, of course, no question of the Princesses broadcasting, nor is it likely to be considered for many years to come.' Derek McCulloch, the originator of the idea that the BBC should broadcast to the evacuated children, had been imploring the Ministry of Information to allow the Princess to broadcast, with little success. Less than two years later, with the

Luftwaffe razing London buildings to the ground, the royal family changed their minds. US support was now vital to the war effort. The Director General of the BBC asked the King's private secretary if the Princess might consider broadcasting to the children of North America. He received a swift assent. Although her words would be ostensibly addressed to children, the import was aimed at adults. As the Director General elucidated, 'it would reach the minds of the millions who heard it with a singular poignancy.' Poignancy and pathos were indeed the theme of the broadcast, bravery through suffering its point.

On 13 October 1940 the Princess read out her script during *Children's Hour* on the BBC. 'Thousands of you in this country have had to leave your homes and be separated from your father and mother,' she announced. 'My sister, Margaret Rose, and I feel so much for you, as we know from experience what it means to be away from those we love most of all.' Comparing life in Windsor, with her parents visiting most evenings, to the sad situation of wartime evacuees was a little tenuous, and the script was sentimental and rather childish for a girl who had reached an age to leave school, but the Princess delivered her words with a precision and clarity that added gravitas to the sentimentality. The close was perhaps most sugary of all. 'My sister is by my side and we are both going to say goodnight to you. Come on, Margaret.' 'Goodnight,' said a rather quieter voice. 'Goodnight and good luck to you all,' concluded the Princess.

According to Derek McCulloch, the King rushed from the room after the first rehearsal crying '*she's* exactly like *her*', meaning that the Princess's voice was very like that of her mother. His daughter had inherited his looks and his stolid devotion to duty, but she was free from his terror of public speaking. Henry Marten had presciently seen that the demands of society would necessitate that the young Princess should broadcast. She had now proved that she had the capacity to do so. At the time, moreover, a little broadcasting was enough. Churchill's great reputation for broadcasting became seemingly unassailable, and yet he only spoke to the nation five times during the war.

The broadcast was a propaganda triumph. 'Princess yesterday huge success here. Some stations report telephone exchanges jammed with requests for repeat,' reported the North American representative of the BBC. *The Times* stated that churches in Canada had installed special wirelesses so that the speech could be heard, and papers across North America put Princess Elizabeth on their front pages. The representation of the Princesses as ordinary girls, suffering displacement and isolation along with their people, proved wildly popular. The BBC eventually turned the broadcast into a gramophone record to be sold in America and the Empire – so that people could play the Princess speaking over and over again. She would not be overused, however – she did not make another radio broadcast until 1944.

The Princess's broadcast was a hit in North America and Britain, but the Blitz continued. On the same evening, the residents of Coronation Mansions in Stoke Newington went down to the basement shelter only for the roof to cave in when the building was hit. It took ten days to dig out the victims, and 154 were killed. In Coventry on 14 November, the city was battered by over 40,000 explosives, leaving it, in the words of one woman, 'a city of the dead and utterly devastated'. For the first time, mass funerals were planned rather than burying each of the 568 dead in turn. The King toured the city alone, to spare the Queen the sight.

★

'This time we are all in the front line,' said the King in his 1940 Christmas broadcast. There were no bombings over the holiday period – 'on the Fuhrer's orders', apparently. But on 27 December, South London was hit again and two days later, the dome of St Paul's Cathedral was caught by a sole bomb, which failed to set it alight.

The sustained bombing of British cities continued until April – 40,000 ordinary people died, half of these in London, and over one million houses were destroyed. In London, the home of roughly one out of every sixth person had been reduced to rubble. Churches, museums, historic houses and the Commons chamber of the Houses of Parliament were ruined. The National Gallery had been hit three times. Helpless families wandered between offices and agencies, desperately looking for shelter and compensation. But the Blitz was a failure as a German operation: it failed to damage British morale significantly and the war industries continued largely unaffected. The Luftwaffe's intelligence was poor and there was a lack of leadership, so industries were bombed in succession, rather than sustained pressure being put upon one. Hitler turned his attention away from Britain and towards Russia.

Although the threat of bombing receded, the war effort continued and the home front was as crucial as ever. Stories about the Princesses became vital to raise spirits. In spring 1941, as the Blitz came to a close, the Princess was announced to be donating a prize open to schoolchildren in Wales for the best essay in English and Welsh on metal salvage. Margaret painted acorns to be made into buttonholes and sold them for the war effort while Elizabeth tried hard to improve her knitting, and both donated half of their pocket money to good causes. In July 1941 the Princesses staged a benefit concert and raised £80 for wool, and their father rewarded them with a ball at the castle – eleven-year-old Margaret's first ball. Margaret stayed dancing until 2.30 a.m. in the morning, and then promptly collapsed in bed with exhaustion for two days.

At Christmas 1940, the Princesses put on a play of *The Christmas Child*, raiding Windsor Castle for bits of old brocade and velvet. Elizabeth was a King in a crown and tunic, along with two evacuees (one with his face covered in cocoa) and Margaret was the Little Child. The play was such a success that at Christmas 1941, the Princesses put on a performance of *Cinderella* in St George's Hall of the castle, pricing the best seats at 7s. 6d. The local children took the smaller roles. The castle became a flurry of costumes, gold paint and choreography as the sisters created costumes and sets, and the King preoccupied himself, as ever, with dress – worrying that Elizabeth's tunic was too short. Unlike many children playing dress up, they had the advantage of years of historical stores. They found an old golden sedan chair from the royal basement and decided it was ideal for Cinderella's coach. A great item that might have carried the courtiers of George III became part of their pantomime. The audience were electrified by Cinderella's entrance as Princess Margaret perched inside the coach, resplendent in white wig, crinoline and patches. Elizabeth, as Principal Boy, wheeled her along. The applause at the sight was deafening. The pantomimes became so successful that the castle post office was besieged with enquiries and some would-be audience members sent blank cheques in the hope of gaining a seat.

The pantomime became a regular occurrence, with *Dick Whittington* particularly successful. In total, the performances raised over £800 for the war effort.

★

The two girls were repeatedly used for photo opportunities such as inspecting bomber planes or shown with their dogs. The hope was that the struggling British public would be encouraged by this publicity to battle on against privation and fear. For it was almost as if life was harder after the Blitz. The risk of loss of life at home had receded but the dreary days dragged on, with insufficient food, poor supplies of water and electricity, nothing to buy and little to hope for.

With the end of the battle in the air came a more concerted German effort by sea. So many ships were lost that Churchill requested the details were no longer given out in the newspapers, because it would affect British morale. Supplies of goods from America, including textiles and foodstuffs, were severely affected and clothes rationing was introduced in June 1941. The Queen and Queen Mary were given larger rations to account for their ceremonial role, but the Princesses, like everyone else, would be allowed one outfit a year. The Queen, however, had laid up great stocks of material for the Princesses before the war, but enthusiastic reports were put about that they were wearing her clothes, altered for them by herself. Food, too, was growing harder to buy. Rice, sugar and tea that had been imported from Asia were no longer available after the Japanese advances in 1941. The Princesses had eggs only on Sunday morning and the fat in which to fry them was scarcer than ever.

Many items were simply impossible to find: the shops were devoid of china and spoons and new books became so rare that reviewers turned to writing accounts of classics by Jane Austen and Charles Dickens. In an attempt to increase the stocks of paper, the Ministry of Supply launched an appeal for old books in 1943. Such was the enthusiasm for new books that 56 million were handed in to be recycled into new paper.

On 18 September 1941, Britain became the first country in the world to introduce conscription for women. Single women and childless widows between twenty and thirty were called up for military service in either the ATS (Auxiliary Territorial Force), the WRNS (Women's Royal Naval Service), the WAAF (Women's Auxiliary Air Force) or the munitions factories. Initially, many women in the services were engaged in clerical and catering work ('those who have been parlourmaids are detailed to wait on officers' declared one publication), but others also worked as drivers of lorries and transport vans. As the war progressed, they were brought into more active roles. Members of the WRNS acted as welders, carpenters, minespotters and crews and WAAFs worked in signals and radar, operated barrage balloons, and trained as pilots so they could deliver fighter planes from the factory to the airfield.

As many of the servants left to work in the factories or the women's services, the palace became more difficult to run. With the shortages, the King's Piper had to assist at table to help. Crawfie considered joining the WRNS but the King informed her that her work at the castle was more important and anyway 'you would be only cooking some old admiral's breakfast'. Such an unedifying view of the women's services suggests why the King was so uninterested in his daughters' academic curriculum and instead fascinated by their dress.

Elizabeth heard the constant appeals for female workers on the wireless and begged to be allowed to join. In 1942 she turned sixteen and signed on at the Labour Exchange, along with other girls of her age. Her father was very dubious. He wished his daughter to be protected, he had a low opinion of women's services and worried that she would be an easy target for the enemy. At the Labour Exchange, Elizabeth was questioned as any girl was on her work experience. As she had no dependents, she was theoretically a 'mobile' woman and could be sent anywhere in the country. But she was, unsurprisingly, not offered work.

In 1942 the Princess was asked to be Honorary Colonel of the Grenadier Guards. The role delighted her for she had become very fond of the Guards at Windsor, and she and Margaret had made friends with some of the officers. On her sixteenth birthday she carried out her first engagement in the role, inspecting the Grenadiers with her father – trailed by thirty reporters and ten photographers. The real serious-ness of the position was very welcome to her, for despite the efforts of her parents and Crawfie to keep her childlike, she was yearning for greater adult responsibility. On inspections she tried to make helpful criticisms, and sometimes, still the little girl who had arranged her shoes under her bed, was a lit-tle too enthusiastic. One major tactfully suggested she might be told that the 'first requisite of a really good officer is to temper justice with mercy'.

As the Honorary Colonel, it was simply not appropriate that Elizabeth was still in the nursery and had nowhere to receive visitors. A room hung in pink tapestry that had been occupied by the Princess Royal was given to her as a sit-ting room and the Princess filled it with her books and orna-ments. Queen Victoria had yearned for her own room and only gained it when she ascended the throne. Elizabeth was more fortunate. But the role as Honorary Colonel and the rooms were not sufficient to satisfy her.

The King agreed to expand his daughter's education. Antoinette de Bellaigue, Belgian wife of a vicomte and educated in Paris, had escaped her home country just over a week before the invasion. A friend of Helen Hardinge, she was summoned to the palace to teach the girls literature and history. Her aim, she said, was to give them 'an awareness of other countries, their way of thought and their customs'. She was a much more intellectually able tutor than Crawfie or Mrs Mountaudon-Smith and the Princesses developed excellent French conversation.

The United States entered the war at the end of 1941 after the Japanese attacked the US Pacific Fleet stationed at Pearl Harbor in Hawaii. From the spring of 1942, the first American soldiers arrived in Britain to train and to protect the country from invasion. Thousands of them packed into cruise liners and passenger ships and arrived to be shocked by the bomb damage, the weather and the poverty. 'NEVER criticise the King and Queen' they were told by a guide published by the US War Departments. 'Don't criticise the food, beer or cigarettes'. By 1944, over 1.5 million were stationed in Britain, mainly in the south of England, all better paid and better fed than their host population. 'They had everything', recalled one envious British soldier, 'money in particular, glamour, boldness, cigarettes, chocolate, nylons, Jeeps' and every girl aspired to have her own 'Yank'.

American soldiers were stationed at the castle and were fascinated by the princesses, saying so often to them 'I have a little girl at home just your age' that Elizabeth and Margaret struggled not to giggle. They collected postcards of the girls and sent them little treats – including a whole box of chocolates on one occasion to Elizabeth, a great treat in rationed Britain.

On the evening of 25 August 1942, the family were dining

at Windsor Castle when a page entered and whispered in the ear of Sir Eric Miéville, the King's private secretary. He left the room and then returned to speak in low tones to the King, who then left the room. The Princesses and the rest of the party sat in silence, terrifying themselves by imagining what had occurred. Finally, the Queen gave the signal for them to leave the table and went to join her husband. Later, they returned and told the Princesses the awful news: their uncle George, Duke of Kent, had been killed in a plane crash in Scotland.

Prince George had been only thirty-nine and his plane had come down in Scotland in poor weather. The youngest of his three children was only seven weeks old. Elizabeth had been bridesmaid to Princess Marina when she married him in 1934, and she and Margaret had been entranced by their glamorous aunt. Playing with their Kent cousins also had the piquant attraction that Marina was the cousin of Prince Philip and had lived in Paris at the same time as he did. The whole royal family grieved deeply. After the death of her husband the thirty-five-year-old Princess Marina devoted her attention to her cousin, receiving him frequently during the war and hoping – like all of the rather rickety family – that he would succeed in vindicating their fortunes by charming the Princess and her parents.

After a slow start, Philip distinguished himself in the war. In the autumn of 1942, at just twenty-one, he became a first lieutenant and was second-in-command of a destroyer. Philip served bravely. He was on HMS *Wallace* when it covered the Allied attacks on Sicily (and had to illuminate the enemy cruisers) and, as part of this, he possibly bombarded one of his brothers-in-law, who was fighting for the

Germans. On his brief shore leaves he stayed in London with his uncle Mountbatten and told stories of derring-do to the pretty girls. Queen Alexandra of Yugoslavia claimed 'the fascination of Philip had spread, like influenza, through a whole string of girls'.

Despite the 'string of girls', Philip still wrote to Elizabeth. In 1941 Alexandra found him writing a letter to 'Lilibet', which he insisted on finishing before they could chat. He spent a weekend in 1941 with the family, impressing George VI with his naval tales. Although he still saw Elizabeth as a child, he was flattered by her interest in him and keen to be friendly with the royal family. She, by contrast, had fallen in love with her handsome correspondent. The King was blissfully unaware of the danger lurking at his doors.

At the end of 1943, Philip was invited to spend Christmas with the royal family at Windsor. 'Who *do* you think is coming to see us act, Crawfie?' demanded Elizabeth excitedly. Miss Crawford thought the Prince much changed, 'weatherbeaten and strained' although still handsome and very well-mannered. Initially Elizabeth was disappointed, for Philip fell ill with flu and was confined to bed during the first two performances of *Aladdin*. He recovered in time for the third performance on Saturday 18 December and sat in the front row, along with the King and Queen and his cousin, the widowed Princess Marina. Princess Elizabeth, a cast of forty and a chorus of twenty-five schoolchildren sang and danced together for *Aladdin*. Philip entered spiritedly into the fun, laughing loudly at all the bad jokes.

The little girl he had met was now seventeen, beloved of the nation and destined to be the richest and most powerful woman in Europe. She was pretty and her figure was mature, but most of all she had a touching innocence that many of the women he had squired had lacked. Philip, who considered himself practically an orphan, had grown up never feeling entirely welcome or at home, and it was impossible not to be envious of the closeness of the royal family. The King and Queen, so intensely devoted to their daughters, were very unlike his own ramshackle parents. He stayed the Christmas weekend with the King and Queen and, as Elizabeth said, 'we had a very gay time, with a film, dinner parties and dancing to the gramophone.' On Boxing Day they played charades, then rolled back the carpet in the Crimson Drawing Room to dance until 1 a.m. – Philip one of the most energetic of all.

After his stay, Philip wrote to the Queen that he hoped his high spirits had not 'got out of hand'. He ventured that he might add Windsor to the homes of the Mountbattens and his cousin, Princess Marina, as his favourite places, that may 'give you some small idea of how much I appreciated the few days you were kind enough to let me spend with you'. Elizabeth may have been a touch unsophisticated, but he was charmed by the artlessness of family life with the Windsors. 'It is the simple pleasure of family pleasures and amusements and the feeling that I am welcome to share them. I am afraid I am not capable of putting this into the right words,' he wrote after a further visit in summer.

Philip returned so enthused by the Windsors that he listened to his Uncle Dickie's pleas to consider the Princess and his cousin, George II of Greece, took it upon himself to intimate Philip's interest to the King and Queen. They were rather shocked by the overture and the King told Queen Mary, a supporter of the young Prince, that although they liked Philip, who 'thinks about things in the right way', they thought Elizabeth 'too young for that now' and were going to tell George of Greece that 'P had better not think any more about it at present'. The King dreaded the thought of Us Four being split apart. Moreover, many in the royal circle believed that the war-battered public would prefer an English aristocrat, such as Hugh Euston, heir to the Duke of Grafton, who had been at Windsor with the Grenadier Guards. The Prince was foreign, penniless and without a home or much of a family and – like Prince Albert before him – was suspected of being something of a fortune hunter. He had not attended Eton, unlike nearly all of the British aristocracy and courtiers, but instead a school viewed as rather oddly progressive and even Germanic. He was much more at home with the manners and mores of itinerant European royalty than the rather more stolid British aristocracy. Some of the palace inner circle called him 'no gentleman'.

Harold Nicolson recorded a courtier as telling him that the royal family thought that Philip was 'rough, ill-mannered, uneducated and would probably not be faithful'. The courtier or Nicolson went a little far, but Philip did have a reputation as a ladies' man and, although appealing and funny, he had a tendency to anger and a forthright and often tactless manner. The King, as a man who was himself prone to rages, recognised the same risky behaviour in another. The Princess, used to excessively delicate courtiers, was charmed by his terse manner and delighted by his energy. The Palace saw him as something of a loose cannon and, moreover, believed Philip to be the creature of Lord Mountbatten and dreaded Uncle Dickie's seemingly insatiable ambition for greater inroads into the Palace and Parliament.

Most disturbing of all was the association of Philip with Germany. The royal family themselves were hardly

183

English – George III and his wife had been German, their son, Edward Duke of Kent, had married a German princess and their daughter Victoria had married a German prince. Edward VII was one of the few royals not to marry a German – for the simple reason that his mother did not judge any of the princesses sufficiently beautiful for his tastes. But the efforts of Queen Mary in particular to show the royal family as perfectly English had paid off. Philip was not much more German than his proposed fiancée, but his tall blond looks made him appear Teutonic – and mistrusted.

Philip was rootless, independent and not easy to control. Nevertheless, Dickie Mountbatten, undeterred, began campaigning for him to gain British citizenship. In August 1944 he suggested to the royal family that Philip should take British nationality – with the excuse that he then might be able to assist them in carrying out their functions. That the King might rely on a distant foreign relative to help him with his duties of visiting hospitals, schools and hosting receptions was very unlikely. Really, Mountbatten was preparing the ground for Philip's eventual marriage, even though the King had already refused the possibility.

Dickie approached courtiers, politicians and civil servants in an attempt to promote his nephew's prospects. However, the King and Queen were still reluctant. With the turmoil in the Balkans, it would not do to seem openly supportive of Greece. It was suggested that any naturalisation of Philip should wait until the following year, after a plebiscite in Greece.

Elizabeth was physically adult, although her stature was small. Those who saw her commented on her regal dignity. Lady Airlie complimented the 'carriage of her head' and noted 'something about her, that indescribable something which Queen Victoria had'. But the publicity showed her repeatedly as a child. She was still dressed in the same outfits as her sister and both were clothed as small children. Crawfie still called them the 'little girls'.

In April 1944 the Princess turned eighteen. Her coming of age was not marked by a great ball or party, but she did finally move from her nursery bedroom to a suite befitting a young lady. She continued to use the sitting room she had been given two years before. The Princess also received her own household, including a lady-in-waiting, a few months later. The question was revived of whether she should receive the title of Princess of Wales – the Welsh were particularly enthusiastic that she should be so named. But, the Palace noted, the Princess was still not heir apparent. If a son were born to the King, the title of Prince of Wales should by rights be his – and his wife would be styled Princess of Wales. The government and Cabinet were enthusiastic about the idea, for they thought it would engender good Anglo-Welsh relations, but the King was not. He wished his little girl to stay Elizabeth. Much to their disappointment, the Welsh remained without a prince or princess.

The Princess had always received a large amount of correspondence, but as she grew into an adult, more and more people in Britain and abroad wrote to her, passing on information, telling her about their lives and, most often of all, begging her for help.

The rules of succession in the British monarchy created an anomalous position: an individual could rule at eighteen, but the legal majority in the country was twenty-one. The 1937 Regency Act had provided that if the monarch were ill or absent abroad, his role could be deputised to five

Counsellors of State – the consort and the four next in line to the throne. These counsellors had to be British subjects and of the age of majority. Thus the Princess could rule the country alone at eighteen but not deputise for her father until she was twenty-one. The King was insistent that his daughter should be a Counsellor of State and the Lord Chancellor pressed the Prime Minister to initiate a change in the law. The justification was that the role would give the Princess valuable experience.

The Act was passed and the Princess became a Counsellor, with her mother, for her father's visit to Italy in July 1944. While he was away she had to sign a reprieve on a murder case and was shocked by the details. 'What makes people do such terrible things,' she asked. 'One ought to know. There should be some way of helping them. I have so much to learn about people!'

Her eighteenth birthday also marked a sea change in the attitude of the Palace. When her presence had previously been requested, the Palace had refused. It was declared that she might occasionally accompany her parents on visits, but otherwise she would remain in the schoolroom. Such responses were not so tenable now that the Princess was eighteen and a Counsellor of State. On 23 May she gave her first public speech at the meeting of Hackney's Queen Elizabeth Hospital for Children and in autumn she launched the huge HMS *Vanguard*, the largest ship ever built in the British Isles. She became President of the National Society for Prevention of Cruelty to Children.

The Princess was not content. Her cousin, Lady Mary Cambridge, was volunteering in the East End of London, and her other cousins, George and Gerald Lascelles, were fighting for their country (Gerald was captured and taken to

Colditz). Prince Philip, of course, was in the thick of battle. 'I ought to do as other girls of my age do,' she said (the conscription age for women was lowered to nineteen in 1943). The government agreed. The Princess would be an excellent propaganda weapon and they did not want any suggestion that the royals were not pulling their weight. The King was still unsure.

German power was fading. British planes donated by people across the country had been pulverising the cities since 1942, attacking Cologne and Hamburg in particular. Throughout the winter and spring of 1943 to 1944, Berlin was continually bombed. In early 1944, the Allies felt sufficiently confident to push back the German advances in Europe. Men arrived from America at the rate of 150,000 per week and villages across the South Coast of England were overrun with troops. On Tuesday 6 June, just after midnight, Allied forces began landing on the coast of Normandy, after an elaborate strategy of subterfuge to fool the Germans into thinking the aim was Calais. Over 23,000 parachutists jumped out and over half landed in the correct place – others drowned in the sea or the ditches the Germans had flooded. At 6.30 a.m., planes soared overhead as the land troops stormed the beaches. 'Paratroopers have landed in Northern France', announced the BBC news at 8 a.m. 'The battle that has now begun will grow constantly in scale and in intensity for many weeks to come, and I shall not attempt to speculate on its course', Churchill told the House of Commons. Newspaper vendors sold out in half an hour and churches opened for round-the-clock prayer.

In June 1944, as the troops moved into France, the people at home learned to fear once more. As Crawfie put it, an 'entirely new affliction came upon us'. The V1 or first pilotless aircraft, also known as the Doodlebug had arrived. 'Vague threats had hung in the air for some time about a new and horrific weapon and we could only suppose this was it', she wrote. Elizabeth and Margaret were terrified of them, worrying that these new weapons made invasion inevitable. They had their first sight of one while cooking sausages with the Girl Guides in Windsor Park. Crawfie lay over Margaret as they watched the craft sail over them and drop onto the Windsor race course. It had missed its target. Many were not so lucky. In February, British bombers razed Dresden in retaliation.

Finally, in early 1945, as the troops were advancing on Germany, Elizabeth was permitted to join the Auxiliary Territorial Service as a trainee driver. By 1943, women had taken over an estimated eighty per cent of the army's driving and the role was ideal for the Princess, for cleaning and cooking was too lowly and clerical work seen as easy (and indeed was generally given to older women). She registered as No. 230873 Second Subaltern Elizabeth Alexandra Mary, and began her training in driving and vehicle mechanics at the No. 1 Mechanical Transport Training Centre in Aldershot. The Princess had a lot to learn. On her first day, 23 March, at the Practical Mechanics lesson, she was shown how to handle a spanner. Asked if she had ever held one before, she 'looked slightly surprised, giggled slightly, and said "No! Never"'. The other eleven girls in training with her felt rather excluded as Elizabeth was whisked away between lectures, lunched in the officers' mess and returned to Windsor every night while they slept in dormitory huts. Within a few days the *Daily Mail* was pronouncing that the Princess was not properly getting her hands dirty and attitudes at Aldershot changed. She was allowed to converse with the other cadets, with the Company Sergeant Major watching. She learned to drive and maintain a car, and became a dab hand at taking an engine apart and reassembling it. 'I've never worked so hard in my life,' said Elizabeth of her experience. 'Everything I learnt was brand-new to me – all the oddities of the inside of a car, and all the intricacies of map-reading.'

Princess Margaret went to visit the mess and was most amused by seeing female officers drinking sherry and smoking cigarettes. Visiting with the King and Queen, Margaret also seized the chance to spot a case of weak compression that her sister had overlooked. 'It's missing,' said Margaret. 'How do you know?' asked Elizabeth. 'Why shouldn't I know?' was Margaret's cheeky response, as she poked one of Elizabeth's buttons.

The Princess was pursued by photographers. More pictures were taken of the Second Subaltern than had been at any time since the Coronation. She appeared on the front cover of *Time* and on the front page of every newspaper and magazine of the Allies. The Princess had become a propaganda weapon once more – her attempt to make herself 'one of the girls' had left her more symbolic than ever. She said later to the politician Barbara Castle that it had been the only time when she had been able to test herself against people of the same age. But it was no more of a level playing field than her Guide pack had been. She simply could not be subordinate. On 27 July she was made a Junior Commander. She also, unlike the other recruits, showed off her skills by driving along Piccadilly in the blackout, then into Buckingham Palace.

Elizabeth had fulfilled her desire to serve, but it was something of a slight victory. Her father permitted her to do so because, privy to Churchill's ear, he knew the war was nearly over – the troops were nearly in Germany. The King had spent almost the entirety of World War One in the sick-room, while his peers were killed in the trenches. He was not about to allow his daughter more heroism than he him-self had experienced. But although the troops were gaining on Germany, there was no guarantee that Hitler might not retaliate. Elizabeth's exercises were a vital morale booster. Hitler had described the Queen Mother as 'the most danger-ous woman in Europe', because of her effect on the national mood; her daughter was not too far behind.

'Poor darlings, they have not had any fun,' said the King of his daughters. He meant that they had not met many people. But Elizabeth had no interest in such 'fun'. She was already in love. In her beloved sitting room the Princess had propped up a photograph of Philip. 'Is that altogether wise?' Crawfie asked her. 'People will begin all sorts of gossip about you.' The Princess looked rueful. 'Oh dear. I suppose they will.' She took down the photograph but promptly replaced it with one of the Prince sporting a large bushy beard. To Elizabeth, he was brilliantly disguised. 'I defy anyone to rec-ognise who that is,' she said. She was wrong. The gossip began – and the news was soon printed in the papers.

On 30 April, Allied troops occupied the Reichstag. On 1 May, Hitler killed himself in his bunker below Berlin, and the entire German forces surrendered six days later. At 7.40 p.m. on 7 May 1945, the BBC interrupted a piano recital to announce that the following day would be hence-forth known as 'Victory in Europe' day and would be treated as a holiday. Few could quite accept that the war was finally over. The terror and tension were no more, the sleepless nights listening for bombs, the fear that friends and relatives had not survived was past. The men would be coming home. Next morning, for the first time since the outbreak of war, the newspapers printed the weather forecast. It was to be a sunny day – with rain to follow.

# 8

# 'After all, she is only nineteen'

*Playing tag with midshipmen on board HMS* Vanguard
*on route to South Africa, 1947*

On 8 May 1945 the crowds around the Victoria memorial outside Buckingham Palace were greater than they had been for the Coronation. Winston Churchill arrived in an open car, briefly spoke to the crowd, then entered the palace for lunch with the King and Queen. The people wanted more. 'We want the King' came the cry. The royal family emerged on to the balcony to tumultuous applause, eight times in total. The King wore his naval uniform and Princess Elizabeth was in her ATS uniform. Each time the people saw them, a great cheer went up – then they began to sing 'For he's a jolly good fellow'. Churchill later appeared and gave the 'V' sign to the crowds.

That night, fourteen-year-old Princess Margaret suggested they venture out on to the street. Swept up in the excitement of the moment, the King and Queen agreed. Margaret and Elizabeth, still proudly wearing her ATS uniform, along with fourteen or so others including Madame de Bellaigue, Crawfie and some Guards officers set off together, escorted by an equerry. Afraid of being recognised, Elizabeth pulled her uniform cap low over her eyes, but one of the officers declared he would not be seen with another officer who was improperly dressed, so she had to adjust her cap. All around them, people were dancing, crying, hugging and kissing and the party wandered to Parliament Square, then Piccadilly and as far as Park Lane, before visiting the Ritz and Dorchester Hotels, crossing Green Park and returning to the palace. For much of the route, they were swept up by the crowds and had to run. After repeated failures to go out incognito the Princess was finally free and unrecognised. All around her were, as she recalled, 'lines of people linking arms and walking down Whitehall and all of us were swept along by tides of happiness and relief'. They danced too – doing the 'Lambeth Walk' and the 'Hokey-Cokey'. They even stood outside the palace and cried 'We want the King' with the crowds. It was a brief and exhilarating moment of freedom.

That night, lights shone around the palace. As Princess Margaret later said in a television interview, 'Suddenly the lights came on and lit up the poor old battle-scarred palace,' she remembered. 'My mother was wearing a white dress with a tiara ... and it all sparkled and there was a great roar from the crowd, which was very exciting. VE Day was a wonderful sunburst of glory.'

On 9 May, the sisters went incognito again. As Elizabeth wrote, 'Out in crowd again – Trafalgar Square, Piccadilly, Pall Mall, walked simply miles. Saw parents on balcony at 12.30 a.m. – ate, partied, bed 3 a.m!' On the following after-noon the Princesses went out to visit bombed-out districts of the East End and appeared once more to the cheering crowds on the balcony that evening.

'It was a nasty shock to live in a town again,' Princess Margaret recalled. London had changed beyond their imag-ining. All around them were broken buildings and roads, wrecked walls and pavements. The palace itself was fragile after its nine attacks. The shops were often sparsely stocked and there were frequent shortages. The teenaged Princesses were emerging to public life in a war-torn city.

The girls had grown up in the war. The King too had become great and Queen Mary had actually gained a little leeway. She wept on leaving Badminton. 'Back in London, I shall have to begin being Queen Mary all over again,' she said. For many people across Britain, life was terrifying in its lack of purpose, now that the victory they had longed for had come.

As the Princesses hurried through the streets outside Buckingham Palace, Prince Philip was sailing east in order to assist with the projected invasion of Japan. But the incursion proceeded more quickly than expected and they were only in the Philippines when the atom bomb devastated Hiroshima. Three days later another bomb hit Nagasaki. Philip arrived on 2 September, in time to witness the formal Japanese surrender.

As the euphoria subsided, the people began to support the need for social reform. In 1941, the economist William Beveridge had carried out an investigation into Britain's social policy and found it sadly lacking. His report recommending more social housing and a welfare state had sold hundreds of thousands of copies. But the seventy-year-old Churchill, who had little time for policies of housing and benefits, was not the man to lead such an endeavour. He resigned as Prime Minister and called for an election. On 26 July, Labour gained a landslide victory and Clement Attlee became Prime Minister.

The naturally conservative King was deeply suspicious of the Attlee government. Yet despite their radical policies of social reform and nationalisation, the new ministers were still respectful of the King. At the first audience with Attlee, the King expressed displeasure that Hugh Dalton, son of George V's tutor, was to be Foreign Secretary. Attlee sent him to the Treasury instead and appointed Ernest Bevin as Foreign Secretary. The government began a policy of housebuilding and instigated moves towards Beveridge's notion of a 'cradle to grave' welfare state. Benefits were introduced, free secondary school education became a right for the first time, key industries and utilities were nationalised and the National Health Service was born.

In the summer after VE Day, the royal family travelled to Balmoral for a holiday. Elizabeth enthusiastically entered into deer stalking, wearing her father's plus-fours. They would travel up to a small house on the moor to picnic on stuffed rolls, ginger snaps and onions fried by the Queen, before washing the pots in the stream. Jock, the Highland pony, carried their belongings to the house, then tried to join them for the food. It was a newly idyllic time for the sisters who had spent so much of the war worrying over their parents. And then at Christmas at Sandringham, Allah died with little warning, much to the shock of the girls. The Princess had grown up with Allah and had spent more time with her than with her own mother in the early days of her life. The loss was profoundly painful.

'Food, fuel and clothes are the main topics of conversation with us all,' wrote the King in 1946. Fuel was scarce and food rationing was intensified as new bread and potato rations were brought in as the state struggled to feed its people. The war machine, the mines, factories and dock-yards had fallen quiet since 1945, Britain was badly in debt to America and its dominions, and the privations seemed so much harder to bear, now the country was no longer at war.

Even unrationed food was scarce – fruit was difficult to find. In 1946 Auberon Waugh's mother managed to buy three bananas for the children. No one had eaten one for seven years and Auberon had never seen one but heard that they had the 'most delicious taste in the world'. His father took them, doused them heavily in thick cream and sugar, and in front of his children happily sliced up and ate each one with relish. For Auberon it was an act of terrible cruelty that permanently damaged his view of his father.

In the post-war palace, it was not easy to hire servants. Many of the men of the traditional servant class had been killed and the women preferred to work elsewhere for higher wages. There were also those industrialists who had been made rich by the war and could pay higher wages to their maids and butlers. Really, the Second World War put an end to the old tradition of devoted royal servants, from Piers Gaveston to John Brown to Allah, who wished for nothing more than to serve the monarch. Bobo was the last of the breed.

The King, like many, discovered that life lost much of its lustre after the thrill of victory had faded. He had found a sense of purpose in being a war king. In a Labour-run Britain suffering austerity and debating public reform, the monarchy seemed much less useful. Bertie began to fall prey to his own bad traits of obstinacy and bad temper. Always irascible, he started flying into rages, or 'gnashes', with very little warning. 'He would explode if he read something in the paper that the Prime Minister hadn't told him about,' one courtier recalled. Princess Margaret could usually laugh him out of his fury, on one occasion throwing a spoon over her shoulder at the dinner table. Without her or his wife to soothe him, he was angry and difficult. One ex-courtier remarked that he 'used to lose his temper with anyone around'.

In the summer after the war, Elizabeth spent less time in the schoolroom and by 1946 she had given up all her lessons other than piano. She spent the mornings in her sitting room at Buckingham Palace, attending to her correspondence, speaking with representatives from her charities, or attended Council Meetings. As in Windsor, she now had receiving rooms in Buckingham Palace and her household was also expanded with her own footman, housemaid and second lady-in-waiting. The Palace appointed Mrs Jean Gibb, a twenty-one-year-old widow of a Grenadier Guard, so that she had someone who could discuss the Grenadier Guards with her and give her informal support in her role as Honorary Colonel.

The Princess was finally permitted adult clothes, which had not been adapted from those of her mother. Mr Hartnell came to the palace with sketches and samples of outfits for the new Princess. This, from her sartorially interested father, was an acknowledgement of her new adulthood.

In post-war Britain, Elizabeth was put on public show. The nineteen-year-old Princess exemplified the greatness that they had all been fighting for. In the summer after the end of the war she opened a library at the Royal College of Nursing, inspected the Fifth Battalion and Training Battalion of the Grenadier Guards, presented prizes at the graduation ceremony of the Royal Free Hospital School of Medicine for Women and addressed 3,000 Girl Guides. Cambridge University suggested the Princess might be the first woman ever to receive an honorary degree, but the offer was refused.

Still, the courtiers were intent that the Princess did not appear too intellectual.

After victory came depression. People contemplated their ruined houses and the miseries they had undergone in the war, men returned to find their wives and children much changed and struggled to find work once more. The Princess herself was joyous. How could she not be? The war was over and her long wait to see Philip once more was almost over.

Philip remained in Japan after the surrender to collect and bring home prisoners of war. In 1946, he returned to Britain and was sent to lecture to petty officers during their naval training in Wales. The photo perched in Elizabeth's sitting room finally became a reality. Philip visited Princess Elizabeth frequently and became a great favourite with Crawfie and Princess Margaret. In contrast to the glamorous evenings he had enjoyed with ladies in Europe, he came up to the old nursery, ate fish and drank orangeade with the sisters, and played card games or ball. Philip and Elizabeth went on outings together to restaurants and dances, often with Margaret and usually in company. After a visit to the musical *Oklahoma*, Crawfie noticed that Elizabeth was play-ing the song 'People will say we're in love'.

The Princess was entirely in love with Philip and, although his wide experience of women made him less romantic, he was charmed by her innocence and loving nature. He kept a photograph of her in his belongings. Matter of fact, organised and cheerful, she was a great contrast to his fragile mother. The Princess was a challenge and Philip, kicking his heels after the end of war, loved a fight. And, importantly, she was incredibly rich. Philip wrote 'of no fixed abode' in visitors' books. That would not be the case if he wed the Princess.

He was very conscious of the collapse in his own family's fortunes and knew how much he would please them by marrying Elizabeth. In May he attended his youngest sister's wedding and told her he was considering getting engaged. Uncle Dickie, he said with some understatement, 'was being helpful'.

'That the heiress to the throne could remain unmarried was unthinkable,' wrote Crawfie. The question was ever more delicate because of her sex. Women still promised to obey their husbands. As in the case of the selection of Prince Albert, the spouse chosen was implicitly supposed to be able to guide the country, as well as the Queen. Various suitors were discussed. But Elizabeth was sure – she was in love with Philip.

Post-war Britain, deep in austerity, was fascinated by a burgeoning royal romance. Elizabeth was distressed to be greeted with shouts of 'Where's Philip?' on a visit to a factory. She began to regard her routine visits with dread. 'Poor Lil,' said Margaret. 'Nothing of your own. Not even your love affair!' There was endless speculation in the papers, many of whom declared him unfit for the Princess because he was foreign.

The King was as unenthusiastic as the newspapers about the match. Philip's German background was a concern, he was impoverished and without a family. As one ex-courtier recalled, 'The kind of people who didn't like Prince Philip were the kind of people who didn't like Mountbatten. It was all bound up in a single word "German".' After the two wars the British Court had become insular. The days of frequent visits from foreign royals were long gone and many would have preferred a British aristocrat as 'one of their own'. Although Queen Mary was a supporter of Philip, some senior courtiers did not like him and the Queen was used to men who fussed around her and flattered her – which Philip did not. Moreover, there were still worries about his love of women, habit of independence and hot temper.

Mountbatten, too, was a problem. He had been assiduous on his nephew's behalf, but his efforts had alienated many. His ambition was just too obvious for some subtle palace courtiers and in addition he was mistrusted as rather left-wing, thanks to his friendships with Labour politicians, and his wife, Edwina, tended to unorthodox behaviour. The King and Queen were fond of Mountbatten but thought him rather too eager to take advantage of his connection with them. By letting in Philip, they would be allowing more space for Mountbatten's overweening ambition.

The King simply did not wish to let the Princess marry. Lady Airlie declared that the Princess was the King's 'constant companion in shooting, riding, walking – in fact in everything'; and after being separated from her for much of the war, he could not let her go. The King and Queen were both guilty of seeing the Princess as much younger than she really was – and they did not think her ready for marriage, even though the Queen had been only a year older when she herself married. As Queen Mary told Lady Airlie, 'They want her to see more of the world before committing herself, and to meet more men. After all, she is only nineteen.'

Really, the King had brought the situation on himself. As young people, he and his wife had socialised widely, and both had had prior romantic entanglements. But Elizabeth had been so intensely sheltered that she had reached her teens with a very small circle of acquaintances. Not allowed to go to school or university, the Princess knew few people of her own age. Without the war, she might have been able to enjoy some of a debutante season – instead she had been hidden away at Windsor Castle. The Guards officers were an opportunity for friendship, but her role as Honorary Colonel only underlined her superior position and made her more unattainable. It is thus hardly surprising that Philip had such a cataclysmic effect on her heart. The Queen hosted dances with Guards officers and the Princess duly did the foxtrot and quickstep with partners – but she thought only of Philip.

The Princess, moreover, was ever dutiful and always hoped to please her country. After the debacle of Mrs Simpson, the heir to the throne was expected not to wait too long to get married. She would be the exact opposite of her playboy, frivolous uncle and show herself as responsible and serious. In June, Philip wrote to the Queen apologising for inviting himself to the palace, for 'however contrite I feel', there 'is always a small voice that keeps saying "nothing ventured, nothing gained" – well I did venture and I gained a wonderful time'.

Philip was invited to summer in Balmoral with the family, perhaps for the King to test his feelings for him. The demands of a family gathering were such that the young people had little time together outside of hunting and trips. But still, Philip raised the question of marriage. As he put it later rather confusedly, 'It was probably then that we, that it became, you know, that we began to think about it seriously, and even talk about it.' Elizabeth was willing. It was the first important matter she had decided on herself, without consulting her mother. But the King and Queen suggested that they wait until at least after the Princess's twenty-first birthday, much to the misery of both – and a harsh sentence for a man who did not like to wait for anything. A planned trip to South

Africa was, the Palace had some hope, a way of expanding the Princess's horizons.

The opposition only intensified Philip's feelings. As a deeply proud young man, he hated the idea that he would not be successful and look foolish to all. As for so many servicemen, life after the war felt dull and directionless, and the royal family offered a role. As he wrote to the Queen after his stay: 'The generous hospitality and the warm friendliness did much to restore my faith in permanent values and brighten up a rather warped view of life.'

In September 1946 Sir Alan Lascelles denied stories that the two were engaged. He refused, however, to deny the possibility that an engagement might occur in the future. The press were then entirely convinced. At the wedding of Lord Brabourne to Patricia, Uncle Dickie's daughter, Philip was a gentleman usher and Elizabeth a bridesmaid. The newsreel caught Philip assisting Elizabeth with her fur wrap and the photo was sent all over the world. Post-war Britain was eager for some news that was not austerity and despair and the marriage prospects of the heiress presumptive were utterly fascinating.

The Greek monarchy was restored after the plebiscite in September. George II was King, but matters still were not simple. There was no guarantee he would remain, the Greek monarchy had been tyrannical and the government worried that uniting Philip with Elizabeth could yet be construed as taking sides in the conflict between monarchy and democracy in Greece.

But without naturalisation Philip's status in Britain was insecure. Finally, after some debate, the Admiralty ruled that he could not remain in the navy without British citizenship. However, many other refugees and foreigners were demanding citizenship and it was surely royal favouritism to allow him to jump the queue. Uncle Mountbatten stepped up his efforts, pressing the King, the Home Secretary and the Prime Minister. Finally, at the end of 1946, Uncle Dickie got his way. Philip became a British citizen. His dynastic name of Schleswig-Holstein-Sonderberg-Glucksburg seemed hardly British, so Philip assumed his uncle's name. In the spring of 1947 Philip, the dog without a basket, became Lieutenant Philip Mountbatten. Uncle Dickie's vaulting ambition had met with success. The children of the Queen should, by all rights, bear his surname. Dickie, always attentive to detail, informed the newspapers that Philip had long been practically British anyway – for he spoke no Greek and had not lived in the country for longer than three months since the age of one. The newspapers cheerfully took his word for it. In actual fact the whole effort towards naturalisation had been unnecessary. As a descendent of Sophia, Electress of Hanover, according to the 1705 Act of Naturalisation of the Most Excellent Princess Sophia, Electress of Hanover, and the Issue of her Body, Philip had been a British subject at birth. It had all been pointless hot air, although it had the benefit that it had provided an outlet for Mountbatten's incessant energies.

Fortuitously for Philip, Mountbatten was offered the role of Viceroy of India in 1946. He was well and truly out of the way.

On 1 February 1947 the royal family set off on a four-month tour of South Africa, on the invitation of Jan Smuts, the Prime Minister. The country was bitterly divided between English speakers and Afrikaners, and the Nationalists were making advances. Many declared Smuts to have invited the royal family only in order to rally his supporters for the forthcoming general election. They were correct. But the King saw himself as a monarch of Empire and he wished the Crown to remain in South Africa. Moreover, he welcomed the prospect of a break from post-war austerity and an escape from Attlee. Most of all, the tour would separate Elizabeth from Philip.

For Elizabeth it was a long period away from Philip, without anything of importance fixed. 'Well, I hope we shall survive, that's all,' she said, looking crossly at the programme. She tried to distract herself with the plans for the wardrobe, the route and rather impressive White Train, in which they would travel the country. The new state train was ivory and gold, a third of a mile long, with a post office and telephone exchange, her only lifelines to Philip during the long tour. To two young people four months seemed an interminable length of time.

The tour was not well organised. The King and Queen would not make the decisions on who would accompany them until the last minute – not thinking that the attendants would quickly have to assemble suitable wardrobes.

Margaret was excited at the thought of leaving Britain for the first time in her life. Elizabeth was anxious. She wished goodbye to the household and there was no gaiety in her eyes. 'Lilibet was sad and we all thought she did not want to go,' Crawfie wrote.

The party arrived in Cape Town at 8.30 on the morning of 17 February to an ecstatic welcome. The state banquet that night was to Sir Alan Lascelles the most miserable and dull dinner he had ever attended in thirty years, but he thought the royal family seemed content. They left behind them the worst winter of the century, in which temperatures did not seem to lift above freezing and there was no fuel to heat the houses.

The Nationalists were too intent on self-government to be won over by the mere visit of the royal family. 'Pleased to have met you, ma'am,' said one Boer to the Queen, 'but we still feel sometimes that we can't forgive the English for having conquered us.' The family were truly a weapon of Smuts: they were due to visit every part of the Union and win loyalty across the country from the Cape to Northern Rhodesia. They attended ceremonies and displays, toured docks, stared in horror at reptiles at the Snake Park in Port Elizabeth (the Queen expressed interest, but Elizabeth clutched herself in terror). It was a long tour with only a few days' rest and it was too much for the King, who was exhausted after the war years, and struggled with the heat and flew into rages. He was essentially touring the country, advertising himself and his value to the people, and it seemed often like arduous and thankless work. The Nationalists infuriated him. 'I'd like to shoot them all!' he declared to the Queen. She replied, 'But Bertie, you can't shoot them *all*.' The people were more delighted by the younger generation than the King and Queen. 'Leave the Princess behind!' they called as she appeared. At a welcoming ball in Cape Town, the night after they arrived, 5,000 people danced to a foxtrot called 'Princess'. Nationalist Stellenbosch, however, stayed silent.

The Princesses had to follow their parents and sit by them at displays. Princess Margaret was fascinated by the countryside and excited by the abundance of food. Lascelles thought Elizabeth 'delightfully enthusiastic and interested'. He was particularly grateful for her attention to time. 'She has her grandmother's passion for punctuality and, to my delight, goes bounding furiously up the stairs to bolt her parents when they are more than usually late.' The Princess frequently took it upon herself to hurry the Queen along by prodding her in the heel with her umbrella when 'time is being wasted in unnecessary conversation'. Still, Elizabeth learned much from watching the Queen in action. 'She can take on the old bores with much of her mother's skill and never spares herself in that exhausting part of royal duty,' said Lascelles. It was almost as if the Princess were King and Queen in one – able to smile and hold hands like a queen and deliver a speech like a king.

The family was due to depart on the 24 April and the Princess's twenty-first birthday fell three days previously. As a consequence, 21 April was announced as a public holiday throughout the Union. The day itself was very different from the quiet family teas of previous birthdays. At a large ceremony attended by the Cabinet, the Princess reviewed various ranks of servicemen, sailors and veterans, gave a speech to a rally of young people and attended a great ball in her honour. General Smuts gave her a necklace of twenty-one gemstones and a golden key to the city.

The greatest moment of the day was when the Princess made a broadcast to the Empire and Commonwealth. The speech had been written by Alan Lascelles and, when the Princess read a draft, she told her father's private secretary, 'It has made me cry' – a rare occurrence. The speech proved greatly touching, as solemnly, on her twenty-first birthday, the Princess dedicated herself to the service of her people.

There is a motto which has been borne by many of my ancestors – a noble motto 'I serve'. Those words were an inspiration to many bygone heirs to the throne when they made their knightly dedication as they came to manhood. I cannot do quite as they did but through the inventions of science I can do what was not possible for any of them. I can make my solemn act of dedication with a whole Empire listening. I should like to make that dedication now. It is very simple.

I declare before you all that my whole life, whether it be long or short, shall be devoted to your service and the service of our great Imperial family to which we all belong, but I shall not have the strength to carry out this resolution alone unless you join in it with me, as I now invite you to do. I know that your support will be unfailingly given. God help me to make good my vow and God bless all of you who are willing to share in it.

The Princess's speech was intended to sell her to the South African people, to the countries of the Empire and the Commonwealth around the world, and to the beleaguered British people who seemed to prefer social welfare to monarchy. In the aftermath of war the Empire was tottering – the economic weakness of Britain made the idea of it governing the world less and less feasible. George VI always saw himself as a King of Empire – but not everyone agreed. The imperial ideology had received its first significant attack in the failure of the British raid on the Boers in 1895. It was fitting that its swansong was in South Africa, as the young Princess toured, she who would not be Empress of India and would judge herself as the Queen of the Commonwealth rather than the Empire.

And yet, despite her broadcasts and her popularity with the people, Elizabeth was still not seen as an adult. As Sir Alan noted, 'For a child of her years, she has got an astonishing solicitude for other people's comfort; such unselfishness is not a normal characteristic of that family.' The Princess was a Counsellor of State and twenty-one – but to Sir Alan she was still a 'child'. His attitude suggests another reason why the Princess was so intent on Philip. Married, she would no longer be a child and she would have her own household.

The tour had seemed like a huge success. But its great purpose had failed. In 1947 Smuts lost to Malan, and the new pro-independence government viewed the Commonwealth with contempt and adopted segregated racial laws. South Africa would withdraw from the Commonwealth in 1960. The ties of Empire were crumbling for those countries who felt they could support themselves and a princess celebrating her twenty-first birthday held a sentimental appeal but little more.

For her twenty-first birthday, despite the shortages, the King and Queen gave the Princess a car with its own numberplate HRH1. Although she enjoyed whipping about London, she spent more time as a passenger in Prince Philip's black sports car. The two were regularly seen out together and he acquired a valet and a detective. The speculation in the press rose and it was clear that there would have to be an announcement either way. Philip's critics machinated against him but they failed. As the Princess's private secretary wrote, they believed that they had not succeeded because 'the Queen's usually good judgement has failed her'. It might just as likely be that 'Princess Elizabeth was so much in love as to overcome her parents' antipathy to the match'. Uncle Dickie had succeeded.

On 8 July the engagement was announced to the people

of Britain, a union to which the King 'has gladly given his consent'. Resentment at privations was replaced by a new story. Royal wedding fever had begun.

The wedding date was fixed for 20 November. Many felt they should wait until the following summer, but the young people felt they had lingered long enough. Letters and telegrams flooded in, including many from brides who planned to marry on the same day, as well as presents, from across the world.

Elizabeth wore an engagement ring of a large square diamond flanked by two smaller diamonds. It was too large for her because she had not been able to try it on in secret. The Welsh sent a piece of Welsh gold for the wedding ring. 'There is enough for two rings,' said Lilibet. 'We can save a piece for Margaret.'

# 9
# 'A flash of colour'

*Elizabeth and Philip at Buckingham Palace*
*after the announcement of their engagement, July 1947*

PHILIP WAS AN OBJECT of national fascination. The newspapers printed endless details about Lieutenant Mountbatten. Everybody knew that he drove a sports car with the registration HDK99. People marvelled at how such an impoverished young man had managed to gain such a victory.

Queen Victoria's marriage to another penniless German prince in 1840 had marked the beginning of perceptions that a royal wedding supplied an opportunity to secure and encourage loyalty to the monarchy and government. Before Victoria's marriage royal weddings had been quiet family affairs, held late at night with no pomp for the people to enjoy. Victoria and her ministers, eager to define her as the queen of purity and duty, in contrast to her rumbustious Hanoverian predecessors, planned a large wedding in which Victoria and her attendants would wear white (previous brides had tended to wear silver, gold or blue, but some wore black) and drive publicly to an afternoon ceremony at St James's Chapel. The gamble paid off: the crowds lined up and cheered, bought pictures of the Queen in her dress in their thousands and the notion of the virtuous, familial monarchy was born.

Since Victoria's celebration the public and government expected to see a royal wedding. Complaints were made that Edward VII, then the Prince of Wales, wed in Windsor –'an obscure village in Berkshire remarkable only for a castle' according to *Punch*. Elizabeth's parents had married in Westminster Abbey and a grand celebration had come to be expected. Still more so, since there had not been a royal wedding since the marriage of Prince George and Princess Marina in 1934 – the marriage of the Queen's other uncle, Prince Henry, had been dramatically curtailed after the death of the bride's father and no one would count the marriage of the Duke of Windsor in France. Nevertheless, many questioned whether a grand royal wedding would alienate the people, burdened as they were by the privations of continued rationing, unemployment and a severe post-war depression that had no end in sight. Some Labour MPs protested about the cost of the wedding, as well as the couple's future living costs. It could hardly be suggested that the groom's family was assisting with the expense. For a Labour government the question was particularly fraught. On one hand they were the party of the people and if the population wished for a good time – they should have it. On the other was it fitting that the party long associated with republican sentiment should devote time and money to celebrating a marriage of a member of an outdated institution?

Britain may have won the war with her Allies, but it was losing its Empire. In June, the Princesses had been among the very last recipients of the Crown of India, an order established by Victoria at the beginning of her rule as Empress. On 1 January 1877, Queen Victoria had been declared Empress of India and ever since then, India had been the Empire's great possession. On 15 August 1947, India gained full independence in the Commonwealth, parted into two states according to proposals agreed to by Dickie Mountbatten.

'Should the Princess's wedding day be selected as the first post-war occasion to restore to Britain the traditional gaiety of a gala public event?' was the rather leading question one newspaper asked of its readers. Nearly ninety per cent agreed. Other newspapers were less enthusiastic. The country was deep in poverty and fuel supplies were verging on crisis levels.

But in the end the decision was made: Elizabeth was the heir to the throne and she must be married in style. It was to be a true royal wedding, paid for by the King from the Privy Purse (his non-governmental income from the Crown Estates), with the exception of some street decorations in the Mall. The public, denied much sight of the Princesses in the war, were eager for the glamour of royalty. A royal wedding would be, as Winston Churchill put it (still playing the spokesman for the people), 'a flash of colour on the hard road we have to travel'. It was a chance to remind the world that the royal family had survived the war and, in many ways, contributed to the country's morale. Great Britain might have lost India, but it was still resurgent. It was still to be feared.

Royalty across Europe began polishing tiaras hidden in coal holes and finding their best gowns from the bottom of their packing cases. Only one was not invited. The Princess was determined that Uncle David should not attend. She still could not forgive him for his behaviour. Moreover, she was still highly influenced by her mother, whose hand was always evident in her actions. As one *Express* journalist wrote, 'It had been the Queen's personality which shaped the wedding.'

The decision was made that 20 November simply could not be declared a public holiday. The economy was too fragile for British workers to down tools for a single day (and no one seems to have thought much of celebrating on a Saturday). What followed was a very careful exercise in pleasing the people. Ever since Queen Victoria's project of strengthening the monarchy by presenting it as a middle-class, essentially bourgeois institution, kings and queens have had to tread a careful road, presenting themselves as fitly grand, without lavish expense. Such an effort was even more intense in 1947.

Elizabeth's dress would have to be made from material purchased with clothing coupons. A large number of women around the country, many of them brides-to-be, donated their coupons to her, in a show of support that seems almost inconceivable now. Almost 3,000 coupons were donated, although all had to be returned for transferring coupons was illegal. Instead, the Privy purse found the money for the silks.

Normal Hartnell designed the wedding dress, taking his inspiration from Botticelli's *Primavera*, imagining clinging lines and flowers symbolising rebirth and reinvigoration after the war. The designs were alive with stars and flowers – and the dress was the most gorgeous in royal history (royal wedding gowns are not always the most beautiful). The ivory silk of the skirt would be embroidered with flowers, crystal and pearls, and the fifteen-foot train decorated with syringa and orange blossom, jasmine and white ears and the white roses of York; 10,000 pearls were imported from America. Hartnell's embroiderers worked around the clock for seven weeks. The cost was estimated at £1,200, a staggering sum for a country still recovering from war. But the greatest question was not one of cost, but provenance. Hartnell was intensely questioned as to the nationality of the worms used to make the dress. He confirmed that they were not Italian, or, even worse, Japanese. They were Chinese – a neutral country in the war.

The people were passionately interested in the gown. The Princess put out a press release declaring her wish that the details remain secret, but the public and the journalists were determined to find them out. The manager had to sleep in the workrooms in case of break-ins from eager photographers. The Princess had received further coupons from the Board of Trade for the trousseau. Fortunately, the palace contained stores of leftover material bought by her mother and grandmother – and there were many offerings of silk from overseas.

The palace postmen had a job on their hands. Almost 3,000 presents poured in from around the world. Previous royal couples had returned all gifts from anyone unknown to the family, but Elizabeth was allowed to keep them. Some dispatched family heirlooms, such as an old lady who sent a Victorian lace underskirt, traditionally worn by the brides of her family. An old man from North Wales provided a rock from Mount Snowdon for good luck. There was a rabbit tea cosy, a Compact personal weighing machine, and two young ladies sent in two soggy pieces of burned toast – quite an offering when bread was on rationing. When they heard the announcement of the wedding on the wireless, they had been so excited that they burned their toast and promptly sent it to the Princess.

The Grenadier Guards busied themselves moving 1,500 presents to St James's Palace to be displayed to the public for the price of 5s. on the first day, 1s. later. The crowds waiting would often stretch for a mile – and Elizabeth watched them in fascination from the palace windows; 200,000 people clustered around dinner services, vases, jewels, silver and materials. Some were impossible to display: the Aga Khan sent a thoroughbred filly (who became Elizabeth's first flat-race winner in 1950); the people of Kenya gave a hunting lodge and two Wiltshire district nurses sent a Siamese kitten; the Earl and Countess Mountbatten a cinema to be fitted up in Clarence House; A Brooklyn woman offered a turkey because there was 'nothing to eat in England' – not entirely untrue – and the Governor of Queensland 500 cans of tinned pineapple; Eleanor Roosevelt towels and cloths for the kitchen.

Gandhi sent a piece of lace, which had been made from yarn he had spun himself, while Elizabeth's mother gave salt cellars and Princess Margaret, Elizabeth's sister, a picnic basket. Other gifts were more useful to a young married couple – a washing machine, a refrigerator, scarves, handkerchiefs and almost 150 pairs of nylon stockings. The latter were considered to be exceedingly generous gifts, as they were still rationed. The Palace also received 10,000 telegrams of congratulation.

Prince Philip celebrated his impending marriage with two stag parties the night before the wedding, one to which the press were invited (at the Dorchester Hotel) and a more private party at the Belfry Club. Many of his naval friends attended, as did his best man, the Marquess of Milford Haven, and his uncle Lord Mountbatten. On the same day Philip had been bestowed with the honorific 'His Royal Highness' by King George and been awarded the Order of the Garter, the highest order of chivalry in the land. Elizabeth had been given membership of the order just over a week previously, to ensure that she had seniority over her husband-to-be. On the morning of the wedding itself Philip was created Duke of Edinburgh, Earl of Merioneth and Baron Greenwich, a slew of titles of which the King said, 'It is a great deal to give a man all at once, but I know Philip understands his new responsibilities.'

The Duke and Duchess of Windsor stayed away. Not only could Elizabeth and her family not forgive him but they also still saw him as a danger to the throne, even after the war. Mary, Princess Royal, Elizabeth's aunt, was absent from the wedding claiming ill health, but there was speculation that she was unhappy at the decision to exclude her brother. Because of their German marriages, Philip's three sisters were not invited – a decision they found upsetting. For everybody else not deemed too German it was a post-war excuse for a jamboree. Dozens of European royals stayed at Claridge's and had cheery dinners where the Queen of Spain, the King of Romania, the King and Queen of Denmark, the Kings of Norway and Iraq, and various other royals sat together round a table. The royals were to take up so many pews that MPs had to hold a ballot to decide which of them would attend the wedding and those who failed were offended to be excluded.

Those who came were determined to enjoy themselves. The King and Queen hosted a dance in the palace two nights before the wedding for the many royals descending. It was, thought Lady Airlie, 'after the years of austerity like a scene from a fairy tale'. As the wine flowed, the fairy-tale atmosphere rather transformed into something more raucous. 'You are the big potato; the other queens are small potatoes', Jan Smuts told Queen Mary. An Indian rajah assaulted the Duke of Devonshire and the King set off on a conga through the state apartments, followed by enthusiastic royalty. 'Saw many old friends,' wrote Queen Mary in her diary. 'I stood from 9.30 until 12.15 a.m.!!! Not bad for 80.'

On the following day the palace was a bustle of chairs

being laid out, flowers arranged, dusting, polishing and preparing outfits. Everywhere smelled of the flowers they had not been able to find during the war. Us Four dined together quietly and then Elizabeth went to bed early. Overnight, the crowds massed in the Mall to secure their position. In the morning, the gardens of the palace smelled of coffee and bacon as they rustled up makeshift breakfasts on their stoves. People flooded in from all over the country – and paid extortionate prices. A view of the procession from a window cost at least ten guineas.

Elizabeth hardly slept and was delighted by all the crowds amassed under her window. 'I can't believe it's really happening, Crawfie,' she said. 'I have to keep pinching myself.' The designer's assistants came at 9 a.m. for a final fitting and then Bobo assisted her to dress.

Not everything went to plan. A delicate tiara broke and had to be swiftly mended, and the bouquet Elizabeth was to carry was temporarily misplaced. Luckily, a footman realised he had put it in a wardrobe to keep cool. The Princess decided that she wished to wear a certain wedding gift of pearls, but the string could not be found. Someone remembered they were on show at St James's Palace, so the Queen's private secretary, Jock Colville, hurried over to get them. The policemen guarding the presents were unconvinced by his story and only allowed him to return with the necklace accompanied by detectives. He dashed back with just minutes to spare.

The Queen travelled with her father in the Irish State Coach. The King wore the uniform of Admiral of the Fleet as he escorted his daughter up the aisle, with Margaret directly behind her, followed by Elizabeth's seven further bridesmaids, all carrying white roses and gardenias.

Prince Michael of Kent and Prince William of Gloucester, Elizabeth's cousins and both five years old, were pageboys in tartan. Elizabeth glittered along the aisle in her 10,000 pearls, 2,000 people crammed into the pews, while 200 million listened around the world to the ceremony broadcast on BBC Radio. The BBC's presence was carefully planned and worked out in advance, because at the previous royal wedding in Westminster Abbey the Abbey cross had banged into a microphone hanging above the altar steps.

The procession was led down the aisle by choirboys of the Chapel Royal and, because the choir stalls were full of wedding guests, the ninety-one singers had to scramble into the organ loft along with the radio commentators. Among the hymns sung during the ceremony was 'The Lord's my Shepherd', which was performed to the tune 'Crimond'. The tune was so unknown at the time that no written score could be found in time – the organist had been summoned to the palace four days previously in order to have Princesses Elizabeth and Margaret perform the descant for him.

The couple knelt before the altar on boxes draped in rose-coloured silk – which were actually orange crates from the previous year, reworked until they were the right height and size.

The Princess, like Queen Victoria and against the advice of many, promised to obey her husband. It was an unlikely vow – as it had been for Queen Victoria.

The signing of the register took place in St Edward's Chapel, a rather small space off the main Abbey. There wasn't enough room for all the planned signatories to crowd inside, so only the bride and groom, the Archbishop of Canterbury, the Dean of Westminster, the King and Queen, Philip's mother (Princess Andrew of Greece) and Queen

Mary made their marks at the Abbey. The other signatures –
from relatives, royalty and bridesmaids – were added back at
Buckingham Palace during the wedding breakfast.

After the ceremony 150 of the party returned to
Buckingham Palace. The gold plate was laid out, the tables
decked with flowers and the King's Piper puffed hard on
the bagpipes, to the discomfort of some of the foreign visitors. The newly-weds sat with their parents, some close relatives and the Kings of Norway, Denmark and Romania and
tucked into main courses named after them – *Filet de Sole
Mountbatten, Bombe Glacée Princesse Elizabeth*. Ice cream was
an incredible treat in post-war Britain and so, to compensate,
the main course was a casserole of partridges, which were not
rationed. The King's speech was characteristically short and
the bridegroom also spoke briefly. It was just as well – many
of the royals complained about the acoustics and could not
hear a word. Philip's unpredictable mother, however, was on
her best behaviour and pleased the royal family. While they
ate and drank, newsreel footage was being packed up and
sent all over the world.

Twelve cakes were made in total, eleven of which were
designed to be given away as presents and mementos. The
cake, much reduced from the original design in keeping with
the need to promote austerity, still weighed in at 500 pounds
and, created with supplies sent by the Australian Girl Guides,
stood nine feet high. Its four tiers were decorated with coats
of arms and sugar figurines depicting the couple's favourite
activities. It was cut with Philip's new sword, which had
been a wedding gift from the King. One layer of this cake
was kept aside to be used at the christening of the first baby
and one was sent back to Australia in thanks for the support
that had helped it be made.

By the evening, the winter rain had begun to fall, but the couple still took up their positions in the open landau, rather than a closed car. Princess Elizabeth, wearing blue, hand in hand with her husband, hurried through the confetti. She later wrote to her mother that her eyes and mouth had been covered in petals and she thought she might easily cry. Crowds lined the route and cried out for them, all the way to Victoria station. Behind them, back in the palace, maids were scrubbing the pots, footmen were stacking the gold chairs and others were cutting up the wedding cakes to send out to hospitals and on to relations. The King and Queen retired to their own apartments, leaving Margaret with Crawfie. The younger Princess was despondent. 'I can't imagine life without her,' she said.

'When I handed your hand to the Archbishop, I felt I had lost something very precious,' the King wrote to his daughter. Their close relationship of We Four had gone for ever, despite his hope that they would have plenty of fun as Us Five. For Elizabeth the day had passed quickly. 'I was so happy and enjoying myself so much, that I became completely selfish and forgot about your feelings or anyone else's!'

# 10

# 'An obedient sitter'

*Elizabeth and Philip with Charles, July 1949*

IN COMMON WITH THOUSANDS of young couples across post-war Britain, Philip and Elizabeth would not be returning from honeymoon to their own home. They had initially chosen Sunninghill Park near Ascot, but it had been badly damaged in a fire in August. They took a lease on Windlesham Moor, in Surrey, but it was only for use at the weekends and would not be available until some months hence. For their London home they were offered Clarence House, on the Mall, but unfortunately it had fallen into a dilapidated state while occupied by the Duke of Connaught, Queen Victoria's last surviving son, who had died in 1942 aged ninety-one. Bombing had added to the chaos: the roof leaked, the plaster was falling in and the only bathroom was very dated.

Lieutenant Mountbatten, a man who had not had his own home since babyhood, was to begin married life in the home of his in-laws at Buckingham Palace, with holidays mostly spent at their households of Balmoral, Windsor and Sandringham.

Elizabeth and Philip had hoped for a private honeymoon. They were to spend the first days at Broadlands, the house of Uncle Dickie, in Romsey near the New Forest. Unfortunately, crowds of royal sightseers had discovered their whereabouts and were hot on their heels. The couple arrived for Matins at Romsey Abbey and the mob surged in behind them, while those outside clambered up ladders, chairs and – bizarrely – a sideboard to peer in and get a better view. After the royal couple had left, the people queued to have an opportunity to sit where they had done. The couple hurried north to Birkhall, where they were allowed more privacy. Elizabeth wrote to her mother: 'It is so lovely and peaceful just now – Susan [the corgi] is stretched out before the fire, Rummy is fast asleep in his box beside the fire, and I am busy writing this in one of the arm chairs near the fire (you see how important the fire is!) It's heaven up here!' Elizabeth was in love, but pragmatic as ever. Philip was more romantic. 'Cherish Lilibet?' he wrote to the Queen. 'I wonder if that word is enough to express what is in me? Does one cherish one's sense of humour or one's musical ear or one's eyes?'

The newlyweds returned for the King's fifty-second birthday on 14 December. 'She was looking very happy and, as a result of three weeks of matrimony, suddenly a woman instead of a girl,' wrote Sir John Colville, her private secretary. Finally, it seemed, the Princess was allowed to be an adult.

Almost immediately, the newspapers began speculating endlessly about a possible pregnancy for Elizabeth. It was according to them her 'dearest wish' and she hoped to be a mother before her first wedding anniversary.

The Princesss was delighted by married life. Philip had a job at the Admiralty and used to walk there along the Mall in the mornings. At 4.30 in the afternoons, Elizabeth would wait by the window to see him trotting past the fountain or turn into the gates in his sports car.

If the courtiers saw the Princess as an adult, her parents still did not. Living at Buckingham Palace, she was at their constant beck and call, and her life was little different from how it had always been. For Philip the palace had the advantage that it was near his work at the Admiralty, but the proximity to the King and Queen, and courtiers he knew had tried to stop him from marrying the Princess, caused him great annoyance. Even more exasperatingly for Philip, the wedding had made Elizabeth yet more fascinating to the people. Her diary of engagements increased and the newspapers devoted pages to her. It was impossible not to feel that he was walking two steps behind her. After his wedding Philip had written to his mother-in-law, 'My ambition is to weld the two of us into a new, combined existence that will not only be able to withstand the shocks directed at us but will also have a positive existence for the good.' But the Princess was still heavily reliant on her mother and frequently popped down to the Queen's apartments to ask her opinion. Although Philip was a royal, he was much less used to running his own life than most aristocrats (a footman at Balmoral before the wedding had been shocked to find that his solitary suitcase contained no spare shoes, pyjamas or slippers).

'Philip is terribly independent and I quite understand the poor darling wanting to start off properly, without everything being done for us,' Elizabeth wrote to her mother from honeymoon. Philip found the constant presence of Bobo Macdonald disconcerting. The key courtiers were not particularly friendly and Lascelles was difficult. Already resentful about the slow acceptance of his marriage, Philip simply could not respond to them with the polite diffidence they expected. Almost immediately after the wedding, Princess Marina, Philip's cousin, had set off to visit his German relations to try to repair their hurt feelings for not being invited. But he was still aggrieved that his family were not welcome and unhappy that his friends were seen as louche.

'I was so comforted to see the truly happy expression on your face and to feel your decision was right from every point of view,' wrote Princess Alice to Prince Philip. It was a decision he would, if not question, sometimes rail against.

Elizabeth was fast overshadowing her father. The iconography of rebirth and renewal with the wedding had been effective. As the economy improved and privation lessened, the young, newly married Princess was seen as the new and quite marvellous focus of the monarchy. For many in Britain she was representative of the next generation. She stood for the many young people who had grown up in the war, suffered privations and now looked forward to a future of hope and prosperity. The King was only fifty-two but he was seen as fading and, although the Palace tried to hide the matter, it was clear to many that his health was not good. Princess Elizabeth was no longer their little girl but their future Queen.

John 'Jock' Colville, the Princess's first private secretary, was ambitious to school the Princess more thoroughly in her political role. A high-flying diplomat, he had become weary of the complicated negotiations of the Balkan countries and accepted a two-year secondment to the household. If, under him, the Princess demanded more than simple ceremonial duties, then his role would also be expanded. He suggested that she receive Foreign Office telegrams – for, as he declared, reading them would give her a greater knowledge of foreign affairs than reading the newspapers. He also took her and the Duke to a debate on foreign affairs in the House of Commons and later to a juvenile court. The Princess met members of the government at a small dinner party hosted by the Prime Minister and his wife. Among those present were Harold Wilson, President of the Board of Trade, and Hugh Gaitskell, Minister of Fuel and Power. The politicians were rather nervous of meeting the Princess. She was no more at ease and was very reserved. 'She had a very pretty voice and an easy manner but is not, I think, very interested in politics or affairs generally,' Gaitskell decided. But although the Princess's light education had not invested her with any particular academic interests, she respected those who did devote themselves to scholarship and learning. She addressed Oxford University in the Sheldonian, declaring that the universities in the country were a 'powerful fortress against the tide of sloth, ignorance and materialism'. By materialism she meant excessive and needless consumption, a great sin in the post-war years.

In February Colville suggested that the royal couple travel to Paris to attend the opening of the Exhibition of Eight Centuries of British Life at the Musée Galliera in Paris. It would be the first official visit since 1939 and a chance to build bridges after the war. The Princess was excited about a trip to a city she had never seen and looked forward to trying out her French, but Philip was reluctant. The city, for him, was a place of sad memories.

Paris in 1948 was even greyer than London. The government worked hard to build up the arrival of the Princess and her husband. Special tablecloths were embroidered with 'E' and 'P' for a great dinner at Versailles, and a triumphal progress was planned down the Seine.

Elizabeth was sick and tired in the early months of pregnancy, but she was delighted to travel abroad in the company of her handsome husband. Philip, who knew Paris well, liked occupying the role of the mentor. His enthusiasm faded somewhat after a painful bout of food poisoning at a dinner at the British Embassy.

'The latent enthusiasm of the French people for the pomp and pageantry of monarchy was clearly revealed,' the British Ambassador wrote to Ernest Bevin. 'It was an unusual experience to see the townsfolk of Paris cheer an English Princess from the Place de la Bastille.' The papers declared that the Norman Conquest had occurred once more, but in reverse: the Princess had subjugated Paris.

The twenty-two-year-old Elizabeth, used to dining with middle-aged courtiers and taking tea with elderly charity representatives, grasped the opportunities in Paris for enjoyment. She and her husband visited a racetrack and a nightclub (much to the despair of Scottish church organisations who believed she set a poor example to the young people of the Empire, who 'look to their Royal Highnesses for guidance and inspiration)'. She also went on a shopping spree to rival those of her mother, rather forgetting that she would have to pay a customs bill on her return.

A few onlookers had reported in Paris that the Princess looked tired and required more rest than usual and in June the matter was confirmed. The announcement of the Princess's pregnancy was finally issued on 4 June, Derby Day. Elizabeth appeared at Epsom Downs, smiling cheerfully at the crowds.

The forthcoming baby became an obsession. People from all over the world sent baby clothes and gifts to the future royal prince or princess, and some were donated to other mothers. Enthusiastic letters even came from Germany. Queen Mary gathered up all the cards for one of her scrapbooks. There were letters full of advice on pregnancy cures and charms suggested by ladies that would tell her if she was having a girl or a boy. The old pram in which Allah had pushed the Princesses was taken from storage, along with the family baby basket and cot. All were decorated in white and yellow, rather than pink or blue, as the latter was not a royal tradition. 'Then,' said Elizabeth, 'no one can guess whether we want a boy or a girl.'

Also in 1948, Crawfie finally left the household to set up home with her husband, George Buthlay, an Aberdeen bank manager. The King gave her a grace and favour cottage, Nottingham Cottage in the grounds of Kensington Palace (then occupied by the Duke and Duchess of Windsor). If it was a pay-off, it failed. Crawfie hoped for more, or at least a position as a lady-in-waiting. At Nottingham Cottage she pondered her relationship with the Princesses and became vulnerable to royal bounty hunters.

The Princess herself waxed ever more enticing to the public. She received letters from all over the world – some purely congratulatory, others wishing for help with problems. The King and Queen were being pushed to the sidelines.

The King was ill and preoccupied by his own bad health. Although fond of exercise, his health was impaired by his heavy smoking and his naturally nervous personality did little to lower his blood pressure. At the end of October he was diagnosed as suffering from early arteriosclerosis and the doctors discussed amputation of his right leg. The forthcoming birth and talks about protocol could not distract him from his gloom. He also became much more difficult for the courtiers to handle. For some time he had found complicated matters hard to comprehend – by 1948 he seemed hardly able to understand. He was still dutiful, responsible and devoted to his family, but politics upset him. His disposition to anger became intense and he was tormented by suspicions that the Court and the Prime Minister were keeping matters from him.

The young couple's renovations to Clarence House proceeded slowly. Parliament had agreed £50,000 to pay for the work, despite an outcry from the newspapers. Philip was quietly persuaded to postpone plans to install a cinema in the basement. Elizabeth and Philip visited, sometimes twice a day, to check on renovations – and the Princess even helped mix up the green paint for the dining room. They were bursting with inspirational ideas – too many, perhaps. The final bill came in nearly £30,000 over budget.

Philip and Elizabeth settled into a regular routine. The corgis would dash into her room first thing and she would take them for a walk across St James's Park, swathed in an old headscarf and raincoat, with a detective trotting unobtrusively behind. In the dining room a footman, resplendent in navy-blue battledress livery, served her with scones, eggs and bacon. Philip, if he had not already left for work, took toast and coffee. She usually attended to her correspondence and official matters. When they dined in, they ate simple food: favourites were cold meat and salad or sausages and mashed potato.

The mother of the future heir to the throne was not simply a wife to a king or prince. When her great-great-grandmother, Queen Victoria, had been due to give birth to her first child, she was discontented at the thought of ministers being at her bedside. Since, she argued, these were the men she had to deal with every day, she wished for them to wait in an adjoining room. Princess Elizabeth, due to be Queen Regnant, was in an equally anomalous position. Both the palace courtiers and the Labour government were uncertain about whether the Home Secretary should attend the birth, as had been the case for her own. The Home Office applied itself to the matter and decided there was no constitutional basis for the tradition – which was less an act of homage than ensuring that the child actually issued from its royal mother. 'The custom is only a custom,' wrote the Home Secretary, Chuter Ede, in June. 'It has no statutory authority behind it and there is no legal requirement for its continuance.' But the King was certain that the Home Secretary should attend. The Queen, apparently, thought such an 'innovation a threat to the dignity of the throne'.

In early November, when the birth was imminent, the Canadian High Commissioner happened to remark, in passing, to Sir Alan Lascelles that he supposed he would be expected to attend the birth – along with the Home Secretary and the other representatives of the dominions. No dominion representative had requested to attend the birth of Princess Elizabeth. But, as Lascelles and the Home Office immediately realised, it was constitutionally incontrovertible that they should be allowed to do so, and if the Canadian High Commissioner made this request, his fellow representatives would ask for the same. As Lascelles pointed out to the King, 'If the old ritual was observed, there would be no less than seven ministers sitting in the passage.' The King was shocked by such an indignity and on 5 November the Palace announced the end of the 'archaic custom'. Sir Alan was satisfied. 'I had long thought that the practice of summoning the Home Secretary to attend, like a sort of supernumerary midwife, at the birth of a royal baby, was out-of-date and ridiculous,' he wrote on his retirement. The public would have to trust that the child was legitimate.

The baby would not automatically be a prince or princess,

because he or she was not the child of the heir apparent. As matters stood, a boy would be styled 'Earl of Merioneth', while a girl would be Lady —— Mountbatten. This would not be acceptable to the people, so the King, despite his ill health, had to rush through a last-minute Letters Patent to ensure that the child would bear a royal title. In doing so he thus raised Princess Elizabeth to the same status as would have been borne by his son and heir.

Elizabeth's family worried about the clamouring crowds in the Mall and encouraged her to move her room to the quieter side of the palace, overlooking the gardens. She had insisted that she would remain. 'I want my baby to be born in my own room, amongst the things I know,' she had declared. On a visit to Crawfie in November, she said she was not afraid of childbirth. 'After all, it's what we're made for,' she said.

The Princess, attended by four doctors, went into labour on the evening of 14 November and gave birth to a 7lb 6oz little boy just after nine o'clock. Prince Philip arrived to see his wife and son fresh from playing squash and to the sound of the crowds cheering outside. His name was decided on as Charles Philip Arthur George. A departure from the preferred names of George and Edward, Charles had been chosen simply because the royal couple liked the sound. There were, however, unfortunate predecessors: the beheaded Charles I and the exiled Bonnie Prince Charlie. Still, there was Charles II, a popular, if lascivious and spendthrift, king.

The heir to the British throne looked like George V, according to Marion Crawford. Queen Mary thought he resembled Prince Albert. The little boy was placed in a gilt crib and every member of the palace staff was invited to admire him The newspapers waxed sentimental about mother and son. 'Prince Charles, as he is to be named, is an obedient sitter,' recalled Cecil Beaton, who was called to the palace to photograph him and the Princess a few days after the birth. The baby Prince was sleeping and opened his eyes 'to stare long and wonderingly into the camera lens, the beginning of a lifetime in the glare of publicity'. The Princess initially nursed her son. Two months after the birth, however, she caught measles and mother and son were isolated from each other for the duration of her illness. It was the beginning of a series of separations.

The flood of correspondence to the Princess was such that the palace opened a special department and hired a dozen typists. People from all over the world sent letters, presents, requests for assistance and copies of their own children's birth certificates – to prove that their offspring had been born on the same day. Elizabeth announced that food parcels would be sent to every other child born on 14 November. On 15 December Charles was christened in the White and Gold Music Room at Buckingham Palace in a ceremony attended by the palace staff and a host of godparents, including the King and Queen, and the King of Norway.

The King's health received little boost from the birth of his grandson. The doctors advised him to cancel a long-planned trip to Australia and New Zealand. In the following March he underwent an operation to his spine in Buckingham Palace. The doctors hoped to restore circulation to his leg. It was partly successful, but it marked the beginning of the King's decline into invalidism. He was sick and often querulous, and his life became taken up with the exhausting round of sickness: treatments, recovery, remission and short periods of relief. No matter what the doctors said, he would not give up his beloved habit of smoking. Everyone had to pretend that he was as healthy as ever. 'The Queen never allowed you to contemplate the fact of the King's illness,' one courtier recalled.

The Princess may have condemned 'self-indulgence' but she was living the most carefree time of her life. She celebrated her twenty-third birthday at the Café de Paris. Laurence Olivier and his wife, Vivien Leigh, were of the party and they then proceeded to a nightclub to dance the night away. It was Princess Margaret, however, who became the leader of the London set of aristocrats and gilded youth. Throughout history young royals have been in demand to head up the *jeunesse dorée*, from the young Henry VII to the sons of George III. Princess Elizabeth was too occupied by her marriage and family, so Margaret fulfilled the role.

Pampered and adored by her father, Margaret had become an independent, glamorous and thoroughly modern Princess. The years after the war were for her a period of exploration and fun as she began to socialise widely, and once her sister was married she became the toast of the newspapers. She mixed with some of the most fashionable aristocrats in London and became a popular icon of style, frequenting coffee bars in the latest gowns and dancing the night away – accompanied by her rather long-suffering lady-in-waiting. Her pose of smoking through a long cigarette holder became her trademark. She was much less interested in outdoor sports than her sister and eagerly assumed the role of metropolitan socialite beloved of her uncle Windsor and grandfather Edward VII before her. Queen Mary described her as *espiègle* – adventurous. She was without occupation, had only a few royal engagements and her education had been curtailed when Crawfie had left in 1948. Miss Crawford, who had recognised Margaret's quick intelligence, was frustrated by the King and Queen's inability to take their second daughter seriously. 'We are only young once,' the Queen had told her. 'We want her to have a good time.'

The Princess loved to joke and entertain. On one occasion, when a Scottish minister was taking tea with the King and Queen, she launched into 'I'm just a girl who can't say no' from *Oklahoma*. The King thought his daughter hilarious. But courtiers' wives were jealous of her and complained how she kept everyone awake too late. Elizabeth played the responsible wife in her headscarf while Margaret, as her cousin Margaret Rhodes put it, 'was the star in the middle, the planet round which everybody revolved.' Her marvellous jewels setting off her luminous eyes, her tiny waist encased in full-skirted couture by Christian Dior and Victor Stiebel, she was invited to every ball, charity fundraiser and reception. Swing was the music of the time and, after the long dancing lessons in the palace as a child, the Princess was an expert dancer, tip-tapping the night away at the top nightclubs, 400 in Leicester Square and the Ambassadeurs and the Milroy in Mayfair. She crept into Buckingham Palace early in the morning, sometimes using the tradesmen's entrance.

No society party was complete without Margaret and the newspapers were festooned with pictures of her nearly every day, flanked by comments about her late nights. Chips Channon saw 'a Marie Antoinette aroma about her'; beautiful, fashionable and seemingly frivolous, she lived for enjoyment, without thought for the consequences. She was consistently voted one of the best dressed women in the world. Lipsticks, perfumes and cocktails were named after her and her dresses and bags were copied for ordinary girls to buy in high street stores. Everybody wanted to be Princess Margaret.

Margaret was beautiful, vivacious and alluring. But like her sister, she found it difficult to meet men. Few dared approach her. Not only had she been promoted to the nation with propaganda reminiscent of the Princesse Lontaine, locked in her tower, it was also inevitable that any young man seen escorting Margaret would immediately be photographed and discussed as a future husband. Philip, of course, came with no brothers or suitable cousins with whom she could mix. As her sister's domestic happiness was blazoned across the newspapers, Margaret felt increasingly isolated in the mornings after her glamorous evenings at the 400 Club. Her father was unwell, her mother wrapped up in his affairs and she was alone. She began to turn for companionship to one of his equerries, Group Captain Peter Townsend.

# 11

# 'Came down a Queen'

*Elizabeth and Margaret in South Africa in 1947;
Peter Townsend is seated far right*

As a child, Margaret had been particularly fond of playing practical jokes on the equerries of her father. She stuffed their shoes with acorns and slipped sticky lime balls into their pockets. Now, there was one who was getting the upper hand over her. Captain Townsend had been a heroic Battle of Britain pilot and had first met the Princesses in February 1944, on his way to an audience with the King. The two girls were waiting eagerly to see their first war hero in the flesh. 'Bad luck,' said Elizabeth to Margaret as they watched him enter. 'He's married.' For Elizabeth, already in love with Philip and not interested in the unobtainable, there was no appeal in a married man. Margaret, just thirteen, was, like her uncle David and many of her relatives before her, particularly attracted by those who were already attached.

Townsend was almost sixteen years her senior and had married the handsome Rosemary Pawle in the war, and they had two small children. After his great successes with the air force he had suffered a severe breakdown – in retrospect his great acts seemed too terrifying almost to contemplate. 'I had gone too far down the hill ever to get to the top again. In my thoughts and visions I saw myself crashing, over and over again, to a horrible death. I was convinced I was going to die – exactly the opposite to what I had felt during the heroic

245

days of 1940, when I was convinced I was going to live.'
Remembering the war induced in him excruciating terror.
After a spell in hospital, he needed an occupation without
strain and the position of equerry was ideal. His role would
be to assist the King in administrative matters and pay particular attention to his visitors, preparing the nervous for the
royal presence and ensuring punctuality.

Townsend was initially appointed for three months.
Gentle, cheerful and willing to please, he became a firm
favourite with the royal family. He was particularly sympathetic to the King's nervous disposition. 'I knew myself the
agonies of a stammerer,' he wrote. Like Margaret, he was
skilled at defusing the King's violent rages. One courtier
described him as 'very attractive' and 'a little bit fey with
rather rigid views, but delightful company'. The Queen
was particularly pleased at having an attractive young man
in close proximity, without considering that her daughters
might have similar feelings. He and his wife moved into
Adelaide Cottage, a grace and favour residence in Windsor.

Unlike the majority of courtiers, who were from families
who had experience of serving the royal family, Townsend
was the son of a colonial administrator and he had attended
Haileybury, a middle-ranking public school – this mattered,
when most of the courtiers had been to Eton. Equerries had
traditionally been appointed from the army and navy but the
King had been insistent that the air force should be similarly
honoured. Townsend's lack of experience of royal service
made him particularly dutiful and eager to please – and also
too willing to devote too much of his soul to his employers.
He misread the King's dependence as friendship. Those, like
Jock Colville, who came from a family of courtiers, knew
that the royals tended to see service in itself as ample reward

and would hardly expect that courtiers would require further recognition, as in the case of the lady-in-waiting of Queen Mary who received nothing from her will. One should not, as experienced courtiers knew, invest one's hopes for happiness in the royal family. As Marion Crawford had suggested, the royals did not always consider their employees as individuals. Like Crawfie, Townsend was dazzled by his proximity to the royal family and quickly convinced he was indispensable.

Equerries and assistants have historically cast a spell over royalty. Queen Victoria's mother, the Duchess of Kent, was emotionally and practically dependent on John Conroy, the man who had been equerry to her husband before he died. The old Queen herself became very fond of John Brown, a servant at Balmoral, after Albert's death, and later became so devoted to her Indian servant, Abdul Karim or 'the Munshi', that guests at a Diamond Jubilee fete watched her retire to a large tent with him, where he busied himself buttering her toast. Toast and condiments were not the limit of the support offered by palace servants. The daughters of George III, isolated from public life with their ailing father and bitter mother at Windsor, derived social and romantic satisfaction from equerries. At least one, Princess Sophia, produced an illegitimate child from a relationship.

Margaret had been an impressionable young girl when Townsend arrived, fresh from the long period of isolation in the war at Windsor. Townsend was the perfect example of the great war hero, with whom any girl might have fallen a little in love. Margaret, like her sister, had longed for a greater role in the war – Captain Townsend had actually experienced action. Margaret was only fifteen when Captain Townsend arrived and still young for her age. It was not until

they travelled together on the lengthy royal tour to South
Africa that she began to see him anew. Her sister was observ-
ing how her father conducted himself on tour and writing
letters to Philip, and the King and Queen were occupied
with plans. Margaret whiled away dull journeys on the train
with Townsend. She was enticing, lovely and innocent, and
it was impossible for Townsend not to be delighted by her.
The country was so preoccupied by Princess Elizabeth that
it failed to notice her sister. The friendship with the 'very
attractive' Townsend continued and no one at the palace
thought to prevent it.

Townsend's marriage was soon only a formality. In August
1950 he was appointed Deputy Master of the Household
with his own office at Buckingham Palace. He was always at
Margaret's side, even leaving the birthday party of one of his
sons when a telephone call came asking him to accompany
her on a ride. 'What ultimately made Princess Margaret so
attractive and lovable was that behind that dazzling facade,
the apparent self-assurance, you could find, if you looked
for it, a rare softness and sincerity,' he said. As he knew, she
had many suitors. 'There were dozens of others, and their
names were in the papers, which vied with each other frantically and futilely, in their forecasts of the one whom she
would marry. Yet I dare say there was not one among them
more touched by the princess's *joie de vivre* than I, for in my
present marital predicament, it gave me what I most lacked
– joy.'

The Princess was sought-after, beautiful, glamorous and
deeply sympathetic to him. As with his comparison of himself to her other suitors, he began increasingly to delude
himself that the King, so fond of him as an equerry, might
look kindly on his romantic interest in his daughter. While

staying with the family in Balmoral in June 1951, the Group Captain was woken from dozing on the moors by Princess Margaret standing over him, gazing very closely at him. He then realised the King was nearby 'leaning on his stick, with a certain look, typical of him: half kind, half amused. I whispered, "You know your father is watching us?" At which she laughed, straightened up and went to his side. Then she took his arm and walked away leaving me to my dreams.'

Townsend's notion that the King was indulging his flirtation was very wide of the mark. The monarch simply would not be able to conceive that his school-aged daughter and his equerry might consider each other in a romantic light. The King and Queen hoped that the Princess might marry one of the young aristocrats in her circle. The young Marquess of Blandford, heir to the Duke of Marlborough, was fond of the Princess, eminently suitable and could have ensured her a life in comfort at Blenheim, a palace much grander than shabby old Windsor or Buckingham Palace. She flirted with him but with little real commitment – and he married one of her friends in 1951. The King and Queen were most enthusiastic about Johnny Dalkeith, heir to the Duke of Buccleuch, one of the wealthiest seats in Britain. But Margaret was unsure. Townsend was exciting, forbidden, a war hero and experienced. Her young friends seemed much more dull in comparison, even if they were due to inherit great estates. 'If the King had lived, he would have made Princess Margaret marry Johnny Dalkeith,' Lord Glenconner declared. 'With his houses and his land, she would have had a virtual state of her own.'

Elizabeth was blind to her sister's danger. In October, just after her husband flew to Malta, she gave a speech to a Mothers' Union rally at Central Hall in Westminster. The

Princess again spoke of the evils of 'growing self-indulgence, of hardening materialism, of falling moral standards'.
The Mothers' Union was conservative on marriage and the
Princess praised their standpoint. As she put it, 'We can have
no doubt that divorce and separation are responsible for
some of the darkest evils in our society today.' The chairman of the Marriage Law Reform Committee protested that
the Princess had taken sides. Her courtiers were attempting
to present her to please her conservative people but she too
fervently believed in the sanctity of marriage. Newly-wed
and a parent, the notion of marital breakdown seemed utterly
impossible to her.

In the summer the Princess, the Duke and Prince Charles
finally moved into their own home at Clarence House. It
was a brief period when they could live together. By October
they were on the move again. Philip gained the position of
First Lieutenant of HMS *Chequers* and leader of the First
Destroyer of the Mediterranean Fleet. He flew out to Malta
on 16 October and the Princess arrived just over a month
later, accompanied by Bobo, a lady-in-waiting and Philip's
equerry and valet. Charles remained in Clarence House with
his nurse.

In Malta, the Princess was free of royal duties and lived a
carefree life. According to the Prince's valet, John Dean, she
spent 'only ten per cent of her time being a princess'. She
visited the beaches for swimming, drove her Daimler around
the island, took tea with the other wives, visited the hair-
dresser, went for walks and dined with her husband at the
local hotel. Uncle Dickie was also living in Malta as commander of the 1st Cruiser Squadron of the Mediterranean
Fleet, and he and his wife entertained the Princess at his

home and took her out on boat trips to the islands around the coast. 'They were so relaxed and free,' recalled John Dean of Elizabeth and Philip. 'I think it was their happiest time.'

Five weeks later the Princess returned home. Rather than going to see Charles immediately, who was staying with the King and Queen at Sandringham, she spent four days at Clarence House attending to correspondence, then visited the races at Hurst Park, where her horse, Monaveen, won 10–1. She had missed Charles's first step and first word. Even when she was at home, her work as heir presumptive was such that she spent an hour with him in the morning and one between tea and bath time. There had been many days when her own parents had done the same, but sensibilities were different in the 1950s and mothers were expected to give more time to their sons.

In April the Palace announced that the Princess was pregnant once more. She returned from Malta in time to give birth on 15 August to a baby girl, Anne Elizabeth Alice Louise, at Clarence House. Thousands waited outside for news and were rewarded when Prince Charles, just over one and a half, was held up at the window to wave.

The Princess was unwell for some time after the birth and found herself unable to fulfil her royal duties in October, and some of the more arduous engagements were cancelled in November. Not long after Charles's second birthday in November, she flew to Malta to spend Christmas with her husband, while Anne and Charles were sent to Sandringham to stay with their grandparents. She accompanied her husband on official naval business to Greece and received a delighted welcome in Athens. The couple stayed with the royal family at Tatoi and Philip was in his element. The wife of the British Ambassador thought her 'very shy and withdrawn, a bit of a shrinking violet in fact, and he [Philip] was young and vigorous and jollied her along'.

In January 1950 the Princess suffered a terrible blow. Her beloved Crawfie published *The Little Princesses*. Crawfie's idealised vision of the Princess's childhood was serialised in the *Ladies Home Journal* in America, and *Woman's Own* ran it in Britain as 'The Loving, Human, Authentic Story of the Little Princesses'. The book brought her and her husband the astronomical sum of £75,000.

It was not a surprise to the Palace. After being approached by a publisher, Crawfie had asked the Queen for permission, but she had refused. Crawfie had included in her contract a proviso that the Palace must approve any stories, but this was a straw clause: the publisher could go ahead whatever was said.

Crawfie, declared the Queen, 'has gone off her head'. The Princesses had not understood the wild fascination with the intimate details of their personal lives. They felt deeply betrayed. Modern scholars who point out the touching, loving tone of the writing miss the point: the Princesses and the royal family were used to absolute obedience and heavy flattery. Crawfie made gentle suggestions that their education had been lacking, noted the paucity of her salary and characterised the royal family as out of touch, easily confused and slightly obtuse. They were difficult employers, giving her little practical help with personal problems and disrupting their children's education.

Royal servants, as Miss Crawford noted throughout the book, were badly paid and prey to often excessive demands for devotion. When Crawfie raised with the Queen the question of her marriage, the response was not congratulatory. The Queen was almost affronted by the suggestion that the governess might leave. 'You must see, Crawfie, that it would not be at all convenient just now. A change at this stage for Margaret is not at all desirable.' They either died in service, like Allah Knight or left with nothing more than a few presents and a box of memories. Possibly it was Crawfie's husband who persuaded her to turn the latter to profit. Certainly, she seemed to have no idea of how distressed her charges would be at the revelations and she was shocked by the fury of the Queen.

Crawfie was immediately ostracised by the royal family. A junior courtier was told not long after the scandal, 'Letters from Marion Crawford should be handled with a very long pair of forceps.' Almost overnight she had gone from being much loved to deeply reviled. Hurt and surprised by the opprobrium, Crawfie retreated to Scotland and began writing 'Crawfie's Column' on royal and society events for *Woman's Own*. The column had to be written six weeks before the event because of the deadlines for the magazine. In 1955 Crawfie gave an enthusiastic description of the Trooping the Colour ceremony and extolled how handsome the Queen had appeared at Ascot. Neither event had occurred, thanks to a rail strike. Crawfie was widely mocked in the newspapers and she disappeared from public life.

After the death of her husband in 1977, Crawfie became a recluse. Her house, situated on the road from Aberdeen to Balmoral, gave her a fine view of the royal cars travelling to the castle. It only gave her more pain. She suffered from depression and tried to commit suicide but was rescued by a neighbour. Her most treasured possession was a box containing letters written to her by the girls, along with paintings, photographs and poems about life in the nursery. Many would have sold them to the press, but Crawfie left them to the Princess in her will. The gesture did not gain her any mercy. The royal family were unforgiving. They received her publishers at Buckingham Palace but she remained an enemy – rather as Uncle David had been. They did not go to her funeral or leave flowers on her grave.

Marion Crawford mourned the end of her friendship with the Princesses, but they perhaps lost more, for she had been their constant companion through their childhood and adolescence. With the break with her, their opportunity to reminisce disappeared, the chance to recall forgotten memories was gone for ever.

The Palace was in part responsible for the wild fascination with the Princesses, which Crawfie had managed to exploit. The courtiers had failed to keep up with the demands of the newspapers in an age of increasingly global media. The King's press secretary, Commander Richard Colville, and Sir Alan Lascelles were infuriated when the press dared to publish anything other than royal announcements. The Crawfie affair also reminded everyone of how the Princesses were more appealing to the public than the ailing King. The Palace response was to attempt to restrict access to the Princess. She was asked to broadcast to the youth of the Empire on Empire Day and was keen to do so. Sir Alan strongly advised against it and the Princess obeyed. He felt that the press and the public should be roundly punished. The Princess would have to wait until she was Queen.

The King's health had been growing steadily weaker for some years. He roused himself to open the Festival of Britain in May 1951, but his frail appearance shocked the onlookers. At the end of that month he took to his bed with an exhausting virus and could not regain his energy. The job of royal representative in Britain would have to be carried out by Elizabeth. The country would expect to see Philip at her side, not in the navy. At thirty he was forced to leave a role he had adored and devote himself to the position of consort. It is possible that his maverick spirit and tendency to outspokenness would have prevented him from reaching the highest levels in the navy, but it seemed at the time to him and others that a hugely promising career had ended prematurely at the age of thirty. He was now to be Elizabeth's helpmate. Jock Colville wondered if he might be a coal miner for a month – an idea rejected on the basis that it would be playing to the gallery. Greece would be his last position of leading the Princess.

The fervent Jock Colville returned to the Foreign Office and was replaced by the more sanguine Major Martin Charteris, who had run military intelligence in Palestine. Calm, devoted and reluctant to rock the boat, Major Charteris became a great favourite of the Queen and would work for her at Clarence House and Buckingham Palace for the next twenty-seven years. He was much less eager to educate Elizabeth in the ways of politics.

The Princess was content. She had trusted servants, her beloved husband and her children. She was taking an increasing interest in national affairs. Along with Foreign Office telegrams, she was also now privy to Cabinet minutes and memoranda, although confidential annexes were excluded. The King was growing increasingly unwell, so the Princess assumed more of his ceremonial duties. In the summer the King had exploratory surgery and the doctors confirmed he had lung cancer. Part of his left lung was removed and he was so ill that the Queen, the two Princesses, the Duke of Gloucester and the Princess Royal were named as Counsellors of State. The Princess wrote to the dress designer, Hardy Amies, in confidence suggesting that in 'view of the unfortunate turn in the King's health', the King would be unable to undertake the projected tour to Australia and New Zealand, and she suggested they begin considering her wardrobe 'as a precaution against any sudden decision for us to go in the King's place'. On 4 October the Princess presided over the Privy Council preceding the dissolution of Parliament before the next General Election.

In October 1951 the Princess and Philip set off for a tour of the United States and Canada. Philip had refused the idea of a tour earlier in their marriage, saying that they should start a family first. Now they had two children and he had given up his naval career – there could be no more excuses. The pair flew across the Atlantic, much to the panic of Winston Churchill. The press crush was such that splinters from flash bulbs were found on Elizabeth's coat. The King's health deteriorated in their absence, so much so that Martin Charteris slept with the accession documents under his bed. The press complained that the Princess was not smiling. Philip tried to cheer her up with practical jokes, chasing her down the corridor wearing false teeth and putting a tin of mixed nuts on her bedside table from which a snake bounced out when she lifted the top. He too, though, found the tour a strain, snapping at her that she was a 'bloody fool' on one occasion.

The Princess, smiling or not, was a grand attraction. At the end of the month they proceeded to Washington. President Truman gave all federal employees time off to welcome the royal couple and delightedly squired the young Princess around to the crowds. The British Ambassador wrote to the King that Truman showed off the Princess in the manner of 'a very proud uncle presenting his favourite niece to his friends', as well as trundling her upstairs in the White House to meet his bedridden old mother-in-law. In a speech in the Rose Garden he declared, 'We have had many distinguished guests here in this city but never before have we had such a wonderful couple, that so completely captured the hearts of both of us.' The President was quite swept away. 'When I was a little boy I dreamt about a fairy princess, and here she is,' he declared to the *Washington Evening Star*.

While the Duke and Princess had been in Canada, an exhausted Labour government had been battling to hold its majority against a belligerent Conservative Party. Labour polled more votes but the Conservatives had a small majority. The King called the seventy-seven-year-old Winston Churchill to the palace and asked him to form a government. It was the first wholly Conservative government since 1929 and Churchill, the war leader, was delighted to be ruling once more. The King was content with the nation's choice: Churchill was Conservative, reliably establishment and childishly delighted by the pomp of royalty. His historic predecessor, Benjamin Disraeli, would have approved of Churchill's method; as he said, everybody likes flattery and with royalty it was best to lay it on with a trowel. Winston's support for Edward VIII was long forgotten. George VI, ill and clinging, welcomed Churchill's return, a reminder of his own finest hour.

Charles turned three while Elizabeth and Philip were away. In his parents' absence the little boy had enjoyed a small tea party at Buckingham Palace followed by an airing in his pram around St James's Park. The royal couple arrived home three days later, to be met by the Queen, Princess Margaret and Prince Charles at Euston. After greeting her mother and sister, the Princess bent to give Charles a kiss. It could not be called the most effusive welcome.

The King rallied on the return of his daughter. At Christmas at Sandringham he managed to go out shooting, and some even thought him gay and carefree. He was still not well enough to travel, so Elizabeth and Philip would replace the King and Queen on a six-month tour of the Commonwealth, beginning in Ceylon. After only a few months with his parents, Prince Charles was to be left with his nannies once more, along with the infant Princess Anne.

Smarting slightly from the failure of the Canadian tour, the Palace decided to allow the Princess and her husband a short stay in Kenya on the way. Not only did this avoid Egypt, which was at the time in political crisis, but also it satisfied the Kenyan white government, who had been asking for a visit. They had given the Princess Sagana Lodge as a wedding present and had been wondering when she might come to use it. She would be a propaganda weapon once more as a tottering colonial government put faith in a royal visit to quell rebellion of the people. It was not from mere generosity that they had given her Sagana Lodge; they wished for her presence in the country. The white settler community were delighted at the news. The governor suggested the royal couple try to come around the time of the full moon and he would reserve a night at Treetops, 'a hotel in the branches of a giant fig tree' about ten miles from the Lodge and overlooking a watering hole. The marvel of Treetops was the sight of animals clustering underneath to drink throughout the night. Elizabeth and Philip agreed eagerly to the suggestion.

At the end of January the royal family went to see *South*

*Pacific* at the Drury Lane Theatre. The evening ended with a rousing rendition of the National Anthem from the cast. The next morning the King travelled with Elizabeth and Philip to London airport. He stood on the tarmac and waved them goodbye as the plane ascended.

# 12
# Regina

*Queen Elizabeth waves to crowds on her way to the*
*House of Lords to open the first Parliament of her reign*

THE YOUNG COUPLE ARRIVED in Nairobi and proceeded the ninety miles up country to Sagana Lodge. They spent two days trout fishing and riding, before travelling to Treetops. It was a trek through countryside and Mau Mau territory (their hotel was later burned down in a rebellion). As soon as they arrived, Elizabeth began filming an elephant suckling her young and giving one a swimming lesson. Philip was in his element. 'All night we were up filming and watching,' said the lady-in-waiting in attendance, Lady Pamela Mountbatten.

Back in London, the King and Queen took Anne and Charles back to Sandringham, after wishing goodbye to the royal couple at the airport. He was feeling much healthier and a tour of South Africa was being mooted. On 5 February the King set off to hunt and shot nine hares. 'Well, Macdonald, we'll go after the hares again tomorrow,' he said to his servant, James Macdonald, at the end of the day. The Queen passed the evening with him in 'tremendous form & looking so well and happy' and he retired cheerful at 10.30 p.m. A watchman saw him adjusting his window at about midnight. It was a final blast of energy. When James Macdonald came to wake the King at 7.30 a.m. with tea he found him dead. He had suffered a coronary thrombosis early in the morning of the 6th. The gamekeepers carried him to the local church to watch over him. 'There were jolly jokes,' said Princess Margaret of the previous evening, 'and he went to bed early because he was convalescing. Then he wasn't there any more.'

Although the King had been seriously ill for months, no one had planned what to do in the event of his death. Macdonald told the Queen, but nearly an hour went by before Edward Ford, the assistant private secretary, was sent to tell the Prime Minister and Queen Mary. Ford drove to Downing Street and arrived in Churchill's bedroom to find the Prime Minister busily writing in bed, puffing on his cigar. 'I've got bad news,' Ford told him and went on to say that the King was dead.

Churchill flung aside his papers in typically dramatic fashion. 'Bad news?' he cried. 'The worst! How unimportant these matters seem. Get me Anthony Eden.' When the call was connected he declared to his Deputy Prime Minister, in a rather vain attempt at secret code, 'Our big chief has gone – we must have a Cabinet.' Jock Colville, now his joint private secretary, found Churchill weeping, and when told he would get on well with the new Queen he would say 'that he did not know her and she was only a child'.

The Princess was the first monarch to be out of the country on her accession since George I in 1714 (who had the excuse of being Elector of Hanover at the time). At Treetops, the party could hardly have been more remote. 'Because of where we were at the time, we were almost the last to know,' recalled Lady Pamela. Unlike George V, surrounded by his family and medical attendants, with his last moments documented, George VI died alone and the exact time of his death is unknown. Kenya is three hours ahead of Britain and the new Queen was probably awake, although this is not certain. At the great moment she might have been eating breakfast or brushing her hair or filming monkeys. Mike Parker, the equerry accompanying Prince Philip, recalled that early in the morning he took the Princess up to a lookout point at the top of the tree to watch the sun rise. An eagle came and hovered over their heads. 'I never thought about it until later,' he told the Queen's biographer, Ben Pimlott, 'but that was roughly the time when the King died.'

The Princess, as Pamela Mountbatten put it, 'had climbed up that ladder as Princess; she was going to have to climb down again as Queen'. While in Britain the shopkeepers put up pictures of the dead King, and the newspapers frantically tried to outdo each other in orgies of black and lengthy eulogies, and the politicians fretted about instability, Elizabeth and Philip, blissfully unaware, went fishing.

Martin Charteris happened to visit the nearby Outspan Hotel for lunch. On the way past the telephone booths he encountered a journalist, white-faced and trembling. 'Is anything wrong?' Charteris enquired. The journalist told him shakily that there had been a Reuters flash saying the King had died.

Charteris immediately hurried to the phone but could not get through to Buckingham Palace. He rang Mike Parker at Sagana Lodge with what he had heard. Parker crept into the sitting room where Elizabeth was sitting at her desk with her back to him, writing letters, and picked up the portable wireless. He found the overseas wavelength of the BBC and heard the news that the King had died. It was 2.45 p.m. local time and Elizabeth had been ruler of Britain and the Commonwealth for at least four and a half hours, probably more than eight, without having the faintest idea.

Philip was having a siesta after being up game watching most of the night. Parker went in with the news. The Prince said nothing, but breathed twice, as if in shock. He looked, Parker recalled, 'as if the world had collapsed on him. He saw immediately that the idyll of their life together had come to an end.' The Prince invited the new Queen to go for a walk in the garden. Lady Pamela and Mike Parker watched anxiously from the window. They were, she remembered, 'doing the naval quarterdeck thing of pacing up and turning back, pacing up and turning back, pacing up, turning back, for a few minutes and then, you know, they came back in and I, thinking that she had lost her father, whom she loved, rushed up and gave her a hug and thought how awful for you, and then I suddenly thought, my God, she's Queen, remember to curtsey. She was always so considerate and she just said, "I'm so sorry, it means we're all going to have to go back home."'

Martin Charteris hurried over from his hotel to find Elizabeth 'very composed, absolute master of her fate', sitting at her desk, drafting letters and telegrams of apology for the curtailment of the tour. The only suggestion of emotion was a faint flush on her face. He asked her what she was going to call herself. Elizabeth did not hesitate: 'My own name, Elizabeth, of course – what else?'

As on the day of the accession of her father, Elizabeth kept her feelings private. Philip's emotions were clearer to all: as she wrote her letters of apology, he lay on the sofa, with a copy of *The Times* covering his face.

Representatives of the world's press hurried to the Lodge and lined the road as the party left, obeying Martin Charteris's request not to take photographs. From Nairobi the new Queen arrived in Entebbe, then embarked for the twenty-four-hour flight. The Queen spoke little and Martin Charteris thought that she had been crying privately. 'What's going to happen when we get home?' she asked him.

The party landed at London airport at dusk on 7 February. The Duke of Gloucester and the Mountbattens came on board, and Philip's equerry handed them a note from Queen Mary. A tearful Churchill, the Leader of the Opposition and a line of ministers dressed in black were waiting to greet her. She was driven in a black palace Rolls-Royce to Clarence House. There, papers were already waiting to be signed – her first related to a case of sodomy in the army. Within half an hour Queen Mary had arrived to pay a visit. 'Her old grannie and subject must be the first to kiss her hand,' said the old Queen (clearly certain that Philip would not have beaten her to it). Elizabeth was shocked by her grandmother's act of homage. Her position had changed beyond her comprehension. Churchill, despite his lack of enthusiasm about the junior Queen, rose to the occasion with pomp. 'Famous have been the reigns of our Queens,' he declared. 'Some of our greatest periods of history have unfolded under their sceptre.'

The next morning Elizabeth walked across the courtyard from Clarence House to St James's Palace for the Accession Council. Many of the councillors had struggled to assemble their mourning clothes in the post-rationing world. Elizabeth read her formal declaration of sovereignty. 'My heart is too full for me to say more today,' she concluded, 'than that I shall always work as my father did throughout his reign, to uphold the constitutional government, and to advance the happiness and prosperity of my peoples ... I pray that God will help me discharge worthily this heavy task that has been laid on me so early in my life.' The Cabinet had already laid out the lines of the Queen's role in the Proclamation. They had decided not to refer to the 'British Dominions' or to the 'Imperial Crown', but to call the Queen the 'Head of the Commonwealth'. She was no longer dubbed 'Queen of the British Dominions beyond the seas' but 'Queen of her other Realms and Territories'.

'Mummy and Margaret have the biggest grief to bear, for their future must seem very blank, while I have a job and family to think of,' wrote the new Queen. The Queen Mother was devastated by grief and could hardly function in a normal fashion. Convinced until the last moment that her husband was recovering, and sure that they deserved some peace after the war years, she found herself a widow in her early fifties, completely lacking a role. She had lost her husband and her status, and she was painfully jealous of her daughter for being Queen. All of a sudden she was no longer important and her daughter took all the attention that had once been hers.

Princess Margaret was in despair. 'He died as he was getting better,' she recalled. The shock was so great that she had to be given bromide to calm her nerves. She felt and registered all the grief that her sister could not allow herself to experience. 'After the King's death, there was an awful sense of being in a black hole,' she recalled. 'I remember feeling tunnel-visioned and didn't really notice things.' Us Four was no more and she was now the Queen's sister, a much lesser role than the King's daughter. The decision of the King and Queen to educate Margaret lightly gave her few resources to fall back on. Her mother was distracted, her sister occupied and she had few friends among the courtiers. Queen Mary had been a particular ally, but her health was frail and Margaret felt desperately alone. Peter Townsend was, it seemed, her only friend.

On the afternoon after the Accession Council, Elizabeth and Philip drove to Sandringham, where the Queen Mother and Princess Margaret met them, and curtseyed to the new Queen. There, her beloved father lay, before he would be taken back to London and become the dead King rather than her father. On 11 February the body travelled from the church at Sandringham to London by train, then it was carried through the London streets by gun carriage to lie in state at Westminster Hall, where 300,000 people filed past to pay their respects. The nation was seized by a genuine outpouring of grief for the King they had never wanted.

The Duke of Windsor heard of the death of the King from newspaper reporters who had hurried to Waldorf Towers, where he and the Duchess were staying. He arrived on the *Queen Mary* and Elizabeth invited him to tea at Clarence House. He found it all friendly, but, he wrote to his wife, 'the intrigues and manoeuvrings backstage must be filling books'. The Windsors were hopeful that they might be able to return and assume the position of grandeur in the country they both desired. 'Now that the door has been opened a crack, try and get your foot in,' Wallis wrote. It was unlikely. Grieving and pained, the Queen Mother had decided that David, by thrusting his brother into the role of king with little warning, was responsible for his early death. Queen Mary wrote hopefully that he 'saw E [the Queen Mother] and the girls. He had not seen them since 1936, so that feud is over, a great relief to me.' She was over-optimistic about the feelings of one of the 'girls'. Elizabeth stopped the yearly £10,000 allowance that her father had been paying the Duke, much to his fury. He had expected his allowance to continue for ever – indeed, he had just bought a new estate. He was desperately attempting to encourage his family to reverse the decision, but although met with politeness from the Queen Mother and friendliness from the Queen, there was no change of heart. Like so many, he had thought the Queen a pushover – their name for her had been 'Shirley' after Shirley Temple, and they now called her 'the girl'. Elizabeth would ensure that his exile was even chillier under her reign than that of her father.

The new Queen had many relatives to receive for the funeral, as well as foreign ministers. On 16 February Elizabeth walked behind the coffin of her father to the funeral at Windsor. Mountbatten had desired the role, but had to be carefully dissuaded. Behind her were her uncles, the Duke of Gloucester and the Duke of Windsor. The crowds wept so for the dead King that they hardly noticed David. The Queen watched her father's coffin being lowered into the vault at Windsor chapel to be stacked alongside generations of royals.

Queen Mary had met the coffin from Sandringham but she was too unwell to attend the King's funeral. She watched the procession pass her windows at Marlborough House, holding the hand of her dear friend Mabell Airlie. 'There *he* goes,' she whispered, thinking of the king as a child. Her health, already poor, was severely impaired by the loss of her son.

The crusty old Churchill was entirely satisfied with the new Queen. 'All the film people in the world, if they had scoured the globe, could not have found anyone so suited to the part.' On 11 February he addressed the House of Commons on the King's death, extolling their new Queen: 'A fair and youthful figure, Princess, wife and mother, is the heir to all our traditions and glories never greater than in her father's days, and to all our perplexities and dangers never greater in peacetime than now. She is also heir to all our united strength and loyalty.'

Churchill was in full, if patronising, flow. The Queen Mother and the King had hoped to enjoy the quietude of peacetime, but the country, even though it mourned him, wished for a new start, a rebirth. Elizabeth, who had dressed herself with symbols of regeneration at her wedding, was young, bursting with health and very attractive to a nation bowed down by post-war austerity. Britain had won the war but it had lost much over the twentieth century: its Empire was gone, and with its loss came that much of its influence and power.

Preoccupied by visits, receptions, meetings and reading her papers, the new Queen was busy, respected and in charge. She felt a great change in her character. 'I no longer feel anxious or worried,' she told a friend. 'I don't know what it is – but I have lost all my timidity somehow in becoming the Sovereign and having to receive the Prime Minister.'

Elizabeth was worried about upsetting her mother. The Queen Mother remained in the palace, in the suite she had always occupied. She simply could not bear the idea of moving and particularly in a 'ghastly hurry'. She wrote rather disingenuously to the Queen that she 'could be quite self-contained upstairs, meals etc., and you would hardly know I was there. It is so angelic of you to say I can stay on at B.P. and I am most grateful for your thoughtfulness. I know it took Granny some months to pack up everything & I fear I shall need some time too. But what is a few months in a lifetime anyway! Thank you darling for being such an angelic daughter.' Elizabeth did her best not to upset her mother, allowing her to walk ahead whenever it was possible and letting her play hostess, as well as asking her for advice, but it was all merely cushioning her from the inevitable. She was simply no longer powerful. The Queen Mother had been relegated to a supporting role at only fifty-two.

While Elizabeth buried herself in work, Margaret was suffering. She turned away from her usual friends and began to spend time at church. Her friend the Marquess of Blandford had married and Johnny Dalkeith, whom the King had hoped for as a son-in-law, was now absorbed with Jane McNeill, an ex-debutante whom he would soon marry. Margaret's close friendship with Peter Townsend intensified. He was always available to her, he was kind and helpful, and he was a strong shoulder for her to weep on. He, who had known the King so intimately through assisting him from day to day, could appreciate her stories. He, too, was feeling emotionally weary. His devotion to Margaret had not helped harmony in his own marriage, and by 1952 it had broken down. While her family, the Court and the world were distracted, the twenty-one-year-old Princess and the thirty-seven-year-old Townsend became romantically involved.

Prince Philip fell into a depression and would barely move from his room in Clarence House. He tried to persuade the Queen that they should remain in their home, so lovingly renovated to suit their tastes, while the business of monarchy continued in Buckingham Palace. The courtiers, led by the Queen's private secretary Alan Lascelles, and with Churchill in agreement, told the Queen forcefully that she must live in Buckingham Palace, as every sovereign had done since Victoria. 'You can imagine what's going to happen now,' Philip said gloomily to his sister Margarita. Despite the hostile courtiers, he had been deferred to and treated as the head of the family. 'I suppose I naturally fulfilled the principal role,' he said. 'In 1952 the whole thing changed, very considerably.' The new Queen kept her rights and privileges to herself. She read the reports of Cabinet meetings and parliamentary proceedings, and met with the Prime Minister, and Philip had no more involvement in the business of governing than her mother had done.

After Easter the new royal family moved into the 'Belgian suite' on the ground floor, where the King and Queen had remained during the war (the couple eventually took up the first- and second-floor apartments on the North Quadrangle, with Anne and Charles in the nursery upstairs). Like Prince Albert before him, the Prince was shocked at the waste at the palace and promptly set off to view every one of the 600 rooms, asking each staff member what he or she was doing. He was particularly struck by the 'miles and miles' of wine cellar under the palace. It was a useful initiative, particularly in British times of austerity, but not one likely to please the stiff courtiers who already found him too interfering. The government and the Palace did not trust him. The Queen might be devoted to him, he might have fathered the heir to the throne, but still, to the old guard he was foreign. Just after the Coronation Philip suggested his idea of the Duke of Edinburgh's award scheme to the Education Secretary, Sir David Eccles. 'I hear you're trying to invent something like the Hitler Youth!' came the response. It was a terrible insult to someone who had fought for Britain in the war and made every effort to downplay his German connections, to the extent of excluding his beloved sisters from the wedding.

Philip and Elizabeth ended the tradition that the monarch's children and spouse should bow or curtsey to the Queen when she entered the room. But he still had to address her as 'Ma'am' in the presence of others and watch the Queen

Mother, Queen Mary and Princess Margaret curtsey to the Queen when they met in public.

Elizabeth was torn. Her adoration of Philip had not lessened, but it was now in competition with her passionate love of the monarchy. She relied heavily for advice on her mother and Queen Mary, whose devotion to their husbands and the monarchy had never been in conflict. The Cabinet and ministers were most nervous of Philip because they dreaded Mountbatten gaining in influence. As the Duke of Windsor noted of his former friend on his visit after the King's death, 'very bossy & never stops talking. All are suspicious & watching his influence on Philip.'

Two days after the death of the King, Mountbatten held a dinner party and toasted the reign of the house of Mountbatten. Prince Ernst of Hanover rushed to pass the gossip to Queen Mary. After a sleepless night dwelling on the horror of upstart Mountbatten, the old Queen summoned Jock Colville in his role as secretary to the Prime Minister. She was certain George V had founded the house of Windsor for the rest of time and no mere Battenberg marriage could change matters. A piece of dinner party gossip not only gained immediate credibility, it continued to be believed. Mountbatten was very unpopular and everybody wished for an excuse to thrust him out of influence. Some were even worried that he wished Philip to be King Consort.

Churchill was furious when Colville passed on the news. He was deeply suspicious of Lord Mountbatten, believing him a political insinuator and influencer who had given away the Indian subcontinent in 1947. He immediately informed Cabinet who concluded that the name Windsor should remain and encouraged him to 'take a suitable opportunity for making their views known to Her Majesty'. Philip, aware of his uncle's reputation for politicking, made the counter suggestion that his children be known as Edinburgh and the royal house that of Windsor and Edinburgh, but this, too, was refused. Churchill told Elizabeth that it would be in the national interest to retain the continuity between her and her predecessors. The Queen made the announcement in April and Philip was very hurt. 'I am the only man in the country not allowed to give his name to his children,' he declared. 'I'm nothing but a bloody amoeba.' It was the worst possible beginning to his relationship with his wife's government. On the birth of Prince Andrew, eight years later, it was decided that the name Mountbatten-Windsor was to be used for those not entitled to be called Royal Highness (although in practice these members are referred to only as 'Windsor'). It was not enough to satisfy the Prince.

Mountbatten was sanguine, eagerly declaring to all and sundry that although the House of Mountbatten only reigned for two months from February to April, it still 'took its place among the reigning houses of the United Kingdom'. Philip remained in his room and nursed his distress. Still, he had consolations, they were no longer in Buckingham Palace.

Philip tried to fill his time. He developed a particular fascination with UFOs, subscribing to the *Flying Saucer Review* and swapping stories of extraterrestrials with Uncle Dickie. 'If they really come over in a big way that may settle the capitalist–communist war,' declared Mountbatten. Various witnesses came to Buckingham Palace to describe their sightings. The Prince even sent his equerry, Sir Peter Horsley, to meet an extraterrestrial being at a house in Ealing. Horsley reported quite an interesting conversation with the being, who declared Prince Philip 'of great importance in future galactic harmony'. Unfortunately, he simply could not describe its appearance, since the room was 'poorly lit by two standard lamps and for the most part he sat in a deep chair by the side of a not very generous fire'.

Elizabeth, by contrast, was constantly preoccupied. Her workload was greater than her father's had been and it began to be mooted that matters might be too much for her. The National Federation of Women's Institutes passed a resolution announcing that the nation 'should endeavour not to overwork our beloved young Queen, remembering she has duties also as a wife and mother'. *The Lancet* suggested she might withdraw from public view until her children were older, in order to protect her 'health and vitality'. Elizabeth was having none of such mollycoddling. It was fortunate that she was so intent on working, for she was a weary Conservative government's best weapon of popularity. The government wished for a coronation as close to the next election as possible, so Churchill suggested it should occur in the summer of 1953. He himself was determined to stay as Premier until the Queen was crowned – much to the frustration of many in his government, who thought him well past his prime.

The young wife called a 'shrinking violet' was now a rather intimidating Queen. 'Not at all,' she replied, when she was asked if the seventy-seven-year-old Churchill was treating her in the same avuncular, solicitous fashion with which Melbourne had dealt with the young Queen Victoria. 'I find him rather obstinate.' He, by contrast, relished his meetings with the lovely young Queen. He arrived looking dapper in a top hat and disappeared into the reception room for hours. 'What do you talk about?' Jock Colville asked.

'Oh, mostly racing,' came the reply.

'He acted upon her lightest word,' said Ford. When she

expressed displeasure at watching *Beau Brummell* at a royal showing in one of their meetings, he charged out declaring 'This must not recur' and the Home Secretary was put in charge of arranging for the films for the next royal showing to be firmly scrutinised.

Prince Philip was given the role of chairing the Coronation Committee, with the Duke of Norfolk as Vice Chairman. If Philip had hoped to bring his modernising instinct to the committee he failed. On 10 July 1952 it was reported that the television cameras would not be permitted into the Abbey. Winston Churchill believed that the cameras would put the young Queen under too much strain and she herself was reluctant to see some of the most sacred parts of the great service televised. The Archbishop of Canterbury and the Abbey clergy fretted that people watching over coffee cups would compromise the dignity of the occasion. The palace worried that the crowds might not turn out to see the Queen at all if they could watch it on television and everybody was anxious that any mistakes would be broadcast to the nation. Coronations, after all, were so difficult to rehearse, and so unfamiliar to most of those taking part, that gaffes were very common – Queen Victoria exited hers at the wrong moment, when misdirected by the Archbishop.

The people were outraged by the decision to hide the Queen from them. Nothing seemed more unfair than that the great spectacle would be viewed only by peers, foreign royals and the upper echelon of officials. The incredible popularity of the wedding on television had raised expectations that the nation should be allowed to watch every royal ceremony. Confronted by a press outcry and public pressure, the Queen and her committee quickly gave in. A compromise was reached: the cameras would film the service and show the crowning and the homage but the anointing, the communion prayers and the Queen's communion would be hidden. In the weeks running up to the Coronation, millions of televisions were sold to an eager public.

The guest list was unwieldy, but Elizabeth had one definite idea for exclusion. 'The girl' may have been 'friendly' to her uncle David, but she did not wish him at the Coronation. She was so adamant when discussing the matter with the Archbishop of Canterbury that he reported she 'would be less willing than anyone to have him here'. It seemed as if the Queen would have to tell him, but the ever-gallant Churchill stepped in. Despite his fondness for the Duke of Windsor he agreed and told David that it would be 'quite inappropriate for a King who had abdicated to be present as an official guest at the Coronation of one of his successors'. With ill grace, Uncle David agreed.

Margaret was now deeply in love with Peter Townsend. Unable to comprehend the ramifications of his actions, he had resisted Palace efforts to move him to the Air Ministry. Instead, he begged the Queen for another position and she made him comptroller of her mother's household. By the end of 1952 he was divorced from Rosemary and thus free to remarry. Even though the consequence of the abdication was plain to see in the exclusion of Uncle David from the family, Margaret was entranced by Townsend and blinded by love.

At the beginning of 1953, Townsend and Margaret informed the Queen and her mother that they wished to marry. According to the Royal Marriages Act of 1772, the sovereign had to consent to all marriages of the descendants of George III (except for those of princesses who had married into foreign families) who were under twenty-five. Margaret was twenty-three. The Queen, sympathetic to her sister, suggested she wait a year before marrying. Perhaps she hoped the romance might cool and knew that opposition could be a potent aphrodisiac. Moreover, when Margaret was twenty-five she would be able to marry without the Queen's consent, provided that Parliament had been informed, and both the House of Lords and the House of Commons agreed. It would have seemed to all of them a far superior solution – Margaret could wait, then the marriage would be agreed by the Commons and the Queen would not have to be involved. Wrapped up in her new role, and not wanting to upset her sister, the Queen did not fully consider the ramifications of her own position. Her uncle had given up the throne to marry a divorcee, and her sister's attachment to a divorced man would make it impossible to keep her royal privileges.

The other courtiers were not as sympathetic as the Queen. Lascelles was furious, declaring 'You must be either mad or bad or both' to Townsend. He rebuffed Townsend's offer to resign, and told the Queen to remove him from her mother's household and give him an overseas position. Instead, she removed him from Clarence House and made him her equerry at Buckingham Palace. Her move only emboldened Margaret and Townsend to hope.

The Queen felt confident that the relationship between the pair bore no great significance, but the other courtiers were less convinced. The fuss about Margaret and Townsend was reminiscent of the abdication of Edward VIII and threatened to overshadow the joyful beginning of the new reign. Many wished the Queen would take firmer action and banish Townsend, but she did not. She was no doubt right not to do so: Margaret and Townsend were so enamoured that he would have refused an overseas position and forbidding Margaret to see him would only have encouraged her.

Queen Mary was the first Queen ever to see a grandchild ascend to the throne. But by the end of February, she was growing extremely ill. Her doctors summoned David from America. He arrived on 11 March on the *Queen Elizabeth* from New York, fretting about leaving the Duchess to the attentions of the notorious New York playboy James Donoghue. 'What I think of having to make this ridiculous and costly trip instead of our being together in Palm Beach is nobody's business,' he wrote to the Duchess. She told him to attempt to influence 'Cookie' (the Queen Mother) and Shirley (the Queen) to continue the allowance. Instead, predictably, he was cold-shouldered by the royal family and stayed with friends. Uncle David stood for fun, irresponsibility, glamour and frivolity – everything Elizabeth had eschewed in order to create her image as the perfect Queen.

The old Queen died aged eighty-five on 24 March, declaring she did not wish to go on living as an 'old crock'. 'A wave of emotion spread over the land,' wrote Chips Channon. The crowds wept outside her home at Marlborough House. When the will was read, it was found that she had left everything to her granddaughter, the new Queen – with the exception of a few candlesticks and boxes for the Duke of Windsor. There was nothing for the Queen Mother, Princess Margaret or any of the ladies-in-waiting. The Duke of Windsor, angered that he received so little, declared 'the fluids in her veins have always been as icy cold as they are now in death'. The candlesticks she had left him did not soften his heart.

The Duke felt further insulted when he was not invited to the dinner following his mother's funeral on 31 March.

He wrote to his wife in high dudgeon: 'What a smug, stinking lot my relations are and you've never seen such a seedy worn-out bunch of old hags most of them have become.'

Queen Mary's body replaced that of her son at Westminster Hall, where another sad ceremony took place, followed by a funeral at St George's Windsor. To the public it seemed as if the old guard really had gone. The government began to plan a Coronation in which notions of rebirth were paramount. The young Queen was the nation's new hope.

Elizabeth had watched her father's Coronation with Queen Mary, giggling and turning over the pages to see how much of the service remained. Now, in quick succession, she had lost her father and her grandmother, and her mother was devastated by grief. Crawfie was gone and her sister was distracted. She threw herself into planning the Coronation.

Elizabeth called Norman Hartnell to the palace and told him to create something in white satin, along the lines of her wedding dress. He returned with plans of a gown embroidered with symbols of the United Kingdom. She asked him if he could figure the Commonwealth and so the traditional rose, leeks, shamrocks and thistle for England, Wales, Northern Ireland and Scotland were interspersed with more exotic plants, including the New Zealand fern, the Canadian maple leaf and the cotton, jute and wheat for Pakistan. The Coronation dress would be reused by Elizabeth in the next few years, twice for receptions and four times at the opening of parliaments in New Zealand, Australia, Ceylon and Canada.

At the same time that Hartnell's embroiderers were working on her dress and those of her maids of honour, Westminster Abbey was being scrubbed, and twelve seamstresses from the Royal College of Needlework were creating the Purple Robe of Estate, thirteen feet of purple silk velvet, edged in ermine and embroidered in gold with olive branches and wheat to symbolise peace and plenty. It took almost 3,500 hours of hard, painstaking sewing to make.

Meanwhile, the government were busying themselves arranging a party. VE Day had been overshadowed by the great sense of loss, so the plan was that the Coronation would be a day of pure celebration across the nation. Churchill decreed that everyone should receive an extra pound of sugar on their sugar ration – much to the horror of officials at the Ministry of Food, who conjured nightmare scenarios of shortages. To the suits in the ministry, Churchill was playing fast and loose with the supplies. He gave more to those who could prove they were organising street parties and gave extra sugar and fat to caterers and restaurateurs, so they could make sweets and pastries, toffee apples and crisps for the crowds. Eggs and sweets were decontrolled – to the delight of shopkeepers, who could suddenly charge much higher prices. Despite rationing still being in place, it was agreed that whole oxen could be roasted for the celebrations – but only if it could be proved that an ox had been roasted in each location at a previous coronation. In the end, only eighty-two applications were approved.

There was a shortage of professional coachmen, due to the rise of the motor car and the death of so many young men during the war. Buckingham Palace let it be known that dignitaries and members of the Coronation party were in need of drivers, and a selection of country squires and rich businessmen – now among the few people who were likely to be able to drive a coach – volunteered their services. They were dressed in the livery of Buckingham Palace servants and were rewarded with the chance to boast that they had been involved in the ceremony.

'Never has there been such excitement,' wrote Jock Colville, 'never has a monarch received so much adulation.' Every newspaper seemed to be full of nothing but Coronation stories; houses across Britain were decked in red, white and blue. According to Churchill, it was joy in the new modern monarchy, since the crown was now 'far more broadly and securely based on the people's love and the nation's will than in the sedate days ... when rank and privilege ruled society'. As Britain's power receded ever more, Churchill and his ministers wanted a large dose of pomp and glamour. The whole occasion was to cost nearly £2 million.

Westminster Abbey was closed almost from the moment of the King's death to begin work on the preparations. The details and organisation were overseen by the Earl Marshal, the 16th Duke of Norfolk (who would later be responsible for the state funeral of Winston Churchill). Elizabeth herself attended two full-scale rehearsals and watched the Duchess of Norfolk, who had been coached by her husband, walk through the ceremony. In her spare time, she busied herself with private rehearsals, parading up and down the palace attached to sheets tied together to mimic her thirteen-foot train and arranging chairs into the layout of the carriage that would carry her on the day. She drank her tea and read the newspapers wearing the huge Imperial State Crown, which was studded with historic jewels: the Black Prince's Ruby, Queen Elizabeth I's pearl earrings, and the Stuart Sapphire from Charles II's crown. As George V said, he knew of few worse ordeals than delivering a speech written by somebody else while balancing a 2.5lb crown on his head. She begged the Bishop of Durham, who would be her chief supporter at her right-hand side, to keep his eyebrows still. He was rather an expressive wiggler and she hoped to persuade him: 'because they made her smile and she did not want to smile in the wrong place'.

'The Coronation was like a phoenix-time,' recalled Princess Margaret. 'Everything was being raised from the ashes. There was this gorgeous-looking, lovely young lady, and nothing to stop anything getting better and better.'

The British public was frantic for a celebration. Towns began planning their decorations: schools started on year-long projects of sticking together crowns, Abbeys and collages of the Commonwealth; shops ordered Coronation merchandise and street parties were planned. The peers of the realm dusted off their old cloaks, the maids of honour practised their curtseys and foreign royals complained they had not been seated with due dignity. By May so many people had flooded into the capital that the police had to restrict any vehicles but those of public service entering within two miles of Westminster. The rest of the world was forgotten: by the end of the month the newspapers gave hardly any space to anything but Coronation news and royal stories.

Coronation Day on 2 June, was wet and cold, but the crowds were undeterred. As they were waiting, the news spread that John Hunt, Edmund Hillary and their team had reached the top of Everest, much to the delight of the people. 'All this – and Everest too!' enthused the *Daily Express*, above images of the crowds huddled in the rain and the Queen's robes. As the young Queen left for Westminster Abbey, the streets around the palace were bursting beyond capacity, crammed with cheering crowds waving souvenir flags and posters, jostling for a glimpse of the carriage. They cried out for their new Queen, and their hope for the country's future, and also to put their own mark on history.

The Abbey had opened at 6 a.m. for the lowliest guests to begin scrambling in. The foreign royals and representatives of Commonwealth parliaments were allowed a lie-in and were required to enter at 8.30. They idled away the time reading newspapers, talking and munching derationed sweets. The various royals arrived in complicated procession. By 11.00, eight thousand guests were waiting. Millions more were watching on television – an estimated twenty-seven million, half the population. Eleven million British wirelesses were tuned in and two and a half million television sets.

Many dignitaries braved the rain to wave at the crowds. Despite the wet morning – and the fact that some carriages were open – the mood was cheerful, with some representatives of foreign nations experiencing their first taste of British tradition in full swing. Of these, the plump Queen Salote III of Tonga was perhaps the most popular with the crowd, smiling and waving from beneath her parasol. The tiny Sultan of Kelantan travelled next to her. 'Who's that?' someone asked Noël Coward. 'Her lunch,' he replied. Philip's three surviving sisters, Theodora, Margarita and Sophie, had demanded to come and it was thought sufficient time had elapsed since the war to dull passions, but they were strictly limited to two accompanying children each.

Charles attended the ceremony, although his sister Princess Anne was considered too young to be there. As such, he was the first child of a monarch to witness his mother being crowned Queen. A hand-painted special invitation was sent to him, as the only child with his own invitation. He had been brought in by his nanny through a side door to sit between the Queen Mother and Princess Margaret, dressed in shirt and shorts, like any other little boy, rather than the regalia of a future king.

Resting on a cushion, St Edward's Crown led the procession into the Abbey, carried by the Lord High Steward of England. He was followed by three peers of the realm, and the whole group passed the Archbishops and Bishops Assistant of the Church of England who were waiting by the Great West Door for Elizabeth to appear.

After processing through the crowds in the Gold State Coach, accompanied by Philip in the uniform of the Admiral of the Fleet, the Queen arrived at Westminster Abbey at eleven. She wore the George IV State Diadem, which had been made for his coronation in 1820. With over 1,300 diamonds and almost 200 pearls, it was a glittering display of the past and hinted strongly at the unbroken chain of succession (it is the one she is depicted wearing on stamps). A quarter of an hour later the Queen entered the Abbey through the West Door, preceded by a great procession of clergy, knights, Churchill, the Prime Ministers of the Commonwealth and the Archbishops of Canterbury and York. The Duke of Edinburgh, further dignitaries, the Earl Marshal, the Lord Stewards and High Constables of the United Kingdom brought up the rear. For the first time the Scottish Church was also involved in the shape of the Moderator of the Church of Scotland. Finally – after the long procession of elderly men – came the young Queen, her train carried by her Mistress of the Robes, the Dowager Duchess of Devonshire, and her six maids of honour, all scions of great families, especially made up by the ladies from Elizabeth Arden to counter the effects of the bright lights. One, Lady Jane Vane-Tempest-Stuart, had travelled with the Lord Privy Purse in the carriage and had been delighted to discover that he had a secret stash of toffees in the Privy Purse. The others battled under the weight of the embroidered gown.

With the Queen came the Bishops of Durham, Bath and Wells as her supporters, then her ladies-in-waiting and members of her household, including Peter Townsend. Many were unimpressed by the decision of Alan Lascelles that Philip should not walk alongside the Queen, as the Queen Mother had with the King.

After a struggle with the gold of her mantle catching on the carpet pile, Elizabeth made it up to the altar and was seated in the Chair of Estate. All of the props and items that would be needed in the ceremony were placed on the altar and the young Queen stood briefly to curtsey to each corner of the congregation – north, south, east and west – after they had cried out 'God Save the Queen' in response to the following request: 'Sirs, I here present unto you Queen Elizabeth, your undoubted Queen: wherefore all you who are come this day to do your homage and service, are you willing to do the same?'

The Queen sat to read out the Coronation Oath, and vowed to protect the United Kingdom and each country of the Commonwealth (although the word Commonwealth was not used), the laws of each country, and the English Church and its clergy. The communion service was then taken, and prayers and various readings echoed among the congregation. The Queen then had her elaborate jewellery and cape removed, in preparation for her anointing.

Behind a silk cloth so the congregation could not see, the Queen was anointed with a specially made holy oil, a mixture of oil of orange, cinnamon, roses, musk and ambergris, blessed and consecrated. There had always been a stash of excess oil kept over from previous coronations, in order to represent a sense of continuity between the monarchs. However, it was discovered during the preparations that the last existing phial had been destroyed by a bomb during the Second World War. The pharmacy that traditionally mixed the anointing oil had gone out of business, but the Coronation Commission were able to track down an elderly chemist, who had kept the recipe as a memento of his work. A batch of oil was made up and consecrated in time for the ceremony.

Elizabeth was now handed all the trappings of state – sword and spurs, which were taken by the monarch and then placed back on the altar, followed by bracelets, robe, ring, orb and two sceptres. With the ring on her finger and holding the sceptres – the Sceptre with the Cross in her right, the Sceptre with the Dove in her left – Elizabeth was finally crowned. Seated on St Edward's Chair, which had been made in 1300 for Edward I and which has been used in every coronation since, the weight of history was pressing on her shoulders. As the Archbishop of Canterbury placed the solid gold St Edward's Crown on her head the crowd shouted 'God Save the Queen', and a twenty-one-gun salute was fired from the Tower of London. After the benediction Queen Elizabeth transferred herself to the throne, where she received promises of loyalty and fealty from the royal family and the members of the House of Lords. The first to offer his allegiance was her husband, Prince Philip.

After all the rituals had been concluded, the congregation set off back to Buckingham Palace. The route had been designed to allow the most people the best chance of seeing their Queen, proudly holding her orb and sceptre, and wearing the Imperial State Crown. Approximately 16,000 people – including guests, servants, footmen and drivers – took part in the procession, which, at almost five miles in length, took almost two hours to complete. Lining the route were men of the Metropolitan Police, 7,000 seconded policemen from other forces, thousands of representatives of the RAF, Royal Navy and the army, members of the royal military police, officers from the Commonwealth and colonies, and over 6,000 reserve troops. Almost 2,000 journalists of various nationalities lined the route of the procession, as well as 500 photographers.

The crowds cried out and the rest of the nation huddled round television screens, often wearing their best clothes. Some bought magnifying glasses which could be attached to the set, allowing a larger but grainier image to be seen. Thirty cameramen had been allowed into the Abbey, some of whom were chosen for their small stature, able to cram into the nooks of the roof.

In order to carry the film, the first ever non-stop flights from the UK to the Canadian mainland were organised. The RAF flew three planes during the ceremony, each carrying another stage of the process, and the flights were met at Goose Bay in Newfoundland by a Canadian air force fighter, which transferred the film to Montreal for broadcast. The Canadian Broadcasting Corporation showed the BBC's film within four hours of the end of the Coronation. The whole ceremony was eventually watched by an audience of 350 million people.

As well as the main BBC cameras, another film crew was allowed into the Abbey, experimenting with a brand-new technology. Pathé News, whose current affairs programmes were a mainstay of cinemas for many years, had developed a means of merging the output from two cameras to provide an effective, if not perfect, 3-D image. Although almost twenty minutes of film was shot, the expense of the process and the drop in popularity of the cinema (ironically, largely driven by the boom in television ownership caused by the Coronation) meant that it was never shown and languished unplayed in the British Film Institute for almost sixty years.

After the Coronation the crowds celebrated all night long. People wore gowns and dressed as everything from royals to Mount Everest and television sets. Souvenir shops, sweet sellers and pubs did a roaring trade. The exhausted maids of honour and the peers returned to rest – Rosemary Spencer-Churchill found them enthusiastically roasting an ox in the grounds of Blenheim Palace. The maids were rather disappointed – Elizabeth managed to forget to curtsey at the right point and they had missed their chance to do the same, losing their moment of glory. As in every grand celebration, there had been mistakes. The Archbishop of Canterbury complained that the Dean of Westminster had given a huge dish for the Queen's offering of a little bag of gold – he could hardly lift it, he grumbled. Everybody who had been anywhere near had been amused by the shabby Baron Mowbray, Segrave and Stourton, who returned from his homage looking most dishevelled – 'moth balls and pieces of ermine flying all over the place,' remarked the Queen. The Abbey in the wake of the distinguished guests was scarcely more ordered: the peers' seats in particular were strewn with newspapers, sweets and sandwich wrappings.

Sir Edmund Hillary famously declared of his success, 'It is not the mountain we have to conquer but ourselves.' The British, watching their young Queen, believed they had already conquered. 'Does not the lesson of Everest stand out as clear?' declared the *Evening Standard* on the day of the

Coronation in an editorial titled 'Onward to Glory'. The message was plain: 'while collectively and acting in unity the men of the Empire can conquer everything, singly they can conquer nothing. Long live the Queen! Long also may there live the Imperial unity which can make her reign one of peace and wondrous glory.' Little could be more deluded. The final embers of Empire had been blown out by the Second World War.

The Queen hosted a luncheon after the ceremony, at which Coronation Chicken was served for the first time. A variation on the recipe for Jubilee Chicken, which had been served at George V's Silver Jubilee celebrations, it was invented by Rosemary Hume and Constance Spry, and was originally called *poulet reine Elizabeth*. A mixture of cold chicken, mayonnaise, cream, curry powder and other spices, the dish quickly became a British favourite. Chicken had been almost impossible to obtain in the war, but now those days were truly over.

Those members of the public who had waited outside the palace were rewarded with an appearance on the balcony – the Queen waved to the crowd after the ceremony, still wearing the Imperial State Crown. The RAF also provided the crowd with some entertainment, as they performed a fly-past down the Mall, despite the overcast weather. The Queen returned to the balcony at 9.45 p.m. to turn on the 'lights of London'. Starting at Buckingham Palace, the lights were switched on down the Mall, through Trafalgar Square and onwards, as far as the Tower of London. It was intended as a potent symbol of the new age that was dawning: no longer austerity Britain, but a country with a new, young, vibrant Head of State, ready to take its place in the new Europe.

★

Five months after her Coronation Elizabeth departed on a six-month tour of the Commonwealth. Unlike her father, who had seen himself as the head of an Empire, she saw her role as that of the head of the Commonwealth and it was as significant for her as the position of Queen of Great Britain. Her long tour marked a new reign. Whereas her father had found foreign travel difficult, Elizabeth was eager to see her dominions.

She began in Bermuda and travelled through the Bahamas and Jamaica, stopped at Belize, sailed the Panama Canal and visited Fiji and Tonga. Christmas was spent in New Zealand, before continuing to Australia and Ceylon. At Tobruk, five-year-old Prince Charles and three-year-old Princess Anne were brought to see her. The greetings in public were formal: Charles shook the Queen's hand. They were met on their arrival in Britain by Churchill, who accompanied them back along the Thames on the royal yacht. 'One saw this dirty commercial river,' Elizabeth recalled, 'and he was describing it as the silver thread which runs through the history of Britain.' His early suspicion of her forgotten, Churchill was captivated. 'I assign no limits to the reinforcement which this royal journey may have brought to the health, the wisdom, the sanity and hopefulness of mankind,' he blustered.

After the ceremony the Queen had departed from Westminster Abbey, escorted by her husband, glorious in her moment of triumph. Margaret was waiting in the porch to be taken by carriage to Buckingham Palace. There, she flicked a piece of fluff from the uniform of Peter Townsend. The photographers caught the moment and the potential new royal romance was blazoned across the front of the newspapers.

Much to the fury of the courtiers, Margaret had seized the limelight from Elizabeth once more.

On 13 June, just a few days after the Coronation, Lascelles drove to Churchill's country house, Chartwell. As the Palace knew, the press had the story and matters must be prevented. There, he informed him that Princess Margaret wished to marry Peter Townsend. Churchill initially saw no objection to the marriage – until his wife pointed out that he was 'making the same mistake as he made at the Abdication'. The Attorney General was sent to investigate the constitutional ramifications of any marriage and to ask Commonwealth prime ministers for their views. The Cabinet refused to sanction the marriage and Lord Salisbury, who had been a friend of the King, declared he would resign.

On 14 June the *People* exposed the 'scandalous rumours' of the romance. Of course, they said, the story could not be true, since no princess so close to the throne would marry a divorced man, even if he had been the innocent party in the divorce. It was, they said, 'quite unthinkable that a Royal Princess, third in line of succession to the throne, should even contemplate marriage with a man who has been through the divorce courts'. The Queen's press secretary suggested to her that Townsend leave the palace. Churchill told her that the Cabinet would not approve the marriage. Perhaps he expected her to infer from this that they would not change their minds and approve it after she was twenty-five, but unfortunately this was not clear, certainly not to Margaret and perhaps not to the Queen. Townsend and Margaret agreed to separate and he consented to go to Brussels as Air Attaché. Outwardly, it seemed as if the storm was over. But, still desperately in love, Margaret and Townsend were convinced that if they simply waited a year they would be allowed to marry. The Queen, the Queen Mother and the courtiers continued to put their heads in the sand. The Queen Mother, according to one friend, rather pretended it was not happening and was 'completely unapproachable and remote, she refused to believe it at all or discuss it with anyone so Princess Margaret could never consult her about it'. Many thought that the Queen simply did not comprehend how threatening a marriage could be. Certainly, she wished to approach matters with scrupulous honesty and so wanted to ensure that her sister made her choice from her own volition and not from concern over the reputation of the Crown or her duty to Church and state. She thus did not make clear to her sister the constitutional ramifications of her desire to marry Townsend and the Princess did not see them. The fact that Townsend had been declared the innocent party in his divorce seemed everything to them. The Princess could see absolutely no comparison between herself and Uncle David and Wallis Simpson. 'She has always despised them as completely beyond the pale,' one friend declared.

At the end of June the Queen Mother and Princess Margaret set off on a tour of Southern Rhodesia. She and Townsend were sure that she would return in time to wish him goodbye as he set off to be Air Attaché, but Churchill insisted he leave before she arrived. Halfway through the tour Margaret was told that he would be gone by the time she came back. Feeling shocked and betrayed, she collapsed with a nervous illness. The Queen Mother had to proceed without her.

Princess Margaret returned to the palace in a state of despair. The loss of her father and lover in quick succession was very difficult to bear. She wrote daily to Townsend and nursed her misery alone, for the Queen Mother would not accept it and Elizabeth was occupied. The newspapers, thrown off the scent by the separation, put about the rumour that she was due to marry Colin Tennant, a friend and the heir of Lord Glenconner, and the gossip made her even more nervous and upset. Her twenty-fourth birthday at Balmoral was a disaster. The Queen Mother wished for the party to dress up and sing a song for the event, just as they used to do when the King was alive. But the sight of her family and friends dressed up as druids and warbling her birthday song as they had done in happier times was too much for the Princess, and she burst into tears.

As Margaret's twenty-fifth birthday approached, the tension grew. In the spring of 1955 she travelled to the West Indies and was widely feted. The attention of the world's newspapers was once more trained on her. The *Daily Sketch* interviewed Peter Townsend in Brussels and asked if he would marry the Princess. He replied, 'Wait and see.' He later claimed he had been misquoted, but the newspaper argued that he had requested the interview. Margaret celebrated her birthday at Balmoral and not long afterwards, Peter Townsend arrived in London. He cut a flamboyant figure in a chauffeur-driven red Daimler and complained vociferously that he had not been invited to Balmoral. Townsend had always been religious, but he was growing ever more dogmatic and had even begun to argue that it was God's will that the marriage should go ahead. He returned to Brussels without any definite answer, but he was determined to succeed.

By October the press speculation had become so intense that it was damaging the reputation of the monarchy. The courtiers began to suspect Townsend of tipping off the editors of his whereabouts. Lord Salisbury, Secretary of State for Commonwealth Relations and Lord President of the Council, who had been a friend of King George VI, told the Queen that she must issue a statement to stop the reports. On 14 October Colville put out a request for the press to stop following Margaret and declared that 'no announcement concerning Princess Margaret's personal future was at present contemplated'. The journalists were only encouraged. Neither the Queen nor the Queen Mother could bear to raise the subject with Margaret. For the Queen Mother the possibility of a marriage had become deeply upsetting and the press speculation reminded her of the misery of the Abdication.

On 18 October the Prime Minister, Anthony Eden, arrived for his audience with the Queen. He told her that Lord Salisbury had not relented on his promise to resign if Margaret married Townsend. As he said, because the marriage could not be sanctioned by Parliament, a bill would have to be introduced depriving her and any children of the right to succeed to the throne, as well as her role as Counsellor of State and her income from the Civil List, which was £6,000. He suggested that the couple would have to live abroad for a period before returning and made it very clear to Elizabeth that her fledgling rule would be damaged by such an action. As *The Times* commented, the Queen was Britain's 'universal representative in whom her people see their better selves ideally reflected; and since part of this ideal is family life, the Queen's family has its own part in the reflection. If the marriage which is now being discussed comes to pass, it is inevitable that this reflection becomes distorted.'

The newspapers engaged in wild speculation. For all the commentators the situation was a repetition of 1936 all over again. Of course, they were exaggerating. Not only was the

Princess not the monarch, but divorce had become more socially acceptable – Eden himself was divorced and had remarried. But the royal family were supposed to be above such activities. For most of their subjects the contract was that they could live in splendour if they accepted their duty to maintain the ideal of monarchy. Any desire that might threaten this ideal should be swiftly quashed.

Elizabeth had condemned divorce to the Mothers' Union in 1949. She had reviled her uncle for his irresponsibility. Now the situation was much closer to home. If Margaret and Townsend married, their life would be very much like that of the Windsors, but on much less money. The Queen was not willing to support her sister abroad, as her father had done for David. Peter and Margaret would have to live off his small salary, from which he also had to contribute to the upkeep of his sons. The Princess, like her Uncle David, loved the luxury and glamour of royal life, the excitable crowds and the position at the top of the social tree, but found the responsibilities more onerous. The life of a humble civil servant's wife in Brussels could have no appeal for her. Her family, who had no idea of the practicalities of living outside the gilded royal bubble, could not help her and, indeed, communicated their own terror of living a life that was not royal. Margaret's despair and confusion were overwhelming. 'We were both exhausted, mentally, physically, emotionally,' Townsend wrote. 'We felt mute and numbed at the centre of this maelstrom.'

The marriage was simply impossible. At the end of October Margaret and Townsend met to draft together their announcement of renunciation. She informed the Archbishop of Canterbury that she would not marry Townsend. They spent the weekend with Lord and Lady Rupert Nevill in their house in Sussex. There was relief in finally coming to a decision. Margaret later said that she had enjoyed the weekend more than any in her life. They met in the afternoon of 31 October at Clarence House to drink to their past and the futures they would not lead together. That evening Margaret issued a statement.

> I would like it to be known that I have decided not to marry Group Captain Peter Townsend. I have been aware that, subject to my renouncing my rights of succession, it might have been possible for me to contract a civil marriage. But, mindful of the Church's teaching that Christian marriage is indissoluble, and conscious of my duty to the Commonwealth, I have resolved to put these considerations before any others.

She spent the rest of the evening on her own. The Queen Mother was at an official engagement. Elizabeth called for a brief telephone conversation. Surprisingly, after what she had given up, the Princess was left alone to nurse her feelings of loss.

The public was deeply sympathetic to Margaret's statement of renunciation. Thousands of people across Britain sent her letters of support – some even told her of their own romantic difficulties. Many felt great compassion for Princess Margaret and began to suggest that she had been treated unfairly. For others the fuss over a divorcé simply showed how out of touch the monarchy truly was. Martin Charteris, the Queen's private secretary, was asked on television if Margaret had been sacrificed to the institution of the monarchy. 'She sacrificed herself,' he replied. But many thought Princess Margaret had been punished for the actions of her uncle.

The Queen, so alert to the importance of public opinion and showing herself as dutiful, hard-working and happily
married, seemed to be unable to see that the journalists would
train a similarly critical eye on the personal lives of her family. Her inability to engage with the problems of Margaret
and how these would seem to the outside world set a pattern
that would be repeated in some of her children's marriages
nearly fifty years later.

For many of the Queen's subjects, the Abdication is a part
of history. But for the royal family itself it is recent memory
– and a horror that must always be avoided. The threat of
being like Uncle David was held over the head of any royal
who seemed likely to waver from the path of duty. Dickie
Mountbatten, busily trying to encourage Prince Charles
towards his granddaughter, Amanda Knatchbull, lost his
temper when the Prince changed plans to stay with the
family. Such selfish behaviour, Mountbatten declared, was
'typical of how your Uncle David started out'. Every day
since the accession of her father has been an opportunity
for the Queen to prove how different she was from Uncle
David.

Queen Elizabeth never expected to be Queen – and she was
not trained to occupy the role – yet she has become one
of our greatest monarchs: hard-working, dutiful and sympathetic to her people. At Victoria's Diamond Jubilee in 1897,
the seventy-eight year old Queen was exhausted and so lame
that the ceremony had to take place on the steps of St Paul's,
because she could not mount them. The current Queen takes
on the workload equal to the younger royals, which would
exhaust many of her subjects. 'It's quite nice', she said of a
portrait sitting before her eightieth birthday. 'Usually one

just sits, and people can't get at you because one's busy doing nothing.' To do nothing is a rare part of her life.

A royal is rather like the old adage about a tree that falls in a forest: if it is not heard, does it make a sound? They have no point unless they are seen. Their job is to represent themselves, and a royal personage who hides themselves away is seen as shirking their duty, even if they are reading papers and answering letters. Queen Victoria began the tradition of royal tours around the country. Previous monarchs, such as George IV and William IV had remained at home, and even those who did travel, such as Elizabeth I, were visiting the homes of their political allies. After Victoria, a monarch, and indeed any royal, had to tour the country. Elizabeth's successors have much to live up to.

On 20 November 1992, just after 11.30 a.m., a spotlight caught a curtain in the Queen's private chapel at Windsor Castle. Within minutes, the heavy material was blazing. The voracious fire spread and soon the State Rooms were ablaze. By midday, fire engines had rushed from Berkshire, Kent and London and over two hundred firefighters battled the flames. Yet the fire was hungry, and would not be stemmed. By 1.30 the roof of the State Apartments was collapsing. The Queen arrived at 3.00 to see her old home in flames. Just after her arrival, the Brunswick Tower collapsed. The fire blazed until 11 p.m. that night, turning the sky bright red for miles around. The people of Windsor, the boys at Eton College and sightseers from all over the country watched in horrified fascination as the fire licked the sky and precious furnishings, art and ornaments inside were destroyed by its insatiable flames.

Two weeks later, the formal separation of Prince Charles

and Diana, Princess of Wales, was announced by the Palace. The years that followed were the most challenging for the Queen and the Royal Family.

On the night of Saturday 30 August 1997, the thirty-six-year-old Diana, Princess of Wales, departed the Ritz Hotel in the Place Vendôme in Paris, accompanied by Dodi Fayed, the son of businessman and then owner of Harrods, Mohamed Fayed. The Princess and Dodi were travelling to Dodi's apartment – but they never arrived. Their car was caught in a terrible crash in a tunnel under the Place de l'Alma. The paparazzi were first to the scene.

'I always believed the press would kill her in the end,' said the Princess's brother, Charles, Earl Spencer, not long after her death.

At 1 a.m. on Sunday, the Queen and Prince Charles, staying at Balmoral, received word of the accident. At 4 a.m., they were told that Diana was dead. That morning the Palace issued a statement: 'The Queen and the Prince of Wales are deeply shocked and distressed at this terrible news.' There was no plan to say anything more – or return to London from Balmoral.

Over the next few days, mourners flooded to London, piling flowers, cards and presents outside Buckingham and Kensington Palaces. The city nearly ran out of flowers. The people were soon demanding the Queen's presence. 'Show Us You Care', cried the *Daily Express* on Thursday. Pressed by her advisors, the Queen agreed to fly to London and address the nation on the following day. She praised the Princess as an 'exceptional and gifted human being' and talked of the family's sorrow.

On the morning of Saturday 6 September, Diana's coffin progressed on a horse-drawn gun carriage to Westminster

Abbey. Behind it walked Prince William, Prince Harry, Prince Charles, Prince Philip and Earl Spencer. As the cortege passed Buckingham Palace, the Queen, standing at the gates of the Palace, bowed to the coffin. The act surprised many, but it reflected the mood of the nation. The Queen's habit of carrying on as normal, ignoring emotions and maintaining routine, had been overturned.

Despite the Queen's response to the people, the period after the death of Diana saw growing criticism against the monarchy and republican sentiment. Suggestions were made that the Golden Jubilee in 2002 would attract little public support. But the people did come to celebrate, and the Queen and her monarchy have survived and now seem stronger than ever.

Born into a time of class turmoil, the Queen lived through the Depression, the Second World War, 1950s austerity, the swinging sixties and the rise of the financial services in the 1980s. In one sense, she *is* the twentieth century. She has been photographed, filmed, painted, drawn and represented in plays, films, satirical sketches and music. She is instantly recognisable and for many people across the world, the Queen is synonymous with the British monarchy. She has weathered the distressing divorces of her children, press campaigns against her non-payment of income tax, the media fallout after the death of the Princess of Wales, and the break-up of the Commonwealth – at the time of publication, Jamaica has expressed its desire to depart. In times of great change, the Queen has been a constant. Even at eighty-six, there is much in her that is reminiscent of the dutiful little girl who lined up her horses outside the nursery and tidied her shoes every night.

On Coronation Day in Paris, the Duke of Windsor

dressed up in a grey pinstriped suit and travelled to attend the 'television lunch' of a wealthy American friend, Margaret Biddle. Along with a hundred of her friends, he watched the broadcast perched on a gilt chair. At the close, he sat back, lit a cigarette and said calmly, 'It was a very impressive ceremony. It's a very moving ceremony and perhaps more moving because she is a woman.' By 1953, he was little more than a spectator.

In November 1998, Charles's press secretary, Mark Bolland, suggested to the newspapers that the Prince would be 'privately delighted' if the Queen relinquished the throne. The Queen asked her son for an explanation and he retracted and said the story was untrue. Media speculation recurs intermittently over whether she will abdicate – but it is all irrelevant. As Elizabeth declared in her Golden Jubilee address to Parliament in 2002, she is driven by 'my resolve to continue, with the support of my family, to serve the people of this great nation of ours to the best of my ability through the changing times ahead.' She has said that she will remain, even if incapacitated through illness Charles would be appointed Regent. The Queen was not born for the role – but she will never give it up.

'My father died much too young and it was all very sudden,' the Queen said, many years after her accession. 'It was a matter of making the best job you can ... and accepting your fate.' It is a fate Queen Elizabeth has accepted with grace and dignity.

*Coronation Day, 2 June 1953*

# Acknowledgements

In writing *Young Elizabeth* I have made particular use of the Cabinet Papers in the National Archives and the Foreign Office Papers in the National Archives, as well as the Admiralty Office Papers in the National Archives, and especially the diary of Ramsay Macdonald. Also vital was the important collection of papers at Churchill College, Cambridge, particularly those of Sir Alan Lascelles. The letters of Earl Baldwin at the Cambridge University Library were also invaluable. I am very grateful to the staff of the British Library, the National Archives in Kew, the British Library Newspaper Library at Colindale, Churchill College, the London Library, Cambridge University Library, the Bodleian Library and the Imperial War Museum. I am very fortunate to have been able to discuss Queen Elizabeth II and many of the events in the book with those who have carried out vital scholarship into the British Royal Family, my friends and fellow royal investigators, Alison Weir, Sarah Gristwood, Siobhan Clarke, Tracy Borman, Philip Eade, Gyles Brandreth, Anne Sebba, Juliet Gardiner, Miranda Carter and Lisa Hilton. I am also grateful to Melvyn Bragg and many other individuals who would prefer to remain nameless.

Queen Elizabeth II has attracted great scholarship in the past and I owe a debt to all those who have produced such important and ground-breaking works, notably Sarah Bradford's *Queen Elizabeth II*, William Shawcross's *Queen Elizabeth, the Queen Mother*, Ben Pimlott's *The Queen*, Jennie Bond's edition of *The Little Princesses*, Anne Sebba's *That Woman*, Philip Eade's *Young Prince Philip*, Elizabeth Longford's *Elizabeth R*, Sarah Bradford's, *George VI*, Philip Ziegler's *Edward VIII and Mountbatten*, Gyles

Brandreth's *Philip and Elizabeth*, Robert Hardman's *Monarchy*, A. N. Wilson's *The Rise and Fall of the House of Windsor* and Christopher Warwick's *Princess Margaret*. I am also grateful to the authors whose works I was able to read just at the final stages of copyediting mine. Andrew Marr's *The Diamond Queen*, Sally Bedell Smith's *Elizabeth the Queen* and Robert Hardman's *Our Queen*. Thank you to all those who have invited me to speak about the Queen on their television programmes, including Huw Edwards, BBC Breakfast, News 24, Jasmin Buttar at *Today* and Liz Gibbons at *Newsnight*. I owe heartfelt thanks to my editor, the extremely patient, judicious and brilliant Bea Hemming, and the inspiring Alan Samson at Weidenfeld & Nicolson, as well as Elizabeth Allen and Sherif Mehmet. My agent, Simon Trewin, was as tireless on my behalf as ever, and Ariella Feiner kind and indomitable. Thank you immeasurably to Marcus Gipps, who has listened to endless stories of princes, kings, wars and governesses, been kindly and patient with the royal books piling up like stalagmites around the sitting room and has been unfailingly interested in the Queen and her life.

If we know the child, we know the adult. This book is an investigation of the Queen's youth, a portrait of an age, an exploration of the impact of the abdication of Edward VIII on her life, and a window into early royal life. In an age when childhood seems to be increasingly squeezed and pressured, as the young are encouraged to become mini adults, early adopters of technologies, dressed as grown-ups, the 1920s and 1930s seem very distant. Most of all, I wanted to explore how it was that a child never intended to become Queen became our most successful, arguably most popular and perhaps, as time will tell, our longest reigning monarch. I am very grateful to all those who have made it possible for me to do so.

For the sources of references and quotations, please see www.kate-williams.com/books/YoungElizabeth/references.htm

# Bibliography

## NEWSPAPERS

*Daily Express*
*Daily Mirror*
*Daily Telegraph*
*Evening News*
*Evening Standard*

*Guardian*
*Picture Post*
*Sunday Dispatch*
*The Times*

## PRIMARY AND SECONDARY SOURCES

Acland, Eric, *The Princess Elizabeth*, The John C. Winston Company, Toronto, 1937

Alexandra, Queen of Yugoslavia, *For a King's Love: The Intimate Recollections of Queen Alexandra of Yugoslavia*, Odhams Press, 1956

Alexandra, Queen of Yugoslavia, *Prince Philip: A Family Portrait*, Hodder & Stoughton, 1960

Airlie, Mabell, Countess of, *Thatched with Gold*, Hutchinson, 1962

Aronson, Theo, *Princess Margaret*, Michael O'Mara, 1997

Bagehot, Walter, *The English Constitution*, Chambers & Hall, 1867

Barrymaine, Norman, *The Peter Townsend Story*, Peter Davies, 1958

Beaton, Cecil, *Self-Portrait with Friends: Selected Diaries of Cecil Beaton, 1926–1974*, Weidenfeld & Nicolson, London, 1979

Beaton, Cecil, *The Unexpurgated Diaries* (ed. Hugo Vickers), Weidenfeld & Nicolson, London, 2002

Beaverbrook, Lord, *The Abdication of King Edward VIII* (ed. A. J. P. Taylor), Hamish Hamilton, London, 1966

Bedell Smith, Sally, *Elizabeth the Queen: The Woman Behind the Throne*, Viking, London, 2012

Birkenhead, 2nd Earl of, *Walter Monckton: The Life of Viscount Monckton of Brenchley*, Weidenfeld & Nicolson, London, 1969

Blackwood, Caroline, *The Last of the Duchess*, Pantheon, New York, 1995

Bloch, Michael (ed.), *Wallis and Edward: Letters 1931–1937: The Intimate Correspondence of the Duke and Duchess of Windsor*, Weidenfeld & Nicolson, London, 1986

Bloch, Michael, *The Secret File of the Duke of Windsor*, Corgi, London, 1988

Bloch, Michael, *The Duchess of Windsor*, Weidenfeld & Nicolson, London, 1996

Bolitho, Hector, *King Edward VIII: His Life and Reign*, Eyre & Spotiswoode, London, 1937

Bonham-Carter, Violet, *Champion Redoubtable: Diaries and Letters of Violet Bonham-Carter 1914–1945* (ed. Mark Pottle), Weidenfeld & Nicolson, London, 1999

Boothroyd, Basil, *Prince Philip: An Informal Biography*, Dutton, London, 1971

Bradford, Sarah, *George VI*, Weidenfeld & Nicolson, London, 1989

Bradford, Sarah, *Elizabeth: A Biography of Her Majesty the Queen*, William Heinemann, London, 1996

Bradford, Sarah, *Elizabeth II: Her Life in Our Times*, Viking, London, 2011

Brandreth, Gyles, *Philip and Elizabeth: Portrait of a Marriage*, Century, London, 2004

Carlton, David, *Anthony Eden*, Allen Lane, London, 1981

Carpenter, Edward, *Archbishop Fisher*, Canterbury Press, Canterbury, 1991

Carrington, Peter, *Reflections on Things Past: The Memoirs of Lord Carrington*, Collins, London, 1988

Carter, Miranda, *The Three Emperors*, Fig Tree, London, 2009

Castle, Barbara, *The Castle Diaries 1964–70*, Weidenfeld & Nicolson, London, 1984

Cathcart, Helen, *The Married Life of the Queen*, W. H. Allen, London, 1970

Chance, Michael, *Our Princesses and Their Dogs*, John Murray, London, 1936

Channon, Sir Henry 'Chips', *Chips: The Diaries of Sir Henry Channon* (ed. Robert Rhodes James), Penguin, London, 1967

Chisholm, Anne, and Michael Davie, *Beaverbrook: A Life*, Pimlico, London, 2003

Christopher of Greece, HRH Prince, *Memoirs of HRH Prince Christopher of Greece*, Hurst & Blackett, London, 1938

Churchill, Sir Winston S., *The World Crisis* (5 volumes), Thornton Butterworth, London, 1931

Churchill, Sir Winston S., *The Second World War* (6 volumes), Cassell, London, 1948–1954

Churchill, Winston and Clementine, *Speaking for Themselves: The Private Letters of Winston and Clementine Churchill* (ed. Mary Soames), Doubleday, London, 1998

Ciano, Galeazzo, *Ciano's Diary, 1939–1943* (ed. Malcolm Muggeridge), Heinemann, London, 1947

Clear, Celia, *Royal Children: From 1840 to 1980*, Barker, London, 1981

Colville, John, *The Fringes of Power: Downing Street Diaries 1939–1955*, Hodder & Stoughton, London, 1985

Cookridge, Edward Henry, *From Battenberg to Mountbatten*, Arthur Barker Ltd, London, 1966

Cooper, Lady Diana, *The Light of Common Day*, Rupert Hart-Davis, Hart Davis, London, 1959

Crawford, Marion, *Queen Elizabeth II*, George Newnes, London, 1952

Crawford, Marion, *Happy and Glorious*, George Newnes, London, 1953

Crawford, Marion, *The Little Princesses* (introduced by Jennie Bond), Orion, London, 2002

Dalton, Hugh, *The Fateful Years, 1931–45*, Frederick Muller, London, 1957

Dalton, Hugh, *The Second World War Diary of Hugh Dalton* (ed. Ben Pimlott), Jonathan Cape, London, 1986

Dean, John, *HRH Prince Philip, Duke of Edinburgh: A Portrait by his Valet*, Robert Hale, London, 1954

Dimbleby, Jonathan, *The Prince of Wales*, Little, Brown, London, 1994

Domville-Fife, Charles William, *King George VI and Queen Elizabeth*, Rankin Brothers, London, 1937

Donaldson, Frances, *Edward VIII*, Weidenfeld & Nicolson, London, 1974

Eade, Philip, *Young Prince Philip: His Turbulent Early Life*, HarperPress, London, 2011

Eden, Clarissa, *Clarissa Eden: A Memoir from Churchill to Eden.* London: Phoenix, 2008

Eden, Sir Anthony, *The Memoirs of the Rt. Hon. Sir Anthony Eden: Full Circle*, Cassell, London, 1980

Edward, Duke of Windsor, *A King's Story*, Cassell, London, 1951

Evans, Harold, *Downing Street Diary: The Macmillan Years, 1957–1963*, Hodder & Stoughton, London, 1981

Evelyn Thomas, Samuel, *Princess Elizabeth: Wife and Mother*, S. Evelyn Thomas, London, 1949

Fareham, Viscount Lee of, *A Good Innings: The Papers of Viscount Lee of Fareham* (ed. Alan Clark), John Murray, London, 1974

Gardiner, Juliet, *Wartime Britain, 1939–1945*, Headline, London, 2004

Gardiner, Juliet, *The Thirties: An Intimate History*, HarperPress, London, 2010

Gilbert, Martin, *Churchill: A Life*, Heinemann, London, 1991

Greatorex, Clifford, *King George VI: The People's Sovereign*, Lutterworth Press, London, 1939

Hall, Philip, *Royal Fortune: Tax, Money and the Monarchy*, Bloomsbury, London, 1992

Hardinge, Helen, *Loyal to Three Kings*, William Kimber, London, 1967

Hardman, Robert, *Monarchy: The Royal Family at Work*, Ebury, London, 2007

Hardman, Robert, *Our Queen*, Hutchinson, London, 2011

Hatch, Alden, *The Mountbattens*, W. H. Allen, London, 1966

Hibbert, Christopher, *The Court at Windsor: A Domestic History*, Longmans, London, 1964

Hibbert, Christopher, *The Court of St. James: The Monarch at Work from Victoria to Elizabeth II*, Weidenfeld & Nicolson, London, 1979

Higham, Charles, and Roy Moseley, *Elizabeth and Philip: The Untold Story*, Sidgwick & Jackson, London, 1991

Howard, Anthony, *Rab: The Life of R. A. Butler*, Jonathan Cape, London, 1987

Hoey, Brian, *All the Queen's Men: Inside the Royal Household*, HarperCollins, London, 1992

Hoey, Brian, *At Home with the Queen*, HarperCollins, London, 2002

Holden, Anthony, *Charles, Prince of Wales*, Weidenfeld & Nicolson, London, 1979

Hough, Richard, *Mountbatten: Hero of our Time*, Weidenfeld & Nicolson, London, 1980

Howard, Anthony, *Rab: The Life of R.A. Butler*, Jonathan Cape, London, 1987

Howard, Philip, *The British Monarchy in the Twentieth Century*, Hamish Hamilton, London, 1977

Hudson, Derek, *Kensington Palace*, Davies, London, 1968

Hunter, Ian, *Malcolm Muggeridge: A Life*, HarperCollins, London, 1980

Hussey, Christopher, *Clarence House*, Country Life Books, London, 1949

James, Paul, *Margaret: A Woman of Conflict*, Sidgwick & Jackson, London, 1990

James, Paul, *Prince Edward: A Life in the Spotlight*, Judy Piatkus, London, 1992

Jenkins, Roy, *European Diary, 1977–1981*, HarperCollins, London, 1989

Jenkins, Roy, *A Life at the Centre*, Macmillan, London, 1991

Jephson, Patrick, *Shadows of a Princess: Diana, Princess of Wales, 1987–1996: An Intimate Account by her Private Secretary*, HarperCollins, London, 2000

Judd, Denis, *Prince Philip: A Biography*, Michael Joseph, London, 1980

Judd, Denis, *King George VI, 1895–1952*, Michael Joseph, London, 1982

Junor, Penny, *Diana Princess of Wales*, Sidgwick & Jackson, London, 1982

Junor, Penny, *The Firm: The Troubled Life of the House of Windsor*. HarperCollins, London, 2005

Keay, Douglas, *Elizabeth II: Portrait of a Monarch*, Ebury, London, 1991

Kynaston, David, *King Labour: The British Working Class, 1850–1914*, Allen & Unwin, London, 1976

Kynaston, David, *Austerity Britain, 1945–51*, Bloomsbury, London, 2007

Kynaston, David, *Family Britain, 1951–1957*, Bloomsbury, London, 2009

Lacey, Robert, *Majesty: Elizabeth II and the House of Windsor*, Hutchinson, London, 1977

Lacey, Robert, *Royal, Her Majesty Queen Elizabeth II*, Little, Brown, London, 2002

Lascelles, Sir Alan, *In Royal Service: The Letters and Journals of Sir Alan Lascelles 1920–1936* (ed. Duff Hart-Davis), Hamish Hamilton, London, 1989

Lascelles, Sir Alan, *The King's Counsellor: Abdication and War – The Diaries of 'Tommy' Lascelles* (ed. Duff Hart-Davis), Weidenfeld & Nicolson, London, 2006

Lees-Milne, James, *Harold Nicolson Volume 1: 1886–1929*, Chatto & Windus, London, 1980

Lees-Milne, James, *Harold Nicolson Volume 2: 1930–1968*, Chatto & Windus, London, 1981

Lockart, John Gilbert, *Cosmo Gordon Lang*, Hodder & Stoughton, London, 1949

Longford, Elizabeth, *The Royal House of Windsor*, Sphere, London, 1974

Longford, Elizabeth, *The Queen Mother*, HarperCollins, London, 1981

Longford, Elizabeth, *Elizabeth R*, Weidenfeld & Nicolson, London, 1983

Lord Moran, *Winston Churchill: The Struggle for Survival, 1940–1965*, Constable, London, 1966

Lowry, Suzanne, *The Princess in the Mirror*, Chatto & Windus, London, 1985

Macmillan, Harold, *The Blast of War, 1939–1945*, Macmillan,

London, 1967

Macmillan, Harold, *Tides of Fortune, 1945–1955*, Macmillan, London, 1969

Macmillan, Harold, *Riding the Storm, 1956–1959*, Macmillan, London, 1971

Macmillan, Harold, *Pointing the Way, 1959–1961*, Macmillan, London, 1972

Macmillan, Harold, *At the End of the Day*, Macmillan, London, 1973

Marie-Louise, Princess, *My Memories of Six Reigns*, Evans Brothers, London, 1956

Marr, Andrew, *The Diamond Queen: Elizabeth II and her People*, Macmillan, London, 2011

Martin, Kingsley, *The Crown and the Establishment*, Hutchinson, London, 1962

McLeish, Kenneth, and Valerie McLeish, *Long to Reign Over Us: Memories of Coronation Day and Life in the 1950s*, Bloomsbury, London, 1992

Mortimer, Penelope, *Queen Elizabeth: A Life of the Queen Mother*, Viking, Harmondsworth, 1986

Morrow, Ann, *The Queen*, Granta, London, 1983

Mosley, Diana, *The Duchess of Windsor*, Sidgwick & Jackson, London, 1980

Muggeridge, Malcolm, *Like It Was: The Diaries of Malcolm Muggeridge* (ed. John Bright-Holmes), HarperCollins, London, 1981

Nairn, Tom, *The Enchanted Glass: Britain and its Monarchy*, Radius, London, 1988

Nickolls, Louis Albert, *The Crowning of Elizabeth II: A Diary of the Coronation Year*, Macdonald & Co, London, 1953

Nicolson, Harold, *King George V*, Constable, London, 1952

Nicolson, Harold, *Diaries and Letters, 1930–1939* (ed. Nigel Nicolson), Athenaeum, London, 1966

Pakula, Hannah, *The Last Romantic: A Biography of Queen Marie of Roumania*, Weidenfeld & Nicolson, London, 1985

Paxman, Jeremy, *On Royalty*, Viking, London, 2006

Pearson, John, *The Ultimate Family: The Making of the Royal House of Windsor*, Michael Joseph, London, 1986

Petropoulos, Jonathan, *Royals and the Reich*, Oxford University Press, Oxford, 2006

Pimlott, Ben, *Hugh Dalton*, Jonathan Cape, London, 1985

Pimlott, Ben, *Harold Wilson*, HarperCollins, London, 1992

Pimlott, Ben, *The Queen: Elizabeth II and the Monarchy*, HarperCollins, London, 2002

Pope-Hennessy, James, *Queen Mary, 1867–1953*, Allen & Unwin, London, 1959

Princess Alice, Duchess of Gloucester, *Memoirs*, HarperCollins, London, 1983

Prochaska, Frank, *Royal Bounty: The Making of a Welfare Monarchy*, Yale University Press, Yale, 1995

Prochaska, Frank, *The Republic of Britain*, Penguin, London, 2000

Prochaska, Frank, *Christianity and Social Service in Modern Britain: The Disinherited Spirit*, Oxford University Press, Oxford, 2006

Pugh, Martin, *We Danced All Night: A Social History of Britain between the Wars*, Vintage, London, 2009

Reith, Lord, *The Reith Diaries* (ed. Charles Stuart), Collins, London, 1975

Rhodes James, Robert, *Anthony Eden*, Weidenfeld & Nicolson, London, 1986

Rhodes, Margaret, *The Final Curtsey*, Umbria Press, London, 2011

Roberts, Andrew, *Eminent Churchillians*, Weidenfeld & Nicolson, London, 1994

Roberts, Andrew, *A History of the English-Speaking Peoples*, Weidenfeld & Nicolson, London, 2006

Rose, Kenneth, *King George V*, Weidenfeld & Nicolson, London, 1983

Sebba, Anne, *That Woman: The Life of Wallis Simpson, Duchess of Windsor*, Weidenfeld & Nicolson, London, 2011

Shawcross, William, *Queen Elizabeth: The Queen Mother*, Macmillan, London, 2009

Sheridan, Lisa, *Princess Elizabeth at Home*, John Murray, London, 1944

Sheridan, Lisa, *From Cabbages to Kings*, Odhams Press, London, 1955

Soames, Mary, *Clementine Churchill*, Cassell, London, 1979

Soames, Mary (ed.), *Speaking for Themselves: The Personal Letters of Winston and Clementine Churchill*, Doubleday, London, 1998

Spoto, Donald, *Dynasty: The Turbulent Saga of the Royal Family from Victoria to Diana*, Simon and Schuster, London, 1995

Thatcher, Margaret, *The Downing Street Years*, HarperCollins, London, 1993

Towers, Frances, *The Two Princesses: The Story of the King's Daughters*, Pilgrim Press, London, 1940

Townsend, Peter, *Time and Chance: An Autobiography*, Collins, London, 1978

Townsend, Peter, *The Last Emperor*, Weidenfeld & Nicolson, London, 1975

Vickers, Hugo, *Alice, Princess Andrew of Greece*, Viking, London, 2000

Vickers, Hugo, *Cecil Beaton: The Authorised Biography*, Weidenfeld & Nicolson, London, 2002

Vickers, Hugo, *Elizabeth, The Queen Mother*, Hutchinson, London, 2005

Von Tunzelmann, Alex, Indian Summer, Simon & Schuster, 2007

Walker, Eric Sherbrooke, *Treetops Hotel*, Robert Hale, London, 1962

Warwick, Christopher, *Princess Margaret: A Life of Contrasts*, André Deutsch, London, 2000

Warwick, Christopher, *Princess Margaret*, Coronet, London, 1983

Warwick, Christopher, *Queen Mary's Photograph Album*, Sidgwick & Jackson, London, 1989

Warwick, Christopher, *Two Centuries of Royal Weddings*, Barker, London, 1980

Warwick, Christopher, *George and Marina, Duke and Duchess of Kent*, Weidenfeld & Nicolson, London, 1988

Watson, Sophia, *Marina: The Story of a Princess*, Weidenfeld & Nicolson, London, 1994

Weir, Alison, *Britain's Royal Families: A Complete Genealogy*, London, Bodley Head, 1989

Weir, Alison, Kate Williams, Tracy Borman and Sarah Gristwood, *The Ring and the Crown*, Hutchinson, London, 2011

Wheeler-Bennett, John W., *King George VI: His Life and Reign*, Macmillan, London, 1958

Wheeler-Bennett, John W., *Friends, Enemies and Sovereigns*, St Martin's Press, London, 1976

Williamson, Philip, *Stanley Baldwin: Conservative Leadership and National Values*, Cambridge University Press, Cambridge, 1999

Williamson, Philip, and Edward Baldwin (eds.), *The Baldwin Papers: A Conservative Statesman 1908–1947*, Cambridge University Press, Cambridge, 2004

Wilson, A. N., *The Rise and Fall of the House of Windsor*, Sinclair-Stevenson, London, 1993

Wilson, Sir Harold, *The Labour Government, 1964–1970: A Personal Record*, Michael Joseph, London, 1971

Wilson, Sir Harold, *The Governance of Britain*, Weidenfeld & Nicolson, London, 1976

Windsor, Wallis, *The Heart Has its Reasons*, Michael Joseph, London, 1956

Young, Kenneth, *Sir Alec Douglas-Home*, J. M. Dent, London, 1970

Ziegler, Philip, *Crown and People*, Collins, London, 1978

Ziegler, Philip, *Mountbatten*, Collins, London, 1985

Ziegler, Philip, *Elizabeth's Britain*, Country Life Books, London, 1986

Ziegler, Philip, *Diana Cooper*, Collins, London, 1987

Ziegler, Philip, *King Edward VIII: The Official Biography*, Collins, London, 1990

# Index

with Elizabeth, 57–8, 73; and fashion,
59–60; disparages Queen Mary, 60;
Crawfie on, 63; babied by Allah, 66;
education, 67, 128; interests and tastes,
70–1; rumoured to be deaf and dumb,
76; and George V's death and funeral,
87–8; Edward visits, 90; swimming
lessons, 95–6; Elizabeth's precedence
over, 109; moves to Buckingham
Palace, 113–14, 116; and parents'
accession, 113; practical jokes, 116, 245;
and George VI's Coronation, 118–22;
Queen Mary takes to museums, 126;
as Brownie, 129; and war precautions,
136; and parents' visit to USA and
Canada, 138–9; asks about Hitler, 148;
at outbreak of war, 149–50; as Girl
Guide, 156–7; dancing lessons, 157; at
Windsor in war, 162–4; in Elizabeth's
wartime broadcast to USA, 171;
wartime activities, 174; attends first
ball, 175; good spoken French, 179;
fear of V1 flying bombs, 188; visits
Elizabeth's army mess, 189; celebrates
VE Day, 195; pacifies father, 199–200;
fondness for Philip, 201; tour of South
Africa (1947), 207–8, 248; wedding
present for Elizabeth, 220; at Elizabeth's
wedding, 222, 225; social life and
fashion-setting, 240–1; romance with
Townsend, 242, 245, 247–9, 269, 272,
278–9, 292–6; on father's death, 264,
268; and Elizabeth's Coronation, 284–5,
292; tour of Southern Rhodesia with
mother, 294; travels to West Indies, 295;
twenty-fourth birthday, 295; renounces
Townsend, 297–8
Margarita, Princess of Greece (later of
Hohenlohe-Langenburg), 272, 285
Marie-Louise, Princess, 65
Marriage Law Reform Committee, 250
Marten, Sir Henry, 126, 143, 151, 156,
171, 173
Martin, Kingsley, 93, 102–7
Mary Adelaide, Princess of Teck, 12
Mary (of Teck), Queen of George V
(May): and birth of Elizabeth, 10,
37; betrothals and marriage, 12–13;
children, 16; marriage and family
relations, 17; and son Bertie's marriage,
33; makes clothes for baby Elizabeth,

40; fondness for Elizabeth, 43, 46, 59;
on housing shortage, 51; activities
and business, 53; Margaret criticises,
60; and Princesses' education, 66, 70,
75, 126, 128, 139; and Elizabeth's
status-consciousness, 75; and Silver
Jubilee, 77; hostility to Wallis Simpson,
84, 107; and husband's death, 87;
and Edward's relations with Wallis,
93; rumoured regency, 96; opposes
Edward's morganatic marriage proposal,
97; in abdication crisis, 99, 101; and
George's reluctance to succeed to
throne, 101; and Edward's farewell
visit, 104; sense of duty, 106; praises
Yorks publicly, 108; accompanies
George VI to Coronation, 118, 121–3;
on Edward–Wallis wedding, 123–4;
evacuated to Badminton in war, 154;
claims royal family to be English, 184;
returns to London at war's end, 197;
and Elizabeth's wedding, 221; and
Elizabeth's pregnancy, 234; and birth
of Prince Charles, 238; on Margaret's
adventurousness, 240; will, 247, 280;
and George VI's death and funeral, 264,
270; and Elizabeth's return from Kenya
as Queen, 267; and Mountbatten's
dynastic ambitions, 274; health decline,
death and funeral, 280–1
Mary, Princess Royal (Countess of
Harewood), 16, 31, 39, 122, 128, 221
Miéville, Sir Eric, 139, 180
Milford Haven, David Mountbatten, 3rd
Marquess of, 220
Milford Haven, George Mountbatten,
2nd Marquess of, 147–8
Milford Haven, Admiral of the Fleet Louis
Mountbatten, 1st Marquess of, 23, 142
Milne, A. A., 60
monarchy: status, 76; and Abdication
crisis, 95, 100, 105, 107; and female
succession, 108; post-war position, 199;
under Victoria, 217
Monckton, Walter, Viscount, 89, 104
Mothers' Union, 249–50, 297
Mountbatten, Edwina (née Ashley; later
Countess), 142, 203, 220
Mountbatten, Lord Louis (later 1st Earl;
'Dickie'): and George VI's reluctance to
accede to throne, 101; and Edward's